Compassion

ESSAYS FROM
THE ENGLISH INSTITUTE

Since 1944, the English Institute has presented work
by distinguished scholars in English and American
literatures, foreign literatures, and related fields.

Also available in the series from Routledge:

Compassion

The Culture and Politics
of an Emotion

EDITED BY
LAUREN BERLANT

Routledge
NEW YORK AND LONDON

Published in 2004 by
Routledge
29 West 35th Street
New York, NY 10001
www.routledge-ny.com

Published in Great Britain by
Routledge
11 New Fetter Lane
London EC4P 4EE
www.routledge.co.uk

Routledge is an imprint of the Taylor & Francis Group.

Printed in the United States of America on acid-free paper.

10 9 8 7 6 5 4 3 2 1

Cataloging-in-Publication Data is available from the Library of Congress.

ISBN 0-415-97051-2 (hb)
ISBN 0-415-97052-0 (pb)

Contents

Contents

Introduction

Compassion (and Withholding)

LAUREN BERLANT

There is nothing clear about compassion except that it implies a so-cial relation between spectators and sufferers, with the emphasis on the spectator's experience of feeling compassion and its subsequent relation to material practice. To open the investigations of compas-sion that follow, I would like to propose a counterintuitive view. You will see that these essays cannot help but be histories of the present: not just because knowledge always shapes and is shaped by the scene of its emergence, but because in the context of the United States where these essays are written, the word *compassion* carries the weight of ongoing debates about the ethics of privilege—in particular about the state as an economic, military, and moral actor that represents and establishes collective norms of obligation, and about individual and collective obligations to read a scene of distress not as a judgment against the distressed but as a claim on the spectator to become an ameliorative actor.

This national dispute about compassion is as old as the United States and has been organized mainly by the gap between its demo-cratic promise and its historic class hierarchies, racial and sexual penalties, and handling of immigrant populations. The current de-bate takes its particular shape from the popular memory of the wel-fare state, whose avatar is Lyndon Johnson's Great Society, with its focus on redressing those legal, civic, and economic inequities that acted, effectively, like disenfranchisement. Now the Republican Party of the twenty-first century brands itself with the phrase "compas-sionate conservatism" and insists that there is a moral imperative to change our image of the kinds of state and personal actions that demonstrate compassion for those people whose suffering can be deemed to be social.

In particular, its advocates seek to replace the grand gestures of the Great Society welfare state with a melodrama of the overtaxed and the underemployed, those whose dignity must be restored to them by tax cuts and welfare-to-work programs. If an expanding liberal state used laws and programs to animate the technology of amelioration, the compassionately conservative state wants to limit these mechanisms severely and in particular to shift its economic obligations from redressing poverty to protecting income by taking less from and giving less back to workers and citizens. Compassion can be said to be at the heart of this shrinkage, because the attendant policies relocate the template of justice from the collective condition of specific populations to that of the individual, whose economic sovereignty the state vows to protect.[1]

Great Society ideology had presumed that the social realities of privilege did not require individual intentions and practices to contribute directly to inequality. Nor were one's particular experiences deemed authentic evidence of whether undemocratic practices were organizing life. Instead, the Johnson administration argued that unjust inequalities were objective and enabled by state sanction, such that the state must alter its economic, juridical, and bureaucratic rules and practices toward equality while also placing demands on smaller institutions to make the same changes.

In contrast, currently reigning Republican thought resituates who the subject of compassionate action ought to be. No longer is the icon of structural damage any member of a historically and structurally subordinated population but rather the working citizen—that is, the person who works for a living, especially for his family's living. (By "his" I point to the crisis of paternal value that this particular state ideology seeks to ameliorate.) But what happens to those who do not work, do not work steadily, or do not belong to heterosexual nuclear families? The aim of current state policy is to impel these people to work harder and to enter nuclear families, at which point state entitlements will step in to protect their economic interests.

The more successful one is at these practices, the more one is protected by the state put forward by this administration.

In other words, compassionate conservatism advocates a sense of dignity to be derived from labor itself—of a particular sort. No longer casting a living wage, public education, affordable housing, and universal access to economic resources as the foundation of the individual and collective good life in the United States, the current state ideology sanctifies the personal labor of reproducing life at work, at home, and in communities. That is, income-producing labor is deemed valuable chiefly in the context of its part in making smaller-scale, face-to-face publics. The Republican view supports the amassing of corporate wealth on the theory that such wealth will produce investments that make the jobs that workers need to maintain their zones of intimacy.

What links these zones conceptually is no longer the American Dream of social mobility as such but faith, faith in the highly symbolized, relatively immobile structures of intimate attachment from the family and the nation to God. Faith in such a project of social membership is seen to provide the moral tone of a state and a nation; at the same time, when compassionate action is necessary to alleviate social suffering, it is seen as at best a local response put out by individuals and smaller institutions toward people who live somewhere, sharing an everyday life. The problem of social interdependence is no longer deemed structural but located in the faith that binds to itself a visible, lived-in community.

In this view all occupants of the United States are local: we cultivate compassion for those lacking the foundations for belonging *where we live,* and where we live is less the United States of promise and progress or rights and resources than it is a community whose fundamental asset is humane recognition. Operating powerfully is a presumption that the local is the same thing as the communal, both experientially and institutionally.[2] This remediation of national life away from the federal state does not blank out the nation but sees patriotism as a feeling of abstract intimacy practiced from the ground up. In asking individuals and local institutions to take up the obligation to ameliorate the suffering that used to be addressed by the state, compassionate conservatives see themselves as moral actors: for rather than imposing solutions from on high, as it were, compassionate conservatives believe that local institutions will best be able to serve the less fortunate persons *who come forward for help.* All social membership is voluntary in this view. By insisting that society's poorest members can achieve the good life through work, family, community participation, and faith, compassionate conservatives rephrase the embodied indignities of structural inequality as opportunities for individuals to reach out to each other, to build concrete human relations.

In the new good life imagined by the contracting state, the capitalist *requirement* that there be a population of poorly remunerated laborers-in-waiting or those who cobble together temporary work is not deemed part of a structural problem but rather a problem of will and ingenuity, and if poverty becomes severe enough for action to be asked for, the individuals caught in that bind are left to themselves and to their community. For more on this topic, see the volume's first three essays: a genealogy of the term "compassion" by Marjorie Garber; an analysis of the current political debate by Kathleen Woodward, with an emphasis on the place of suffering in liberal theory and its egregious absence in the Right's Compassionate Conservatism; and, through Emerson and Poe, an ethical inquiry into the modern American compassionate imaginary by Candace Vogler.

Although any emphasis on communal interdependence as the scene of democratic collective life has much positive to be said for it, it is worth noting that none of the essays in this volume admire the project of compassionate conservatism; rather, they create new genealogies and archives of compassion, seeking to understand the concept as *an emotion in operation.* In operation, compassion is a term denoting privilege: the sufferer is *over there.* You, the compassionate one, have a resource that would alleviate someone else's suffering. But if the obligation to recognize and alleviate suffering is more than a demand on consciousness—more than a demand to *feel right,* as Harriet Beecher Stowe exhorted of her white readers—then it is crucial to appreciate the multitude of conventions around the relation of feeling to practice where compassion is concerned.[3] In a given scene of suffering, how do we know what does and what should constitute sympathetic agency?[4]

Not only is this volume about the present moment, but the present moment haunts its investigations of the compassionate emotions, their aesthetic conventions, their place in political theories, and their centrality to modern subjectivites. This is a peculiarly modern topic, because members of mass society witness suffering not just in concretely local spaces but in the elsewheres brought home and made intimate by sensationalist media, where documentary realness about the pain of strangers is increasingly at the center of both fictional and nonfictional events.[5] The Freudian notion of *Schadenfreude,* the pleasure one takes in the pain of another, only begins to tell the unfinished story of the modern incitement to feel compassionately—even while being entertained.

Some readers might feel that to think about compassion as a social and aesthetic technology of belonging and not an organic emotion is to demean its authenticity and its centrality to social life. No one in this volume says that compassion is merely stupid, naïve, or a narcissistic mirror in which the privileged can express to themselves their worthiness. This worry—that critique seeks to befoul its object—is especially acute in response to writing on what we might call the humanizing emotions: compassion, sentimentality, empathy, love, and so on. But scholarly critique and investigation do not necessarily or even usually entail nullifying the value of an affirmative phrase or relation of affinity. It is more likely that a project of critique seeks not to destroy its object but to explain the dynamics of its optimism and exclusions.[6] If we challenge the affirmative forms of culture, it is not to call affirmation wrong but to see how it has worked that forms of progress also and at the same time support destructive practices of social antagonism. Social optimism has costs when its conventional images involve enforcing normative projects of orderliness or truth. This kind of bargaining demands scrutiny, in that desires for progress in some places are so often accompanied by comfort with other social wrongs. Such contradictions were as much a part of the Great Society as of the compassionately conservative one.

Nonetheless, it makes sense that people object when analysis of the intimate emotions makes those desires for attachment seem equally like instruments of suffering. In the liberal society that sanctions individuality as sovereign, we like our positive emotions to feel

well intentioned and we like our good intentions to constitute the
meaning of our acts. We do not like to hear that our good intentions
can sometimes be said to be aggressive, although anyone versed in,
say, the history of love or imperialism knows volumes about the ways
in which genuinely good intentions have involved forms of ordinary
terror (think about missionary education) and control (think of state
military, carceral, and police practices). We do not like to be held responsible for consequences we did not mean to enact. We can feel
bad about it; we can feel compassionately toward those who suffer:
why isn't it enough to have meant well, or not to have meant badly?

The authors of the essays in this volume look at scenes of compassion and ask what kinds of obligation are being entailed when we
witness the theatrical scene of suffering that makes, minimally, moral
demands of our bodies—our hearts and tears—as well as, sometimes,
political and economic demands on the people and institutions that
house that suffering. For brilliant readings of different aspects of
compassion's aesthetic ethics, see the essays on George Eliot by Neil
Hertz (on *Adam Bede*), Carolyn Williams (on *Daniel Deronda* and
melodrama's theatrical conventions), and Mary Ann O'Farrell (on
Eliot, ethics, and style). In this section we see that if compassion is a
simple emotion ideally, intending a clear program of amelioration or
justice to follow, in context its power involves myriad anxieties about
who among the sufferers deserves to be positively or negatively
judged, and why, and whether there is any adequate solution to the
problem at hand not only within the work but in the reader's sense of
what is to be done. Indeed, the scale of the response is often what is
at stake in the experience of what Lee Edelman so accurately calls
"compassion's compulsion": Does a scene involve one person's suffering, or a population's? What kinds of exemplification are involved
when a scene of compassion circulates in order to organize a public
response, whether aesthetic, economic, or political? When we want
to rescue X, are we thinking of rescuing everyone like X, or is it a singular case that we see? When a multitude is symbolized by an individual case, how can we keep from being overwhelmed by the
necessary scale that an ethical response would take? The third section
of this volume contains essays on the difficulty of maintaining compassion in the scene of judgment framed by the law, politics, and the

human sciences; see Lee Edelman (on Lacan and Hitchcock), Neville Hoad (on Freud, Darwin, and *The Island of Dr. Moreau*), and Deborah Nelson (on Hannah Arendt).

Each essay takes these questions very seriously as aesthetic, intellectual, and ethical problems to be opened up by analysis. Each can be read as a case study in suffering and the aesthetics and politics of compassionate responses to it. But this very analytical seriousness works against the desire for the good to feel simple. When people read about the positive, world-building social emotions, they want to feel part of the world of goodness described therein. No one of these authors claims that sentiments of compassion are *at root* ethically false, destructive, or sadistic, just that they derive from social training, emerge at historical moments, are shaped by aesthetic conventions, and take place in scenes that are anxious, volatile, surprising, and contradictory. We can conclude from reading this volume that there is nothing simple about compassion apart from the desire for it to be taken as simple, as a true expression of human attachment and recognition.

But I have not yet described the counterintuitive perspective on compassion advertised at this essay's beginning. Instead, I have laid out for you the geopolitical scene in which this volume emerges, where another counterintuitive position was advanced and gained political and institutional purchase. No doubt many readers of this volume will not feel comfortable in the faith-based society that is now being offered as the ground of the good. But this does not mean that they are somehow superior to or untouched by the contemporary culture of true feeling that places suffering at the center of being and organizes images of ethical or honorable sociality in response.[7] When the response to suffering's scene is compassion—as opposed to, say, pleasure, fascination, hopelessness, or resentment—compassion measures one's value (or one's government's value) in terms of the demonstrated capacity not to turn one's head away but to embrace a sense of obligation to remember what one has seen and, in response to that haunting, to become involved in a story of rescue or amelioration: to take a sad song and make it better.

Needless to say, not all responses to social suffering that might be called "compassion" take the same shape or envision the same just world. For a salutary—and in its own way, equally polemical—mirror to that offered by the shrinking republic of compassionate conservatism, see the massive ethnographic theoretical work by Pierre Bourdieu and colleagues, *The Weight of the World: Social Suffering in Contemporary Society*.[8] This volume catalogs the local, embodied struggles of workers in the contemporary global economy; the weight of the volume devastates with an archive of the subjective experience of inequality so powerful and intricate that it is hard to know how to respond. This is often as true for the subjects interviewed as it will be for any close reader. Loïc J. D. Wacquant writes:

> Under such conditions of relentless and all-pervading social and economic insecurity, where existence becomes reduced to the craft of day-to-day survival and where one must continually do one's best with whatever is at hand, that is, precious little, the present becomes so uncertain that it devours the future and prohibits thinking about it except as fantasy . . . in its own way, a *labor of social mourning* that does not say its name.[9]

Homosexuality, the love that dare not speak its name, echoes within this phrasing of the labor of social mourning: both phrases are about what must remain veiled in order that a scene of social belonging may still be experienced as such. Such euphemisms protect the vulnerable subjects and the social order that ejects them from appropriateness. In Waquant's case, social mourning amidst poverty must remain unstated directly, on behalf of not feeling defeated, of remaining optimistic. Hence, paradoxically, his ethnographic interlocutor manifests mourning without feeling it in an explicit way as hopelessness but is distracted by his own projection of unworkable fantasy. Compassion would seem beyond the point—or, more accurately, before the point, since no one in the text, the ethnographers or their interviewees, asks for compassion. Still, if one blames the people on the bottom of so many social hierarchies for their residence there, one has not made the fundamental connection between the structural conditions that buoy some people and relegate others to treading water.

The various contributors to *The Weight of the World* refuse their readers the pleasure of learning of social suffering by not asking for fellow feeling or extracting a feeling of uplift at the refusal of their subjects to be defeated by the project of living amidst inequality. But the kinds of dignity and indignity produced by the project of survival under the pressure of national and transnational capitalism's inequalities demand of the reader and the interviewers both analytic and affective presence. Susan Sontag argues that compassion is what you feel when you feel impotent, overwhelmed by the enormity of painful spectacle; but one could also say the opposite: that when suffering is presented to you in a way that invites the gift of your compassion, compassion can feel like the apex of affective agency among strangers.[10] In the case of *The Weight of the World*, neither affective position seems appropriate; to feel compassion for people who struggle or fail is at best to take the first step toward forging a personal relation to a politics of the practice of equality.

All of this is to say, then, that the aesthetics of compassion—the cultivation of the senses toward a more nuanced and capacious engagement with scenes of human activity—opens a hornet's nest of problems about what responses should be desired and when private responses are not only insufficient but a part of the practice of injustice. Compassion turns out not to be so effective or a good in itself. It turns out merely to describe a particular kind of social relation, as I suggested in this essay's first sentence. Indeed, it would be possible to make an argument about the image of the human the compassion archive provides for us that could bring down on our heads the whole project of feeling committed to compassion.

As I have worked through this volume, I have been struck by an undertone accompanying the performance of compassion: that scenes of vulnerability produce a desire to withhold compassionate attachment, to be irritated by the scene of suffering in some way. Repeatedly, we witness someone's desire to not connect, sympathize, or recognize an obligation to the sufferer; to refuse engagement with the scene or to minimize its effects; to misread it conveniently; to snuff or drown it out with pedantically shaped phrases or carefully designed apartheids; not to rescue or help; to go on blithely without conscience; to feel bad for the sufferers, but only so that they will go away quickly. In this book's archive, the aesthetic and political spectacle of suffering vulnerability seems to bring out something terrible, a drive not to feel compassion or sympathy, an aversion to a moral claim on the spectator to engage, when all the spectator wants to do is to turn away quickly and harshly.

I thought about calling this volume *Coldness and Cruelty,* but that title has been taken and it might confuse the issue by making compassion seem like a bad thing.[11] Yet the relation of compassion to sadism seen generally cannot be overlooked. There was no way to call this volume *Withholding,* either: there is no elastic enough affective term for the variety of refusals archived here. Let me list some of the forms that withholding compassion takes in the following pages: Neil Hertz's crisp representation of George Eliot's refusal to feel compassion for her characters' stupidity; Neville Hoad's representation of the aversion to compassion for the animals and the captive humans on the Island of Dr. Moreau; Deborah Nelson's review of Hannah Arendt's theoretically consequential distaste for moral softness.

Some theorists, such as Veena Das, use the publicness of politically silenced subjects and the alternative modes of spectatorship those subjects make through bodily performance as a way of talking about not the transparency of pain nor the need for compassion but the fundamental break in the "human" that manifests itself in scenes of structural violence. In this book too, again and again, as we track the training in compassionate action that each essay conveys and queries, we must also track the training in aversion we receive, which must take place simultaneously. When we are taught, from the time we are taught anything, to measure the scale of pain and attachment, to feel *appropriately* compassionate, we are being trained in stinginess, in not caring, in not knowing what we know about the claim on us to act, as Nietzsche would say scathingly, all too human.

What about that? What is the relation between becoming capaciously compassionate and becoming distant from responsibility for what one experiences directly and indirectly about the populations relegated to social negativity? What if it turns out that compassion and coldness are not opposite at all but are two sides of a bargain that the subjects of modernity have struck with structural inequality? Normatively, the bargain would go like this: the experience of pain is pre-ideological, the universal sign of membership in humanity, and so we are obligated to be responsible to it; but since some pain is more compelling than some other pain, we must make judgments about which cases deserve attention. Justice is objective; it seeks out the cold, hard facts against the incoherent mess of feeling. But we must be compelled to feel right, to overcome our aversions to others' suffering by training ourselves in compassionate practice. This discipline is a discipline of our judgment, phrased as the cultivation of our visceral sense of right. This logic only seems circular. Actually, the moral elevation of compassion is reversed when we raise questions about the scale of suffering, the measures of justice, or the fault of the sufferers. The modern social logic of compassion can as easily provide an alibi for an ethical or political betrayal as it can initiate a circuit of practical relief.

This, then, is a book not just about the optimism of fellow feeling nor the privileged pedagogies of social coldness. It is about an emotional complex that has powerfully material and personal consequences. As George Eliot demonstrates in *Middlemarch:*

> Some discouragement, some faintness of heart at the new real future which replaces the imaginary, is not unusual, and we do not expect people to be deeply moved by what is not unusual. The element of tragedy which lies in the very fact of frequency, has not yet wrought itself into the coarse emotion of mankind; and perhaps our frames could hardly bear much of it. If we had a keen vision and feeling of all ordinary human life, it would be like hearing the grass grow and the squirrel's heart beat, and we should die of that roar which lies on the other side of silence. As it is, the quickest of us walk about well wadded with stupidity.[12]

Notes

1. The emergence of a culturally dominant discourse requires less a beautiful mission statement and more countless commentaries on the production of this as a fully intelligible discourse within what passes as "common sense." What follows is a list of works that participated strongly in the normalization of compassionate conservatism as a social referent posited against the traditional association of compassion with personal and state practices of recognition and redistribution. For performances of traditional liberal affectivity, see John Rawls, *A Theory of Justice* (Oxford: Oxford University Press, 1971) and *Political Liberalism* (New York: Columbia University Press, 1993); Martha Nussbaum, "Compassion: The Basic Social Emotion," *Social Philosophy and Policy* 13 (1996), 27–38; and,

more recently, the Compassionate Listening Project, available at
http://www.compassionatelistening.com. On behalf of Compassionate
Conservatism, see the White House archive at
http://www.whitehouse.gov/news/releases/2002/04/20020430.html; the
Heritage Foundation archive beginning with
http://www.heritage.org/Research/PoliticalPhilosophy/hl676.cfm; the
Hoover Institute input at http://www-hoover.stanford.edu/publica-
tions/digest/004/goldsmith.html; the Cato Institute at
http://www.cato.org/events/010220apf.html; and a general middlebrow
bibliography at http://www.compassionateconservativism.org/. For cri-
tiques of the Republican view see, for a start, Dana Milbank, "President's
Compassionate Agenda Lags," at http://www.washingtonpost.com/wp-
dyn/articles/A37908-2002Dec25.html; Bob Herbert, "The True Believer," at http://www.nytimes.com/2000/11/30/opinion/30HERB.html;
John J. DiIulio, Jr., "The Future of Compassion," at
http://www.philly.com/mld/philly/4636962.htm; and Robert Kuttner,
"The Compassionate Conservative's Bait-and-Switch Budget," at
http://www.businessweek.com/magazine/content/03_10/b3823036_mz0
07.htm. In contrast to the substantial bibliography of antiliberal, procom-
passionate conservative books and despite much liberal and progressive
ranting against it, there is as yet no really full anticonservative book-
length study of compassionate conservatism as theory and practice.

2. On the antidemocratic nature of the idea of a community of consensus,
see Jacques Rancière, *Disagreement,* trans. Julie Rose (Minneapolis: University of Minnesota Press, 1998). Rancière argues that democracy, the
practice of equality, requires public antagonism and a destabilization of
the identity forms derived from citizenship; in his view, the translation
of everything into pseudotransparent and pseudoconsensual normative
categories is postdemocratic, dressing up as good fellow feeling a disciplinary regime.

3. Harriet Beecher Stowe, *Uncle Tom's Cabin: Or, Life Among the Lowly,* ed.
Ann Douglass (New York: Penguin USA, 1986), p. 624.

4. Page Du Bois has recently argued that compassion initially described any
adverse event that befell one, and only with the advent of Jesus did the
concept turn to the scene of one mind reaching out to another, suffering
one, and alleviating that suffering through recognition. See "A Passion
for the Dead: Ancient Objects and Everyday Life," in *Representing the
Passions: Histories, Bodies, Visions,* ed. Richard Meyer (Los Angeles:
Getty Research Institute, 2003), p. 270.

5. The contemporary trauma bibliography is huge; this particular selection
is shaped by discussions of the public sphere. See Mark Seltzer, *Serial
Killers: Death and Life in America's Wound Culture* (New York: Routledge,
1998); Hal Foster, "Death in America" *October* 75 (Winter 1996): 37–60;
Avital Ronell, "Trauma TV," in *Finitude's Score: Essays for the End of the
Millennium* (Lincoln, NE: University of Nebraska Press, 1999), and *Stupidity* (Urbana, IL: University of Illinois Press, 2003); Veena Das, "Language and Body: Transactions in the Construction of Pain," in *Social
Suffering,* ed. Arthur Kleinman, Veena Das, and Margaret Lock (Berkeley, CA: University of California Press, 1997), pp. 67–91; Veena Das,

Arthur Kleinman, Mamphela Ramphele, Pamela Reynolds, eds., *Violence and Subjectivity* (Berkeley, CA: University of California Press, 1998), and *Remaking a World: Violence, Social Suffering, and Recovery* (Berkeley: University of California Press, 2001); Susan Sontag, *Regarding the Pain of Others* (New York: Farrar, Straus and Giroux, 2002).

6. I have just described, in slightly different terms, what Gayatri Spivak calls "affirmative deconstruction"; see her "Subaltern Studies: Deconstructing Historiography," *Selected Subaltern Studies,* ed. Ranajit Guha and Gayatri Chakravorty Spivak (Oxford: Oxford University Press, 1988), p. 16.

7. Lauren Berlant, *The Queen of America Goes to Washington City: Essays on Sex and Citizenship* (Durham, NC: Duke University Press, 1997), and "The Subject of True Feeling: Pain, Privacy, and Politics" in *Cultural Studies and Political Theory,* ed. Jodi Dean (Ithaca, NY: Cornell University Press, 200), pp. 42–62.

8. Pierre Bourdieu, et al., *The Weight of the World: Social Suffering in Contemporary Society,* trans. Priscilla Parkhurst Ferguson, et al., (Stanford, CA: Stanford University Press, 1999).

9. Loïc J. D. Wacquant, "Inside 'The Zone': The Social Art of the Hustler in the American Ghetto," in Bourdieu, et al., p. 156.

10. Sontag, *Regarding the Pain of Others.*

11. Gilles Deleuze and Leopold von Sacher-Masoch, *Masochism: Coldness and Cruelty,* trans. Jean McNeil (New York: Zone Books, 1991).

12. George Eliot, *Middlemarch,* ed. David Caroll (Oxford: Clarendon Press, 1986 [1871]), p. 226.

1

Compassion

MARJORIE GARBER

"Either out of humility or out of self-respect (one or the other) the Court should decline to answer this incredibly difficult and incredibly silly question," Justice Antonin Scalia responded to the issues posed by *PGA Tour Inc. v. Martin,* a case of a professional golfer's fight for permission to ride in a golf cart while competing on the PGA tour. Comparing the majority's decision to grant Martin's request to "misty-eyed judicial supervision," Justice Scalia's acerbic dissent began: "In my view today's opinion exercises a benevolent compassion that the law does not place it within our power to impose."[1]

Since Justices (and their clerks) are conscious stylists, often attentive to the opening and closing phrases of their opinions, the phrase "benevolent compassion" caught the eye of some experienced readers. The executive editor of the now-defunct Inside.com, Noam Cohen, a former copy editor at the *New York Times,* wrote to his friend and former colleague at the *Times,* William Safire, to inquire whether Safire did not find "benevolent compassion" redundant. Could there, he asked, be such a thing as "malevolent compassion"? Safire's subsequent correspondence on the question with Justice Scalia formed the basis of a Sunday column.

Scribal joustings between such elevated wordsmiths cannot always avoid a certain archness of tone. Here is Justice Scalia's response to the question, posed to him by his friend Safire, about whether he was being redundant or "differentiating from some other kind of compassion":

I shall assume that such differentiation is impossible—that compassion is always benevolent—though that may not be true. (People sometimes identify with others' suffering, "suffer with" them—track the Latin root of compassion—not because they particularly love the others or "wish them well"—to track the Latin root of benevolence—but because they shudder at the prospect of the same things happening to themselves. "There, but for the grace of God, go I." This is arguably not benevolence, but self-love.)

But assuming the premise, is it redundancy to attribute to a noun a quality that it always possesses? Surely not. We speak of "admirable courage" (is courage ever not admirable?) [and] "a cold New England winter" (is a New England winter ever not cold?). . . . It seems to me perfectly acceptable to use an adjective to emphasize one of the qualities that a noun possesses, even if it always possesses it. The writer wants to stress the coldness of the New England winter, rather than its interminable length, its gloominess, its snowiness and many other qualities that it always possesses. And that is what I was doing with "benevolent compassion"—stressing the social-outreach, maternalistic, goo-goo character of the Court's compassion."[2]

Safire, transcribing this document with manifest readerly pleasure, here interrupts to footnote "goo-goo," which, he says, "some may mistakenly take as akin to 'gooey.'" Instead, he explains, it is short for "good government," since "goo-goo" was "the derisive appellation given by the *New York Sun* in the 1890s to local action groups calling themselves 'Good Government Clubs.'" The phrase, says Safire, is Theodore Roosevelt's from the latter's time as New York City police commissioner, when he railed at fellow reformers who voted independent as "those prize idiots, the Goo-Goos."

I am willing to believe that this is the meaning of "goo-goo," since it comes from a virtually unimpeachable source in the language business. But perhaps Safire will not mind if I also have recourse to one of his favorite tools, the *Oxford English Dictionary*, where a researcher in diligent quest of "goo-goo" finds "goo-goo, a." goo-goo eyes, "an amorous glance, a 'glad-eye' (from *goggle*)," and "goo-goo, int." (echoic), "to talk in the manner of a baby," but no "goo-goo, a" from Good Government clubs. I do not doubt that the robust Roosevelt, the legendary personification of everything that was not "social-outreach" and "maternalistic," might have thought his contemporary Goo-Goos were guilty of excessively benevolent idealism.

Yet Justice Scalia's list of condemnatory terms for "the Court's compassion" fits just as well with spoony glances and baby talk as with the politics of reform. Indeed, the contiguity of "maternalistic" and "goo-goo" in his playful sentence suggests that he was thinking of the high chair as much as the high court. And this association of "compassion" with the ironically inflected "maternalistic" (the opposite of "paternalistic," plainly regarded as a buzzword of liberal-speak) suggests where some of the judicial animus may lie; for "compassion" these days is a "liberal" word, damned with faint praise from both the right and the left. To see how this has come about, despite the high regard with which the concept of compassion is nominally held, is my objective here.

The suit on behalf of Casey Martin was brought under the Americans with Disabilities Act of 1990. Martin suffers from a rare circulatory condition in his right leg and sought to pursue his career as a professional golfer on the PGA Tour with the assistance of a cart. Justice Scalia, whose scathing dissent was joined by Justice Clarence Thomas, derided the Court's "solemn duty" to "decide What Is Golf."[3] The majority opinion was written by Justice Paul Stevens, who is one of the Court's two members to have shot a hole in one; the other is Justice Sandra Day O'Conner.

The word compassion was, perhaps inevitably, picked up and bandied about in the wake of the Court's 7-2 decision. Conservative columnist George Will wrote dismissively of what he called "a moral theory in vogue" in prestigious law schools, "that one virtue trumps all competing considerations. That virtue, compassion, is a feeling that confers upon the person feeling it a duty to do whatever is necessary to ameliorate distress." Will imagined a flood of other disability suits arising from this one, like the suit against the San Francisco Ballet by a mother who charged that the ballet company's height and weight standards discriminated against her daughter. "The work of compassionate courts never ends," he concluded with heavy irony.[4]

Others had contrary views, like the veteran golfer Chi Chi Rodriguez, a star of the Senior PGA Tour. Rodriguez thought Martin was right to sue. "The tour is played for charity," he noted. "It's supposed to be a compassionate tour, but when it came to compassion everyone went against him."[5] A letter to the editor of the *Chicago-Sun Times* shared Justice Scalia's view that it was unnecessary to spend the Court's time on this question, but the writer saw the matter from a different perspective: if Martin needed a cart he should have the use of one. In that event, to even up the odds, all the other players should have the option of using carts: "Instead of tying up our judicial system and wasting mega-money on lawyers' fees, this could all have been settled in 30 seconds with common sense and compassion."[6]

Who would have thought that compassion could become a two-edged sword in national debate? When George Will and Antonin Scalia both come close to ridiculing it at the very time that the president of the United States (and the leader of the Republican Party) describes himself as a "compassionate conservative," something interesting is happening at the level of political—and religious—rhetoric.

Indeed, both of our two most recent presidents have sought to associate themselves, at least rhetorically, with the concept of compassion. When George W. Bush campaigned as a "compassionate conservative," the phrase seemed to convey, in its insistent and alliterating adjective, traces of an intrinsic uneasiness. What would the alternative be, one was left to wonder: A *dis*passionate conservative? An *unfeeling* conservative? A *cruel* conservative? Where "compassionate liberal" seemed virtually pleonastic, the term "compassionate conservative" appeared to fend off or hold at bay intimations of oxymoron. As for Bill Clinton, his compassionate catchphrase—so celebrated that it has entered the world as a seriocomic cliché—was the affective, even bathetic, but consistently successful "I feel your pain," an expression unsurprisingly labeled "feminine" by early media critics:

> If other presidents tended to speak by lecturing the American public ("We have nothing to fear but fear itself" or "Ask not what your country can do for you"), Clinton often communicates by listening ("I feel your pain"). . . . Call it New Age if you wish. But the Clinton style is really a textbook example of a leader who communicates in ways often more characteristic of women than men. . . . A woman tends to say, "I feel your pain." A man might say, "Let me tell you why you feel pain and what you should do about it." And then he might look at his watch.
>
> This is not to say that displaying a "feminine" style is bad. . . .[7]

This debased version of Carol Gilligan or Deborah Tannen, circa 1993, is one of the first analyses of what would become a famous Clinton watchword.

A few years earlier media analysts had begun tracking what they labeled "compassion fatigue," a term presumably coined on the model of "metal fatigue" or more likely "combat fatigue." The combat in this case was the war against poverty and the cause of human rights. By the mid-1980s, the term was in regular use among disaster relief agencies and United Nations officials, though the U.S. media kept "rediscovering" it through the early 1990s, as donations to famine relief in Ethiopia, cyclone relief in Bangladesh, and homeless shelters in New York City began to wane. In this context, "compassion" clearly meant donations as well as volunteer aid; "compassion fatigue" was well glossed by one editorial, headed "Compassion Overload," as: "the weariness with which Americans are reacting to suffering abroad and the unwillingness to respond to yet another disaster."[8]

"Compassion fatigue" entered modern dictionaries such as *Chambers* and became an example of late-twentieth-century language innovation, with its typical compression of noun plus noun, the noun-as-adjective so familiar from headline practice. Susan Moeller's 1999 book *Compassion Fatigue: How the Media Sell Disease, Famine, War, and Death* described what was in effect the commodification of compassion, its use and misuse by a journalism more concerned with celebrity culture— including its own—than committed, in-depth coverage of "unsexy news."[9] But in fact the *fatigue* had affected the word *compassion* itself.

Once in regular use to describe human kindness, one of the very "virtues" celebrated in William Bennett's *Book of Virtues*—which contains, indeed, a section on compassion wherein Bennett offers the unexceptionable view that we should treat no one with "callous disregard"—*compassion* has increasingly become associated with issues like human rights, children's rights, animal rights, and multiculturalism. Hence, for example, Herbert Kohl, an educator and writer, responds to Bennett in *A Call to Character: A Family Treasury* (coedited with Colin Green), suggesting that Bennett's "family values" are too rigid and underemphasize compassion and social responsibility. Bennett's book includes the text of the Boy Scout Oath; Kohl's reprint instead includes the International Declaration of the Rights of Children.[10]

The problem with compassion begins with its etymology and history. From the fourteenth century to the beginning of the seventeenth, the word (deriving from Latin *com,* together, and *pati,* to suffer) was used to describe both *suffering together with one another,* or "fellow feeling," and an emotion felt *on behalf of another who suffers.* In the second sense, compassion was felt not between equals but from a distance—in effect, from high to low: "shown towards a person in distress by one who is free from it, who is, in this respect, his superior." When the first sense fell out of use, which it did fairly quickly, the remaining sense hovered between charity and condescension.

Later usages, especially in a religious context, stress the emotional benefits to the nonsufferer. Here is a symptomatic example from a university sermon of 1876: "Compassion . . . gives the person who feels it pleasure even in the very act of ministering to and succouring pain."[11] One does not have to be a card-carrying Freudian to see that pleasure and pain are intermingled here in a way that is satisfactorily both simple and complex: the pain of someone else provides an access of pleasure for the compassionate one.

The phrase "the compassionate one," indeed, invokes one of the most familiar uses of this notion, the idea that compassion is one of the attributes of God (e.g., from the apocryphal book Ecclesiasticus 30:33: "For the Lord is full of compassion and mercy, long-suffering, and very pitiful"). By extension, compassion could be regarded as a normative and desirable prerequisite of monarchs who ruled by "divine right"—as God's deputies—at least in theory (e.g., "By the compassioned mercy of Queene Elizabeth"; John Speed's *History of Great Britain,* 1611). The aspect of fellow suffering led to some specific religious uses, notably in a term like *compassivity,* which described the feelings of a saint on beholding in a vision the sufferings of Christ, "whereby his soul is transpierced with the sword of a compassive pain."[12] As was the case with *compassion* as a kind of emotionally gratifying condescension, this sense of the word carries with it a certain occluded erotics.

Although Samuel Johnson called the transitive verb (*to*) *compassion* "a word scarcely used," it does appear in references from the sixteenth century to the nineteenth. The use of the verb in Shakespeare's *Titus Andronicus* gives a clear sense of its function: "Can you heare a good man grone / And not relent, or not compassion him?" (4.1.24). To compassion is to have compassion about something or someone, to pity him or them. In a letter written in 1838, John Quincy Adams expressed himself "In charity to all mankind, bearing no malice or ill will to any human being, and even compassionating those who hold in bondage their fellow men, not knowing what they do."[13] These words, later adopted by Abraham Lincoln, suggest the crucial role of "compassionating" as both activity and belief.

The best-known biblical example here is that of the "good Samaritan," who offered succor to a stranger:

> A certain man went down from Jerusalem to Jericho and fell among thieves, which stripped him of his raiment, and wounded him, and departed, leaving him half dead. And by chance there came down a certain priest that way: and when he saw him, he passed him by on the other side. And likewise a Levite, when he was at the place, came and looked on him, and passed by on the other side. But a certain Samaritan, as he journeyed, came where he was: and when he saw him, he had compassion on him. And went to him, and bound up his wounds, pouring in oil and wine, and set him on his own beast, and brought him to an inn, and took care of him. And on the morrow when he departed, he took out two pence, and gave them to the host, and said unto him, Take care of him; and whatsoever thou spendest more, when I come again, I will repay thee. (Luke 10:25–37)

This parable is told to a lawyer who asks Jesus skeptically how he can attain eternal life. He is told to love God with all his heart, with all his soul, and with all his might (a literal invocation of the language of Deuteronomy 4, the prayer known to Jews as the "Shema," the standard Jewish declaration of faith) and to love his neighbor as himself. The lawyer in true form then demands, "Who is my neighbor?" and the story of the Samaritan is his answer. "Which of the three was the neighbor to him who fell among thieves?" asks Jesus, and the lawyer responds, the one who showed mercy. "Go thou and do likewise," is the reply.

There is much to detain us in this parable, which seems to depict the high-ranking Jews as more indifferent to the lot of the unfortunate man than the Samaritan, who is a despised member of another sect.

(Hence the paradox in the identification of the "neighbor.") The Samaritan's compassion is generosity but also, by implication, fellow feeling. The definition of a true neighbor derives from the behavior of the helpful passerby, who does not cross the road to avoid involvement.

We can know little about this particular Samaritan and his motivations; for one thing, he is in all probability a fictional character summoned to life to play a part in the parable of instruction rather than a "real" individual with knowable motives. Structurally speaking, what we are given is the story of two "high-status" insiders versus one "low-status" outsider, with the actions of the third acting as a rebuke to the selfishness of the first two. The Samaritan is the third in a series of three; the priest and the Levite, like Cinderella's two wicked stepsisters, are examples of privileged persons who behave selfishly or ignobly, in contrast to the humbler and more virtuous third. A similar sentiment can be deduced from this symptomatic phrase from the Epistle of John: "Whoso hath this world's good, and seeth his brother have need, and shutteth up his bowels of compassion from him, how dwelleth the love of God in him?" (3:17). Again, "brotherhood" (like "neighbor-hood") is a matter of feeling, not blood.

It is worth noting that the phrase "good Samaritan" is itself not biblical but, rather, developed over time as a way of interpreting the parable. Most English translations call him "a certain Samaritan"; the *New Living Translation* reads "a despised Samaritan." The implication of the adjective *good* when attached to "Samaritan" is oxymoronic (like "compassionate conservative"), and must once have been stressed ("the *good* Samaritan") to emphasize the surprising fact that generosity in this case came from an outsider, from whom little was to be expected. (Matthew Henry's *Commentary on the Bible* calls the Samaritans "That nation which of all others the Jews most despised and detested and would have no dealing with."[14]) The usual modern emphasis on the second term rather than the first ("good *Samaritan*") forgets this history of anomaly and turns an oxymoron into something like a redundancy.

The terms *Samaritan* and *good Samaritan* have had their own history, becoming not only proverbial shorthand for a disinterested do-gooder but also the honored name of hospitals, organizations, help lines and missions dedicated to the care of the sick, the suicidal, the homeless, and the despairing. The organization called the Samaritans, founded in 1953 to offer telephone counseling to those in distress, dropped the word "good," as presumably implied in the term; by this point the sense of redundancy was so fully established that all sense of surprise at the "goodness" of a Samaritan had been definitively lost. In any case, those who took the name of Samaritan in this sense, like those compassionate passersby so labeled in newspaper accounts, intervened with acts of compassion like their biblical namesake: compassion extended from the better-off to the worse-off, as the Samaritan of the parable gave his own beast, his own money, and his own kindness to the man who fell among thieves. The sense that the Samaritan himself might have deserved "compassion" because he was a member of a disliked outsider sect has completely dropped away.

Where *compassion* quickly tipped in the direction of inequality, charity, or patronage (the nonsufferer showing compassion to the sufferer), *sympathy* remained historically a condition of equality or affinity, whether between the body and the soul, between two bodily organs, or, increasingly, between persons with similar feelings, inclinations, and temperaments. *Sympathy*'s roots are Greek and Latin: it literally translates as "having a fellow feeling," from *sym* plus *pathos*, "suffering together." (The word *pathos*, of course, survives in English, where it has become a word more often encountered in aesthetic criticism than in ordinary life.)

To be sure, there was a sense of *sympathy* that was analogous or even identical to *compassion* ("the quality or state of being . . . affected by the suffering or sorrow of another; a feeling of compassion or commiseration"), a sense that became especially prominent in the late eighteenth and nineteenth centuries and which survives in the material form of the "sympathy card" or "sympathy note" expressing condolence on a bereavement. An example from Edmund Burke's speech on Charles James Fox's East India Bill—"To awaken something of sympathy for the unfortunate natives"—makes clear how close this kind of sympathy came to compassion. One could also sympathize with a political party, ideological stance, or philosophical position: again the angle of incidence, so to speak, might be one of *equality* ("he had no sympathy with the anti-opium party") or of *inequality*, again in the sense we have already noted from *compassion*—that is, the sympathizers were not themselves suffering the same ills as those with whom they sympathized. Here the clearest example is that of the "sympathy strike" engaged in by workers or students on behalf of an embattled group elsewhere.

Empathy, we might note, is a modern word, although it has a Greek analogue. Coined in the early years of the twentieth century as a translation of German *Einfühlung*, it has come to denote the power of projecting one's personality into the object of contemplation and has been a useful technical term in both psychology and aesthetics. It seems possible that the need for this word arose as the strongest sense of *sympathy* began to decline or become merged with *compassion*. But *empathy* also seems to stress the matter of personal agency and individual emotion. A person who displays empathy is, it appears, to be congratulated for having fine feelings; a person who shows or expresses sympathy has good cultural instincts and training; a person who shows compassion seems motivated, at least in part, by values and precepts, often those learned from religion, philosophy, or politics.

It is arguably this question of the abject other in need of assistance that has been the undoing of *compassion* as well as its proudest boast. "Rallying the armies of compassion" is what George W. Bush called it on the campaign stump. "Compassion is a miserable basis for American politics," declared Mickey Kaus in the *New York Times*. "It was a bad idea when liberals were selling it, and it's no less bad now that conservatives are embracing it." Kaus, the author of *The End of Equality*, found three fundamental flaws in compassion: it was "inegalitarian, carrying the condescending implication of charity, inferiority, and helplessness"; it was sentimental, tending "to override traditional, and sensible, moral distinctions," as between, for example, a young working father and a drug addict or a prisoner; and it was fragile, since it "appeals to essentially charitable impulses" and thus can fall victim to market forces. Citizens will give generously when times are good but not when they themselves feel the necessity to economize. Kaus applauded Al Gore's description of Bush's *no-*

blesse oblige as "the crumbs of compassion" and declared "So the Republicans now have compassion? They can keep it."[15]

In fact, no party seems to want to keep it. Justice Scalia's confident tone of scorn about "benevolent compassion" and governmental over-regulation is right in the spirit of George Will's allergic reaction to unlimited government. Compassion has become the default currency of nongovernmental organizations and other "goo-goo" agencies, especially those concerned with children's and animal rights and social services. Indeed, despite its high-sounding name, compassion is fast becoming an *alternative* virtue associated with persons and practices outside the mainstream. Californians for Compassionate Use works to reform laws concerning cannabis. The Compassionate Club provides marijuana to chronically ill patients in Vancouver. *Compassionate Souls* is a book about raising your children as vegetarians. *Love! Valour! Compassion!* is the title of a hit play about eight gay men.

Although numerous religious groups—Catholic, Jewish, Unitarian-Universalist, and Christian nondenominational—also continue to reiterate their commitment to compassion, it may be symptomatic that most current books in print on the topic are voiced from the perspective of Tibetan Buddhism,[16] for this connection between an Eastern religion and a disempowered religious and cultural leader of great moral power offers a useful example of the pitfalls of "compassion." George W. Bush, we are told by the Associated Press, "extended a carefully measured welcome to the Dalai Lama" when the exiled Buddhist leader visited the White House.[17] The Chinese government objected to the visit, and the United States did what it could to minimize its "official" nature: Bush greeted the Dalai Lama not in the Oval Office but in the White House residence. This spatial decision in itself (taken together, perhaps, with the choice of a woman, National Security Advisor Condoleezza Rice, rather than Secretary of State Colin Powell to join the welcoming delegation) seemed to place the concerns of the Dalai Lama all too clearly on the side of what Justice Scalia called the "maternalistic," the admirable but perhaps ultimately inadvisable claims of that worrisome neopleonasm, "benevolent compassion," rather than on the side of expedient political action.

Compassion seems to waver politically between two forms of inequality: the benevolence of those who have (the power of the rich) and the entitlement of those who need (the power of the poor). The insoluble problem for society—and for government and law—is to behave as if there were no competition between the two. And in some quarters, at least, "compassionate government" is regarded as either a contradiction in terms or a category mistake. Compassion, it appears, is a good campaign slogan but not necessarily a winning political strategy. It seems clear that for Bush, as for Scalia, implementing it in any kind of international policy would represent putting the (golf) cart before the horse.

Notes

1. *PGA Tour Inc. v. Martin,* certoriari to the United States Court of Appeals for the Ninth Circuit, No. 00-24. Argued January 17, 2001. Decided May 29, 2001. Available at http://laws.findlaw.com/us/000/00-24.html.
2. William Safire, "On Language: Compassion," *New York Times Magazine,* July 1, 2001, p. 22.
3. Justice Clarence Thomas, quoted in Linda Greenhouse, "Disabled Golfer May Use a Cart on the PGA Tour, Justices Affirm," *New York Times,* May 30, 2001, p. A1.
4. George F. Will, "Compassionate Courts," *Washington Post,* June 3, 2001, p. B7.
5. Joe Gordon, "FleetBoston Classic: Notebook," *Boston Herald,* June 24, 2001, p. B4.
6. Charles Chi Haleri, "'Golf's Handicap' A Lack of Compassion, Logic," letter to the editor, *Chicago-Sun Times,* June 5, 2001, p. 30.
7. Steven D. Stark, "Practicing Inclusion, Consensus: Clinton's Feminization of Politics," *Los Angeles Times,* March 14, 1993, p. M2.
8. H. D. S. Greenway, "Compassion Overload," *Boston Globe,* May 17, 1991, p. 19.
9. Susan Moeller, *Compassion Fatigue: How the Media Sell Disease, Famine, War, and Death* (New York: Routledge, 1999), p. 321.
10. Herbert Kohl and Colin Green, eds., *A Call to Character: A Family Treasury* (New York: HarperCollins, 1996).
11. *Oxford English Dictionary,* "Compassion," vol. 2, ed. Mozley (New York: Oxford University Press, 1989), p. 597.
12. Rev. James Gardner, *Faiths of the World: A Dictionary of All Religions and Religious Sects, Their Doctrines, Rights, Ceremonies, and Customs,* Div. 3 (London: Fullarton, 1857), p. 570.
13. John Quincy Adams to A. Bronson, July 30, 1838, in *Bartlett's Familiar Quotations,* 10th ed. (Boston: Little, Brown, and Company), p. 458.

14. In John 4:9, the woman of Samaria anticipates scorn from Jesus since "the Jews have no dealings with the Samaritans."

15. Mickey Kaus, "Compassion, the Political Liability," *New York Times,* June 25, 1999, A23.

16. See, e.g., *Buddhist Acts of Compassion; Compassion: the Key to Great Awakening; Thought Training and the Bodhissattva Practices; Cultivating Compassion: A Buddhist Perspective; Mediation, Compassion and Loving Kindness: An Approach to Vipassana Practice; Science and Compassion: Dialogues between Biobehavioral Scientists and the Dalai Lama.*

17. Associated Press, "Dalai Lama Meets with Bush; China Lodges Formal Protest," *Newsday* (New York), May 24, 2001, p. A16.

2

Much of Madness and More of Sin

Compassion, for Ligeia

CANDACE VOGLER

Have a Heart

Sometimes it's important to state the obvious. This is one of those times. America is a great country. There are many reasons for this, foremost among them our long tradition of personal responsibility, the demand for high standards and clear values, and the central importance of family in social and economic progress. . . . We're coming to understand that a good and civil society cannot be packaged into government programs but must originate in our homes, in our neighborhoods, and in private institutions that bring us together, in all our diversity, for the works of mercy and the labors of love. . . . We approach [America's] challenges with compassionate conservatism, a concept that is as old as the pioneers heading West, in which everyone had responsibility to follow the rules, but no one would be left behind.[1]

A recent Republican Party platform announces compassion within the limits of rule-following as the spirit of American moral progress and the key to sound social reform. The territory charted and claimed in this document is what Lauren Berlant calls "the intimate public sphere," the ideology that "recognizes a public good only in a particularly constricted nation of simultaneously lived private worlds."[2] Berlant argues that representations of pain play a special role in reproducing intimate public social relations: public outcry in response to the evidence that injustice hurts simultaneously produces a sense of shared concern for the common weal and prevents politicized, movement-building work in the service of securing it.

Now, some conservatives are suspicious of compassionate conservatism.[3] As Jonah Goldberg puts it, "the phrase 'compassionate conservatism' . . . does a disservice to both concepts." Goldberg continues:

Emerson commented on the fact that there is a certain meanness to conservatism coupled with a certain superiority of fact. But that alleged meanness is in the eye of the beholder who would also blame the concrete for not offering a nicer bounce after a twelve-story fall.[4]

Emerson's contemporary, Edgar Poe, an author fascinated by things that fall, had this to say about travel in the other direction:

In looking at the world *as it is,* we shall find it folly to deny that, to worldly success, a surer path is Villainy than Virtue. What the Scriptures mean by the "*leaven* of unrighteousness" is that leaven by which men *rise.*[5]

The meanness that Poe saw as one ingredient of worldly success and that Emerson located in conservatism need not be *entirely* uprooted by compassion, however. Of the many species of tenderness directed toward others' troubles, compassion falls squarely in the range of affective orientations with a built-in clean-hands clause. This is, I would suggest, an important distinguishing mark of compassionate receptivity to others' misfortune. One *regrets* injuries done to others as an accidental by-product of one's own just and reasonable acts. One has *remorse* when others have suffered unjustly by one's own hand. One is called to *mercy* when one has the power to ease burdens that others have brought upon themselves, to *forgiveness* when their acts injured one's own interests. But the compassionate person sympathizes with misfortunes that she did not cause and that would not otherwise touch her life. Accordingly, any intervention that she undertakes from compassion, beyond expressing condolence, will involve generosity or kindness, which likewise takes good people beyond the strict limits of what the platform authors called *responsibility.*[6] While it's good to help strangers now and then, you do not *owe* aid and comfort to particular strangers.

The absence of obligation suits compassion and generosity to the political landscape that Berlant charts. In the intimate public sphere, interpersonal duties are few. Such institutions as taxes and law mediate any obligatory relations among citizens as such. Voluntary undertakings, like joining a church or a profession or making a contract, generate attendant responsibilities to one's fellows. Starting a family brings the burdens of family—at least to parents, at least as long as their own minor children are on the scene (obligation toward one's parents, grandparents, siblings, and other kin in the North American middle classes has gradually been replaced by an image of familial interdependence as rooted in mutual affection; relations among adult family members, however emotionally charged, are not exactly required but are prompted by guilt, ambivalent longing, hope, love). For all that, there are very many strangers to whom we owe nothing directly, and our private stake in their good is most naturally lodged first in the bowels of compassion.

Interestingly enough, the sentence in which compassion becomes a platform plank displays this lack of imagination for relations among strangers. Compassionate conservatism is "a concept that is as old as the pioneers heading West, in which everyone had responsibility to follow the rules, but no one would be left behind." The suggestion that the contemporary ideal of compassionate, fiscally sound social policy finds its first concrete manifestation in conquest is fascinating. "No one would be left behind" in the great push westward. Likewise, no one would be left standing out in front.

The juxtaposition of a moral call to compassion with a remark suggestive of ethical blindness is not, I think, a simple blunder. The authors are thinking: We stand together, self-reliant, bound one to another by ties of duty and affection, in our common pursuit of prosperity, just like those pioneers of old. *Compassion* is their name for how to respond to the aggregate and ongoing human costs of pursuit of property in this part of the world. And the reader made uneasy by the invitation to go along may be sensing, however dimly, that these self-proclaimed new pioneers are standing on the shifting heap of damaged and decaying things that have always been generated by and crucial to the colonial and neocolonial predations of capital.[7] The ferment of the pile is the impersonal leaven by which men rise—an ethically charged aspect of capital's material foundation that is hard to theorize if we focus on such individual matters as villainy or virtue, duties, or, more generally, intended act and consequence.

In this sense, to accuse the platform authors of some injustice for failing to notice their implication is unfair.[8] The wealth made possible by North American capitalist landgrabs, genocidal policy, and race-slavery is not the special province of any party. Neither, for that matter, is an image of the common weal as the aggregate outcome of simultaneously lived private worlds. What makes the call to compassion by contemporary conservative ideologues noteworthy is that it inadvertently points to a shared subtext—the *sine qua non* of nineteenth-century North American capitalist expansion.

In this essay, I will be shifting through the wreckage of this *sine qua non,* trafficking in compassion, melancholy, loss, death, and the threat posed by revenants. My guide will be Edgar Poe. His counterpoint will be Ralph Waldo Emerson. I will read both as responding to what was then a special problem for American ethics (and has since developed a wider sphere of influence). The problem is this: Given a shared practical orientation that treats the individual person as the fundamental unit for ethics, how ought one to respond to a man-made injustice that is neither any one person's fault nor the sort of thing that any one person can remedy?

As I say, it is an American problem along the North Atlantic in the first half of the nineteenth century. By contrast, across the ocean, working at about the same time as my chosen men of letters, John Stuart Mill argues that there are hardly any individuals at all, that Englishmen do not know how even to estimate the value of individuality, and that, nevertheless, his countrymen ought to pursue major social reform for the sake of making England a place where self-made persons might emerge from the human herd and thrive.[9] Stateside, for Poe and Emerson, the individual is instead the flat baseline from which we proceed, the given, plain parameter for ethics.

In Poe and Emerson, the masculine individual stands in need of some feminine element to live well. In Emerson, the feminine supplements masculinity, producing a form of alterity in sameness conducive to masculine maturity and adaptive functioning in a complex social and cultural milieu. What the woman brings is kin to compassion. Things are less straight in Poe. In Poe, the woman is death's intimate who cannot be laid to rest. Through her figure and the trouble she makes for her man, I will return to the ethical problem and the urgent situation. That situation will focus initially on race, but race will open onto more general questions about colonial and neocolonial social relations and the ideologies that reproduce them.

Remembrance

Emerson once complained that "when men die we do not mention them."[10] The charge seems to have been somewhat inaccurate in the first decades of the nineteenth century on the northeastern seaboard. Then, in cities like Boston, middle-class women were in near-perpetual mourning. The good woman treasured objects associated with her deceased kin and was fond of decorating her house and her person with remains of the body—with locks of hair, for example, braided and mounted.

There must have been pleasure in parading what Poe identified as "that sorrow which the living love to cherish for the dead."[11] There may have been multiple, conflicting modes of aggression in the tactics of renunciation and memory that marked feminine displays of bereavement. Officially, there was insistence on the spiritual dimension of life. Kenneth Silverman writes:

> American culture [preached] from every quarter the duty of remembering the dead. This so-called cult of memory helped to allay anxieties about the continued vitality of Christian ideas of immortality, and concern that commercial and industrial values had begun to prevail in personal and domestic life.[12]

The mode of remembrance at issue is, I think, closer to compassion than one might expect. On Silverman's reading, the cult of memory produces the middle-class woman's body as at once melancholy archive and testament of faith, a place where pain is carried without working it through and where supernatural hope is indirectly registered. Compassion, too, holds close others' troubles in an imitation of woe without working through the associated sorrow. When I have compassion for you, your unhappiness disturbs me. I open myself to your misfortune by skillfully tracing the contours of its occasion in imagination, by letting your suffering weigh down my shoulders, by telling myself stories about you. Taken to an extreme, compassion can betray a thirst for indefinitely multiplied sites of pain made one's own by choice or inadvertent largess. And while condolence is less disturbing than private grief, this may merely involve our tendency to stand further back from the losses that occasion compassion. As Berlant argues, affective receptivity to other people's misfortunes even carries a kind of spiritual charge, becoming nowadays a symptom of universal humanity. My voluntary or spontaneous unhappiness at your loss, like my grief at my own, indexes the survival of my own heart, which you might as well call my own *soul*—the terms *humanity* and *heart* function pretty much as current secular alternatives for whatever is sympathetic about people generally.

The nineteenth-century northeasterners no longer imagined themselves bearers of forces bright and dark charged with doing the Lord's work in a devilish land—*that* image belonged to colonial Puritanism. Still they were steadfast in following the prescribed forms of remembrance, thereby showing that the dead person was more than an organism. At least, this was their approach with the intimate dead. Remembrance of such of the dead as bore extrafamilial socially or nationally significant ties to the living was a different matter. And that may have been what Emerson was driving at in charging his contemporaries with inappropriate muteness. One of his most important topics was how to think the personal, ethical significance of social history.

Emerson's circumnavigation of this topic is perhaps most direct in the lecture to which Goldberg alluded, "The Conservative." There Emerson identifies two tendencies: conservatism, which "makes no poetry, breathes no prayer, has no invention," and reform, which "inclines to asinine resistance, to kick with hoofs," running "to egotism and bloated self-conceit . . . to a bodiless pretension . . . which ends in hypocrisy and sensual reaction."[13] Conservatism "is all memory."[14] Reform stakes all its hopes on a possible future unlike anything we have known before. The woman in mourning would seem to straddle this divide. But women are not Emerson's concern in this lecture. Addressing conservative and reformer alike, Emerson says, "each is a good half, but an impossible whole," hence, "in a true man, both must combine."[15]

Emerson has good intentions. He wants to help men make themselves true. His intended audience, being educable, is immature and primed for development. The specific target seems to be the masculine youth who would take the energy of reform to its radical edge, because the talk begins in a meditation on how the spirit of innovation itself is very old, and merely "renews itself as if for the first time, under new names and hot personalities."[16] This may surprise the young.[17] Conservatism, Emerson insists right from the start, is likewise demonstrably old, but radical youth knew that already. What do you give the young man called upon to fight for right in a world built of and upon wrongs? Advice:

> Who put things on this false basis? No single man, but all men. No man voluntarily and knowingly; but it is the result of that degree of culture there is in the planet. . . . Consider it as the work of a great and beneficent and progressive necessity, which, from the first pulsation of the first animal life, up to the present high culture of the best nations, has advanced thus far. Thank the rude fostermother though she has taught you better wisdom than her own, and has set hopes in your heart which shall be history in the next ages. You are yourself the result of this manner of living, this foul compromise, this vituperated Sodom. It nourished you with care and love on its breast, as it has nourished many a lover of the right, and many a poet, and prophet, and teacher of men.[18]

Radical youth rails against the "mountainous load of . . . violence and vice of society."[19] The conservative insists that these are inevitable, telling youth, "so deep is the foundation of the existing social system, that it leaves no one out of it. . . . As you cannot jump from the ground without using the resistance of the ground . . . you are betrayed by your own nature."[20] Both are postures of masculine assertion, the friction between them involving seemingly irreconcilable differences. The lubricant needed to combine conservatism and reform is not exactly compassion. Rather, it is philosophy. Philosophy is, Emerson insists, feminine insofar as it is receptive. Making men true requires awakening men's receptive potential. Stanley Cavell takes up this point in his reading of Emerson's "Fate":

[Emerson writes], 'So women, as most susceptible, are the best index of the coming hour. So the great man, that is, the man most imbued with the spirit of the time, is the impressionable man'—which seems to divine that the great man is a woman. . . . Emerson's thought here is that this makes knowledge difficult in a particular way, not because it is hard to understand, exactly, but because it is hard to bear; and his suggestion, accordingly, is that something prepares the woman for this relation to pain, whereas a man must be great to attain it.[21]

In the true great man, developed powers of feminine receptivity temper masculine assertiveness to produce a balanced, thoughtful self. True history, for Emerson, finds its model in one key outgrowth of a sexual division of labor, that is, in a family's intergenerational continuities.[22]

The implicit teleology that shapes both Emerson's discussion of individual maturity and his discussion of social growth is gendered, familial, and developmental. It is made possible in part by the textual strands that license Cavell's claim that the Emersonian great man both is and is not a woman. Femininity in the masculine self becomes here a deconstructive supplement—a mode of alterity in sameness that requires, exceeds, and limits the core whose imaginary coherence is made such by the contaminating supplement. Masculinity, the chief attribute of men, is all presence and assertion. This must be in part replaced by absence—by a lack-poised-to-be-filled, by receptivity—if the man is to make himself true. And what is receptivity receptive to? To knowledge—that is, to the substance at issue in assertiveness.

Philosophical, feminine receptivity enables the combination, for example, of conservatism and reform—the two good halves, each of which (*qua* half rather than a whole) is apparently lacking something—something that can be acquired through developing receptivity, that is, directed lack. The absent absence—a kind of intellectual variant on the affective receptivity in compassion—is the femininity whose presence would allow a pair of impossible men to couple (impossible insofar as incomplete, incomplete insofar as lacking the lack whose presence might be filled by something of the other man). The whole process of completion is painful, and the feminine in this process is also the capacity to endure pain. On Cavell's reading of the sexual division of labor in Emersonian self-culture, it turns out that woman is suited to bearing more than one kind of pain—not just the pain of bereavement or of childbirth, not just the pain of knowing things, but also the pain of penetration by a half-cocked man. The woman becomes the gap through which foreign masculinity enters domestic masculinity, allowing for the birth of true masculinity. That is what I mean by saying that we have here entered the territory of deconstructive supplement. Femininity simultaneously completes and undoes (masculine) self-culture.[23]

The endless return of Emerson's prose, the wide, flat compass of his lists, the avuncular rhetoric, productive, paragraph by paragraph, of starting points emblematic of the ends of the essay—all draw the wagons into a circle around an emerging masculine self that must be understood, especially in North America, as an individual whose associations always already are and should remain familial or voluntary.[24] The preordained loneness of this figure poses a special conundrum for Emersonian ethics. His empire is established in violence by his fellow citizens on his home turf and thereby produces and continually reproduces that turf as his home. That turf is still being wrested from other people by means Emerson finds scandalous, and slave labor still accounts for much of its productivity. The question is how on earth to model ethical relations between individuals in this scenario. The substance of self-culture as an answer to that question remains elusive.

Bad Air

At this point, compassion turns back on itself. And we might, if we did not know better, side with Poe's suggestion that there is good reason to limit its scope because, "To be *thoroughly* conversant with Man's heart, is to take our final lesson in the iron-clasped volume of Despair."[25]

Poe makes the remark in his final "Marginalia," a collection of *aperçus* that Silverman finds "Ecclesiastes-like."[26] Iron and despair, of course, intersect in the discourse of colonial Puritanism.[27] In Poe, one can scarcely keep from forging a link between these figures and southern scenes of bondage. Poe was born in Boston and spent most of his adult life shuttling between northern cities, but he was raised in Richmond, and his brief career at the *Southern Literary Messenger* put him in an office two blocks from the slave market.

Now, Poe's attitude toward treatment of indigenous peoples was not that far from Emerson's.[28] Poe's explicit writings on slavery, by contrast, are scarcely more than southern apologetics in the form of enthusiastic reviews of the same. And Poe reviled the educated New England abolitionist set as "Frogpondians" and members of "the Humanity *clique*," a diverse group whose opinions on ethical topics were somehow still marked by fixation on figures of falling, spiritual progress, and whatever could be salvaged of redemption when grace was superceded by works and membership in the company of pilgrims gave way to self-culture. Poe placed the most prominent Frogpondian, Emerson, among "a class of gentlemen with whom we have no patience whatever—the mystic for mysticism's sake."[29]

Mysticism to some good purpose, however, was another story. Poe claimed that his was in the service of such earthly matters as producing sadness or terror in readers. This it does. It is also useful in ways unanticipated by Poe's philosophy. Joan Dayan argues that Poe's textual infusion of spirit in matter manages the crises of southern interracial intimacies; his tropes reverberate with white apprehension about miscegenation, about African and African-American religion, about the activities and status of white ladies, and about relations between the white sexes.[30]

The reason that these interracial intimacies were possible, actual, and threatening was North American capitalist slavery and the concomitant, complex, lived amalgam of institution, practice, self-representation, erasure, misrecognition, and such—"ideology" for short—that daily reproduced the relevant social relations of production by interpellating relevantly race-marked subjects. Building upon Dayan's work, we might say that Poe's transcendental passages, like many dominant cultural representations fixed upon carnality in the spiritual practices of subject peoples, rise and fall in the fetid air of colonial relations of production.

Traditional Marxism teaches us that the ideology reproductive of wage labor naturalizes the relations that it misrepresents. Think here of Emerson's plea to bring the culturally and historically charged parts of an individual personality into harmonious organization for the sake of adaptive functioning, of the need to add the woman to make self-consciousness possible and bearable, thereby allowing man to give birth to his true self, of the simultaneous stress on self-culture and family. But now rock backward in the migration of the term *fetishism* from Hegel to Marx: capitalist colonial ideologies as often *super*naturalize the relations that they misrepresent, sometimes relations of conquest or occupation, sometimes relations of illegitimate contract, always relations productive of profit. These are treated not by analogy to the part-whole constitution of organisms and adaptive principles of development and intergenerational continuity, but rather with reference to spiritual orders that move through man and nature without being strictly human or otherwise natural. Think of the New World pilgrims' divine moral cartography. Think of the terror of polluted blood, drumming, and violent uprisings. Think of accounts of adult subject persons as having prehuman bodies animated by infantile minds or less than infantile instincts. By the lights of these strands of dominant cultural representation, colonized bodies are so corporeal that they are no longer bodies, that is, no longer material aspects of functional wholes marked by traditional European mind-body dualism. Their supernatural aspects are so overwhelming as to be no longer minds or souls.

What we find in discourse about the alarming vigor of subject bodies, then, exceeds the deconstructive supplement. The vitality of subject peoples is not a trace of precapitalist past in a colonial capitalist present. The teleological order suggested by "pre-" is precisely what cannot be ascribed in contexts of conquest or colonization.[31] It is not the other side of some cultural coin whose abstracted value is in principle measurable using the standards of dominant culture, although it becomes a source of such stuff. These congeries of disparate remains can neither reproduce a singular, organized form of life, nor be set to rest, nor be reanimated by being returned to the forms of life from which they came. As Gayatri Spivak remarks, where dominant cultural representation touches subaltern lives, lives conducted in spaces of difference without access to established paths of social mobility, "there are no test cases . . . singularities overflow definitive determinations."[32]

Spivak uses the figure of the spectral to read the break with teleology signaled in discourse about the bodies and practices of subaltern subjects and about their economic immobility, aspiration, and exclusion; I am about to read Poe's traffic in the spectral as a much more crude register of related pressures.[33] And, like a typical male figure in Poe, one finds oneself better able to say what such remains are *not* than to give any positive characterization of them (nay-saying is the mode of assertiveness most comfortable for Poe's men).

What collects the discursive particles of special interest here (representations of various indigenous North American peoples and of members of divergent African groups), making the term "congeries" available for describing them, is not that the subjects came from the same place, had similar histories or cultures, had similar practices, or anything "internal" like that, but rather that they were differently related to making the raw materials for capitalist "development" in North America. Like Emerson,[34] Poe is perched on a pile of residue from these processes (what Emerson's reformist youth experienced as a "mountainous load of violence and vice" constitutive of a "vituperated Sodom"). But when Emerson says, "Every man must begin where he is and move forward," Poe says, "It smells bad here!"

Both are, I think, ethical responses. It is hard to navigate the ethical from the first-person perspective when you are registering horrors (however inchoately, however unwillingly) that can be neither laid on any individual's doorstep nor laid to rest by any individual's act. It is harder still if, like these two, you neither can nor want to sever all ties to the benefits secured for you by your forefathers. It is hardest of all if, unlike Emerson, in spite of your longing to take advantage of your position, you cannot quite bring yourself to straighten up and fly right. This was Poe's predicament, I think.

At the least I ask that, just for once, we do not immediately look to trouble in that most beloved of private institutions, the one traditionally theorized as the ur-scene of prepolitical voluntary association, the site of conservative optimism and Emersonian radical disappointment—the family—in order to unlock the secrets of Poe. In doing so I will be tacitly urging us to pause and think diagnostically about the near-perfect fit between sophisticated Freudianism and Poe's corpus. In Poe we seem to find some version of a return of the repressed without a prior repression, phallic mothers who never gave birth to the infantile masculine figures standing or falling, in love and dread, before them, libidinal cathexes as attachments to mortality, scenes of masculine mourning in which nothing of the departed is ever successfully incorporated, where grief is instead made exterior and dead women threaten always to perform independent feats of re-vivification from some beyond that is far too close for comfort. It is an analyst's paradise, this stuff.[35] But, as we know, psychoanalysis makes its topic the modes of violence and misrecognition that enable production of a functioning individual self well suited to the world as we know it. It may be that Poe is fantastically available for analysis precisely *because* he cannot quite manage the screens needed to view historical circumstance through the lens of family affairs and individ-ual maturity as settling down.

I am not saying here that there is anything wrong with Freud or with Freudian readings of Poe. The point is one about emphasis. Compare: in much work on trauma, trauma is modeled as a force that takes something away from the traumatized subject, as loss. Psycho-logical work on trauma, accordingly, sometimes works by analogy with psychological work on bereavement. But in some cases at least, for example, infantile sex abuse, there was nothing in place that was taken away by traumatic encounters. Rather, the traumatized subject is not shielded from subsequent experiences in the way that an imag-inary untraumatized subject would or should be. Instead of straight-forward "loss," we find here a failed opportunity to develop "normal" defenses against active awareness of vulnerability. The traumatized subject "loses" out on a developmental trajectory designed to resist "gain." It would be interesting to think trauma as getting more than you can handle rather than losing something that you already had. I am urging a similar shift in emphasis in psychoanalytic work on Poe.

In short, the teleology of ego psychology is familial and develop-mental; the teleology of high-end psychoanalysis is dynamically adaptive. Stable or stabilizing selfhood can emerge from working through troubles in either perspective. Poe is transfixed by the possi-bility of selfhood, of family, of settling down—yes—but their attain-ment belongs to a conjuring trick beyond his powers. In his fiction, for instance, he seems to have simply refused the seductions of self-culture, specializing in short stories in part because "in the tale proper . . . there is no space for development of character."[36] And I should like us to read masculinity in Poe as nondevelopmental without being maladaptive, the corresponding femininity as carrying remainder toward no clear destination, a strange twist on representation of femininity as the capacity to bear pain. This twist happens when Poe animates the miseries borne by feminine receptivity in the body of the woman. It is as if rather than wear jewelry fashioned from a lock of a familiar dead person's hair, women in Poe are themselves all made of remains taken from many different sources.

The Jingle-Man

Poe is a conservative who cannot keep a grip on anything, much less serve as steward and husband. In the face of the apparent impossibility of looking after his own interests, his own claims on others' aid and affection, begun in postures of abjection, often turn into outright demands insinuating that debts are owed.[37] Since compassion and generosity both rely, recall, on the presumption that nothing given is owed, Poe's suggestion that his associates are obliged to help him makes the plea decidedly unsympathetic. This is no isolated problem. Poe is generally provoking—a gadfly with no effective will to progressive reform whose bad moods are more clearly associated with plain morbidity than the finer compromises of melancholia. He is tender and funny. But nothing wears a smiling face in Poe, or else every smiling face resolves itself into a grin or a leer—gallows humor, you might say. Of course, the failure of death to resolve anything satisfactorily is one of his themes. And the ethical in Poe is, accordingly, a nightmare.

It is not so much that, in Poe, everything is good in some respects, bad in others. Nor is it that some things are just plain good, others irredeemably bad, and the subject poised between the two, tempted. We find in Poe neither a happy pluralism of incommensurable good things nor a lukewarm sense that, after all, nothing is *all* bad. Instead, the contrasts of good and evil remain shattering throughout, and all strength is often on the side of the shadow. But however deep the pit and however bright the star (and we go to extremes whenever we make an ethical journey in Poe), neither legal fear of just punishment nor conviction of sin, nor tenderest love nor loftiest aspiration, can make an impact on the will in sufficient strength to produce character. It is as if, deprived of the delusional moral map that informed colonial Puritan ideology, unable fully to incorporate the morals of racial hierarchy, and lacking all capacity for proper mourning, there is no way to produce a mode of selfhood adequate to the task of embodying the ethical charge of the text. Poe's men and women cannot produce the interior walls prerequisite to taking the Emersonian high road to the good life. That is, they cannot make of themselves reliable selves. Neither do they have the will, wish, or power to imagine effective collectivities, not even of the homely sort inscribed by middle-class sex/gender systems. The result is moral disaster.

Poe registers the impossibility of ethical self-culture by tracking groundless but still goal-directed surges of volition, affection, and intellection in his men. He registers the uselessness of collective enterprise by invoking images of lost civilizations, foreign faiths, and Empire and family in decay. And these figures revolve around strange and beautiful women who only really come into their own postmortem.

Everywhere Women Are Dying

Poe's women, most of them disturbed, dead, or dying, notoriously resist the grave. They died under mysterious circumstances. They died too soon. They lived somehow illicitly. Or, all appearances to the contrary, they may never have died at all. In Poe, feminine figures are at once elusive and omnipresent. I have announced an intention to show compassion for one feminine figment of Poe's imagination. I suggested earlier that compassion could be interpreted as unmotivated, melancholic mimicry with a moral flair. But we cannot so much as accurately express our condolences for Poe's men and women without understanding ourselves as inadvertently stuck in an ethical predicament related to the ethical nightmare of the text. Accordingly, I will read the female figure in question as a kind of peer.

She is the titular heroine of "Ligeia," a name Poe invented in an early poem called "Al Araaf," apparently because he wanted a word that would rhyme with "idea." In a footnote to the poem, Poe likens some species of the sorrow living men love to conserve for dead women to "the delirium of opium."[38] The point is developed and made indefinite in Ligeia's story. There we find an indirect representation of a compromise that learned women sometimes make involving femininity, masculinity, and will. It is hard to classify this compromise. In a Nietzschean spirit, one might call it hypertrophy of the volitional function, a disorder marked by overattachment to the intact liberty of an unsubmissive will—directed now at mental matters, now at bodily mastery. The force of the will in such cases is so great as to threaten to sever all ties between acts of volition and the practical point of willing. Ligeia's tale is one of the very few of Poe's fictions where it is left to the reader to suppose that we have been given no more than the hallucinations of a male narrator addicted to opiates. Poe thought that it was his best story.

Above the tale hangs one of Poe's misquotations—some lines attributed to Joseph Glanvill. The bulk of it reads: "And the will therein lieth, which dieth not. Who knoweth the mysteries of the will and its vigor. . . . Man doth not yield himself to the angels, nor unto death utterly, save only through the weakness of his feeble will" (1984a, 262).[39] But man is not the creature notable for volition in the tale. That distinction belongs to Ligeia, whose "*intensity* in thought, action, or speech, was possibly, in her, a result, or at least an index, of that gigantic volition which, during our long intercourse, failed to give other and more immediate evidence of its existence" (1984a, 265). This stuttering, cautious, multiply hedged and qualified description of her power comes through the "feeble" memory of her bereaved husband, the unnamed narrator of the story (1984a, 262). He introduces the topic of his wife's volitional magnitude by giving the misquotation again in the body of the text and telling us that these lines "never failed to inspire . . . the sentiment" he felt looking into Ligeia's eyes (1984a, 265).

Like many of Poe's mournful men—like Poe himself, for that matter—our narrator's will is caught in a strange loop. We might diagnose him as displaying the early form of a malady called *psychasthenia*.[40] John King argues that psychasthenia was the godless, spiritual heir of pilgrim melancholy.[41] The disorder entered North American psychological theory through William James's attempts to explain what was wrong with his father. The hallmarks of psychasthenia were dread and fixation on a handful of ill-formed thoughts, compulsive flurries of activity somehow expressive of an attempt to buy salvation through works, drunkenness, addiction, an overweening, underdeveloped ethical sensibility, and the experience of worldly fortune (or its absence) as immoral.

The North American psychasthenics were mostly men of letters who lacked both faith that their lives had a meaningful place in God's plan and any academic or commercial context in and against which to read their labors and lassitude as productive activity punctuated by leisure. They either had or felt they ought to have inherited small fortunes, normally through their fathers. (Ligeia's husband's money comes from her.) The psychasthenics were united in regarding forthright, methodical engagement in productive intellectual or managerial work which brought a satisfactory market return as a wondrous good thing, however far from their lives it seemed at any given moment.

We enter the tale proper through the psychasthenic husband's absentmindedness: "I cannot, for my soul, remember how, when, or even precisely where, I first became acquainted with the lady Ligeia" (1984a, 262). Nor does he know her origins: "Of her family—I have surely never heard her speak"; "I have *never known* the paternal name of her who was my friend and my betrothed, and who later became the partner of my studies, and finally the wife of my bosom" (1984a, 262). But he remembers what she looked like: a tall, thin, pale woman whose person was composed of fragments one might acquire in some dryly fertile Orientalist archive.[42] His descriptions of her read like a catalog of relics from lost civilizations.[43] Her skin was ivory and marble (1984a, 263). Her forehead and black hair were Homeric, "hyacinthine" (1984a, 263). Her profile echoed "the graceful medallions of the Hebrews" (1984a, 263). Her eyes were "fuller than the fullest of the gazelle eyes of the tribe of the valley of Nourjahad," beautiful like "the beauty of the fabulous Houri of the Turk," black and "more profound than the well of Democritus" (1984a, 264). It is her eyes that both fix and unhinge his memory: "They were, I must believe, far larger than the ordinary eyes of our own race" (1984a, 264).

Dayan finds in the description of Ligeia's body and eyes Poe's rendering of "the favorite fiction of white readers: the 'tragic mulatta' or 'octoroon mistress.'"[44] She asks:

How can you detect color in a white "suspect"? As colors faded and hair
and eyes became closer to those of "pure" whites, new distinctions had to
be invented. The attempt to name, label, and classify the degrees of color
between extremes of black and white resulted in fantastic taxonomies of
a uniquely racialized enlightenment. . . . And since it was not always
possible to detect black blood in light skin, natural historians assured
their readers that the tone of whiteness was different: unnatural, less animated, dull, or faded, white but pale or closer to yellow, . . . yellowish-
white like ivory.[45]

The taxonomic aspect of the account is especially interesting in light
of our narrator's insistence that virtually everything about Ligeia is
deliberate. In a way, Ligeia threatens not a predictable return of the
repressed but, rather, a willed return of the variously oppressed. She
was the source of the narrator's fortune. Her vitality, her will, the
force that forges the undetached relics of her person into a mixed-
race-marked body, inspires equal measures of need and dread in him.

The result is suspiciously insubstantial, its bits nothing but incommensurate remains, its movements as a whole hard to detect. The living body of Ligeia is already haunting, this thing forged of stolen
fragments that secured the fortunes of a psychasthenic American:[46]

I would in vain attempt to portray the majesty, the quiet ease of her de-
meanor, or the incomprehensible lightness and elasticity of her footfall.
She came and departed as a shadow. I was never made aware of her entrance into my closed study save by the dear music of her low sweet
voice, as she placed her marble hand upon my shoulder. In beauty of
face no maiden ever equaled her. It was the radiance of an opium
dream. (1984a, 263)

Her voice betrays the materialized mastery of breath associated
with poetry. This much our narrator remembers. And he remembers
that she knew everything and was both mathematician (i.e., a genius
of proportionality) and metaphysician. But Ligeia's knowledge is
rather different from the knowledge philosophy holds in its Emersonian receptacle. She is made of remains that do not belong together
and, anyway, were supposed to be long gone. Her truly alarming wisdom shows itself in knowing how to animate these, breathe through
them, and move about undetected when she wants to. She is a genius

at materialization. And the specter of this life (supposedly vanquished) returning to take hold of valuable matter and occupy closed chambers from which it cannot be entirely barred—our narrator has no real inclination to keep the undead out, in truth—becomes the crux of horror in Ligeia's story.

What happens in "Ligeia" is this. Ligeia writes a poem, asks her husband to read it to her, says the lines (subsequently?) attributed to Glanvill, and dies. Her husband uses the fortune she leaves him to buy a decaying abbey and convert it into a single-family dwelling, lavishing his attention on furnishing the place. The catalog of its appointments is isomorphic with the account of Ligeia's bodily attributes, save for her eyes. In their place, in a pentagonal chamber high in a turret, is a single-paned window, "an immense sheet of unbroken glass from Venice . . . tinted of a leaden hue, so that the rays of either the sun or moon, passing through it, fell with a ghastly lustre on the objects within" (1984a, 270). The incoherence of the design makes it a room without any organizing principle, requiring something on the order of Ligeia's will to make it seem like one sort of place. In her absence, color is drained from the scene, the black-in-white of the marble-skinned, dark-eyed Ligeia replaced by dull gray light settling like a shroud over the room.

Having seen to domestic arrangements of a sort, our narrator remarries a normal woman, "the fair-haired and blue-eyed Lady Rowena Trevanion, of Tremaine," whom he loathes and who does not love him. Having entered into his second marriage in a "moment of mental alienation," he moves his bride into the pentagonal room. To whatever extent Poe's figures carry the colonial charge, to whatever extent there is a hint of colonial allegory here, what is supposed to happen next is this: against all odds, the couple will live well. The narrator will snap out of it. Rowena will be his mate. Ligeia will have been set to rest after yielding her treasures to the couple and so will have miraculously made possible a fledgling family. Of course, this is not how things go.

Ligeia has also moved into the bridal chamber, aided, no doubt, by her husband's choice in furniture. Perhaps because the couple has taken up residence in something like her body, perhaps because she is no longer the force that invisibly knits the bits together, her bodily presence has been enhanced by death. Utterly ethereal in life, Ligeia becomes a noisy ghost, rustling wall hangings and stepping heavily enough on the carpet to make discordant sounds as she moves through the newlyweds' room.

Over the course of three nights about two months after the remarriage, when Ligeia's specter is especially active, the narrator uses drugs and drinks while Rowena dies of a strange fever at the other end of their room. On the fourth night, as he keeps an increasingly tense vigil by the enshrouded corpse, it begins to seem that the lady has not died. There is color in her cheeks. She moans. He does not dare leave the room. He watches and ministers to subsequent signs of life, thinking that the detested bride is coming back. But throughout the fourth night, we learn, it is *Ligeia* who repeatedly revivifies and transmogrifies Rowena's body, and dies and dies and dies. Rowena's feminine receptivity, here identified with illness or weakness of will, may facilitate this process. Whatever the case, she is no match for a psychasthenic husband and his strong-willed, undead, first wife. The luxurious reminiscence and forgetfulness with which the tale begins occurs after Ligeia is, finally, dead.

We might note in passing that it is possible to read the story as involving a husband who murders his second wife. Hardly anyone does, I suspect because he seems incapable of completing any duly motivated course of action. The one thing to which he applies himself steadily is the painstaking realization of his interior-decorating scheme. He writes his story alone in the turret room, staring at the results of his one great project, and laments: "I have said that I minutely remember the details of the chamber—yet I am sadly forgetful on topics of deep moment—and here there was no system, no keeping in the fantastic display, to take hold upon memory" (1984a, 270). What is left for Poe's man when Ligeia is gone is forgetfulness, nay-saying, and plain paralysis in the face of congeries of items that only ever seemed to belong together because of Ligeia's vitality.

The poem he reads on Ligeia's deathbed, Ligeia's poem, is about life, death, and the spectacle of moral imitation, staged as a play performed by God's mimes—men—for an angelic audience. In the drama, the players "come and go/At the bidding of vast formless things/That shift the scenery to and fro/Flapping from out their Condor wings/Invisible Wo!"—just as Ligeia's memory and specter seem to have moved things into place and around in the bridal chamber. The play of men moved by potentially deadly forces unseen is, it turns out, precisely the stuff of the ineffectual, ethically charged memory that is by its very nature absolved from accountability for its content:

> That motley drama!—oh, be sure
> It shall not be forgot!
> With its Phantom chased forevermore,
> By a crowd that seize it not,
> Through a circle that ever returneth in
> To the self-same spot,
> And much of Madness and more of Sin,
> And Horror the soul of the plot. (1984a, 268)

What men and their companions can say in Poe is "nevermore," the word that seals "The Raven" from its first inception, according to "The Philosophy of Composition," whose human significance is indeterminate because it is first uttered by a bird.[47] Ligeia's word is the word that will not die, "Forevermore." And the men's "plot" is no ordinary plot at all, but rather a peculiarly adaptive repetition of key points, impersonal ones, which return eternally to the spot of self-sameness.[48] This is what is carried by sounds whose source is unseen, misunderstood, essentially elusive. The image calls to mind Poe's bizarre definition of plot as "that, in which nothing can be disarranged, or from which nothing can be removed, without ruin to the mass—as that, in which we are never able to determine whether any one point depends upon or sustains any other."[49] The result is a congealing of subject and event that has more to do with echoes than with memory, with the arresting moment than with end-directed movement and development. Repetition, sometimes with mortal rupture, is what the men can perform, suggesting powerful parallels between the staged mimicry and the operations of compassion.

Neither is much to Ligeia's liking, one surmises. She knows better than to go there. Her poem turns on an event that displaces the staged strutting and fretting and gives the angels cause to weep. Have a look at the dénouement of Ligeia's play:

> But see, amid the mimic rout,
> A crawling shape intrude!
> A blood-red thing that writhes from out
> The scenic solitude!
> It writhes!—it writhes!—with mortal pangs
> The mimes become its food,
> And the seraphs sob at vermin fangs
> In human gore imbued.
>
> Out—out are the lights—out all!
> And over each quivering form,
> The curtain, a funeral pall,
> Comes down with the rush of a storm,
> And the angels, all pallid and wan,
> Uprising, unveiling, affirm
> That the play is the tragedy, "Man,"
> And its hero the Conqueror Worm.

In her poem, Ligeia offs men wholesale. As she is dying, just after she has had her husband read the poem, she adds insult to injury by repeating that *no* man yields to death "save only through the weakness of his feeble will." Indeed, as near as one can tell, Ligeia's subsequent brief career as a revenant in possession of Rowena's matter (suitably reinformed) may be no more than her way of illustrating the point.

Bad Women, Good Morals

J. Gerald Kennedy remarked that Ligeia's "denial of death seems an inherently masculine response to the problem of dying."[50] At the very least, it is not an ordinary response. She neither mourns herself nor enacts the rituals of remembrance and renunciation for the sake of dead kin. She will not so much as reveal her paternal name to her husband, much less describe her family. She may herself be to blame for the death of the narrator's second wife. The parts of her living body are not the natural parts of a single organism at all. They are relics, remains, reminders—the sorts of things that bear a mathematically functional one-to-one correspondence with a tasteless accumulation of furniture but lack the unities of organic or cultural system. They also lack the productive relation to some normal required to make this femininity a supplement. The kind of ethical space that Ligeia can occupy, accordingly, is a space of insistent assertion of life in death, productivity from decay. Whatever recuperative force she carries arrests the flow of events, insists on the presence of the past without seeking to conserve it, makes things wobble and move in unpredicted ways, has no obvious, contentful agenda.

Her bigness, in turn, makes her an ideal mate for our narrator, who is either unwilling or incapable of producing a functioning version of himself, instead keeping himself occupied with tasks that are somehow not to the point. Ligeia provides and provides for him; he even detects her hand in the removal of his bad object choice. He is ill fitted to productive engagements with his world, adapted not to family or established institutions of law and property, not even to the work of self-subsistence, but to the need for repetitive insistence that things have been lost, that there is always human cost in the operation of ordinariness. Forgetful of how or why or when things happened, he clings to relics whose significance is no longer clear and engineers circumstances that hold him suspended in dreams. Ligeia, on the other hand, carries the remains with possibly lethal direction, incarnates things without incorporating the parts into a new, organically sound whole, produces an ephemeral presence that is somehow all past set in disruptive motion. Whatever sexual division of labor this is, it is not the one that praises feminine receptivity and masculine assertion, charging women with domesticity and mourning, men with progress within the limits of giving other men their due. It is instead, I think, the best that Poe could manage, given what he had to work with, however difficult it is to give any positive account of the "it." And it may be that this is exactly what it will look like if a couple carries the ethical charge, however unwittingly, that I have tried to read in Poe.

Masculine poetry finds itself in the repetitive "nevermore," somehow evacuated of its significance by the impersonality of its first utterance. Feminine poetry, on the other hand, says "forevermore," and postulates an offstage conqueror worm, a movement of death in life, that makes a mockery of the undead woman's own best feature, individual will. Our narrator is his own man in the end, sitting in a bad room, recording the taking of a white woman's body by a woman of questionable origins. He thinks that this is a passionate and compassionate love story. But his attachment to Ligeia is represented as a function of her inscrutable designs, not his warm heart, and Rowena's plight leaves him cold.

The apparent pointlessness of masculine or feminine action in Poe is, I would urge, a function of precisely the seemingly axiomatic input that is at work in privatized accounts of citizenship and Emersonian urgings to self-culture, the thought that ethics begins and ends with individuals, that agency is the causal nexus of individual attitude, intention, act, and consequence. You cannot theorize the injustices indirectly registered in Poe from this perspective. Neither can you imagine a remedy for them. To think past such alternatives, we would need to think modes of agency in which the parts of an agent are not necessarily the parts of a person and in which fellow feeling does not exhaust the possibilities of ethically motivated solidarity.

Acknowledgments

An earlier version of this paper was given as a talk at the English Institute in September 2000. I am grateful to Jane Gallop, Barbara Johnson, Marjorie Garber, Lise Jardine, Christina Zwarg, and Alan Parker for their extended discussions of the paper there. Correspondence with Neil Hertz afterwards helped me begin revisions. Ian Mueller and Jeremy Bendik-Keymer read a later draft and helped me to pinpoint trouble spots, and Neville Hoad gave me criticism and encouragement throughout the revision. Tim Reid has been an invaluable interlocutor on Emerson for me. And I want especially to thank Lauren Berlant for her editorial help, advice, conversation, and friendship.

Notes

1. Republican National Committee, 2000 Platform, "A Responsibility Era": http://www.rnc.org/GOPinfo/Platform/2000platform3.htm
2. Berlant, *The Queen of America Goes to Washington City* (Durham, NC: Duke University Press, 1997), p. 5. Berlant develops her discussion of the place of representation of pain in liberal norms of personhood in "The Subject of True Feeling: Pain, Privacy, and Politics," in *Feminist*

Consequences ed. Elizabeth Bronfen and Misha Kavka (New York: Columbia University Press, 2001), pp. 126–160.

3. William F. Buckley asks, "Why are we so determined to 'understand' those whose behavior is anti-social, whether sowing disruptions in classrooms or seeds of life in lackadaisical engagements?" He continues, quoting John O'Sullivan with approval and insinuating that compassion is not a proper stance for Republicans: "When Bill Clinton feels our pain, his real emotion is mild self-satisfaction at his own sensitivity"; see Buckley, "On the Right," *Daily Tease Newsletter,* July 30, 1999.

4. "The Goldberg File," *National Review Online,* December 4, 1998. http://www.nationalreview.com/goldberg/goldberg120498.html

5. Marginalia (June 1849), in *Edgar Allan Poe: Essays and Reviews* (New York: Library of America, 1984), p. 1457. Not that Poe thought it preferable to make policy in the service of virtue instead: "The fact is, that in efforts to soar above our nature, we invariably fall below it. Your reformist demigods are merely devils turned inside out"; Marginalia (June 1849), in *Edgar Allan Poe: Essays and Reviews,* p. 1456.

6. What the platform authors meant was something like what some ethicists mean by *perfect* duty. Perfect duties enjoin specific acts. For example, I have a perfect duty to pay the debts that I have voluntarily incurred, to look after my children, to refrain from such acts as perjury, murder, and rape, to pay my taxes. According to this tradition, I also have imperfect duties to help strangers now and then, to develop my talents, and in general to improve things around me by seeing to others' happiness and the development of my own better nature. There need be no specific acts at issue in discharging imperfect duties. I might, for example, never give anyone a jump start in a parking lot, never give a sandwich to a street person, and never volunteer to work toward a good cause, but instead discharge my imperfect duties of benevolence by giving money to charity, donating canned goods to a food kitchen, and so on. I owe humanity the occasional act of benevolence. I do not owe kindness to particular strangers.

7. *Capital* traditionally calls to mind wage labor and some means-of-production-controlling other of wage labor. By invoking wagon trains and such, the platform draws attention to other faces of capital. The crucial aspects of North American colonial capital for the purposes of this essay are the institutions of race-slave-based agricultural production and relations with indigenous peoples in North America.

8. Not, I think, because it treats a bit of propaganda as if it was a train of thought. I am unconcerned about taking the platform seriously. While I do not expect party platforms to be well argued, I am trying to catch hold of a series of associations, and this one opens the series in two ways—first, as an occasion for reflecting on the place of compassion in contemporary American politics, and second as an occasion for thinking about its relation to colonial and neocolonial ideology.

9. See *On Liberty,* in *Collected Works of John Stuart Mill,* vol. 18, ed. John M. Robson (Toronto: University of Toronto Press, 1977), pp. 260–276.

10. Quoted in Kenneth Silverman, *Edgar A. Poe: Mournful and Never-Ending Remembrance* (New York: Harper Collins, 1991), pp. 72–73.

11. Edgar Poe, "Al Araaf," in *Edgar Allan Poe: Poetry and Tales* (New York: Library of America, 1984), fn., p. 49.
12. Silverman, *Edgar A. Poe,* p. 72.
13. Emerson, "The Conservative," in *Emerson: Essays and Poems,* ed. Joel Porte, Harold Bloom, and Paul Kane (New York: Library of America, 1996), p. 175.
14. Emerson, "The Conservative," p. 175.
15. Emerson, "The Conservative," p. 175.
16. Emerson, "The Conservative," p. 173.
17. It may also calm the old, I suppose, but the lecture's occasion suggests a youthful audience.
18. Emerson, "The Conservative," p. 182.
19. Emerson, "The Conservative," p. 174.
20. Emerson, "The Conservative," p. 174.
21. Cavell, "Emerson's Constitutional Amending," in *Philosophical Passages* (Oxford: Basil Blackwell, 1995), p. 30.
22. In this spirit, he marked the anniversary of emancipation in the British West Indies by announcing that with the freeing of slaves, "A man is added to the human family"; see "An Address Delivered in the Court-House in Concord, Massachusetts, on 1st August, 1844, on the Anniversary of the Emancipation of the Negroes in the British West Indies," in *Emerson: Essays and Poems,* p. 988. For fascinating discussion of Emerson's various ambivalences in the Concord address, see Christina Zwarg, *Feminist Conversations* (Ithaca, NY: Cornell University Press, 1995), pp. 133–137.
23. To some extent, Emerson knows this. At least, he seems to have known this through his intimacy with Margaret Fuller (who saw tremendous potential energy for social reform in the intolerably unstable place of woman in western culture, an energy that might fuel feminist collective political action if women were better educated). There is good reason to think that the impossible association of masculine and feminine that I have traced found its model for Emerson in his intercourse with Fuller, and its sexual anxiety in the trouble each had in finding an appropriate place for sexuality in thought about social justice. For an excellent reading of these intersections and formations, see Zwarg, *Feminist Conversations.* Her commentary on Cavell's reading of "Fate" is especially sensitive and acute. See *Feminist Conversations,* pp. 272–274.
24. For a fascinating meditation on the loneness of self-consciousness in Emerson, see Cavell, "Being Odd, Getting Even," in *The American Face of Edgar Allan Poe,* ed. Shawn Rosenheim and Stephen Rachman (Baltimore, MD: Johns Hopkins University Press, 1995), pp. 3–36, esp. pp. 4–13, where Cavell reads Emerson alongside Descartes and Nietzsche.
25. Marginalia (June 1849), in *Edgar Allan Poe: Essays and Reviews,* p. 1457.
26. Silverman, *Edgar A. Poe,* p. 397.
27. Hayden White makes the point by tracing an association between *ferus* (wild) and *ferrum* (iron), an association between the allegorical appropriation of the New England landscape as the desert of Christ's temptation, an understanding of temptation as a trial that ought to engender melancholy, and despair as an iron cage or rod. See White, "The Forms of

Wildness: Archaeology of an Idea," in his *Tropics of Discourse: Essays in Cultural Criticism* (Baltimore, MD: Johns Hopkins University Press, 1978), p. 181, n. 25.

28. Emerson found U.S. policy toward indigenous peoples outrageous. His intellectual intimate, Fuller, found in law and frontier practice a site for thinking cross-cultural catastrophe, but seems to have accepted the thought that the Native American was a tragic figure doomed to demise. Poe shared something of these views. He argued that our country's nickname should be *Appalachia* rather than *America,* partly because South America was also America and partly as a kind of epitaph: "in employing [*Appalachia*] we do honor to the Aborigines, whom, hitherto, we have at all points unmercifully despoiled, assassinated, and dishonored." Drawing on his own work on the sounds suited to remembrance, he also extols *Appalachia* for its mournful music—"Nothing," he writes, "could be more sonorous, more liquid, or of fuller volume, while its length is sufficient for dignity"; in *The Unknown Poe,* ed. Raymond Foye (San Francisco: City Lights Books, 1980) p. 47.

29. Quoted in Arthur Hobson Quinn, *Edgar Allan Poe: A Critical Biography* (Baltimore, MD: Johns Hopkins University Press, 1941/1998), p. 328. Poe seems not to have read much Emerson. And Poe was touchy about mysticism and transcendentalism, his own tales containing elements of both and sometimes being derided as German on that account, so little of northeastern American sensibility was there in his spiritual edge.

30. See Dayan, "Amorous Bondage: Poe, Ladies, and Slaves," in *The American Face of Edgar Allan Poe,* ed. Shawn Rosenheim and Stephen Rachman (Baltimore, MD: Johns Hopkins University Press, 1995), pp. 179–209. To read Poe in this frame is to give him the backhanded benefit of the doubt, which may itself comprise an act of compassion toward him. For example, it makes it possible to sense unsuspected acuity in his notoriously self-serving, often libelous accusations of conspiracy and villainous cruelty, fired off at the slightest provocation against Northern and Southern gentlemen alike. Charges of "conspiracy" and "cruelty" become ways of personalizing the impersonal politicoeconomic context.

31. There is some suggestion of the "pre"human in it. As Neville Hoad suggested in conversation on the topic, the pathology of the colonized body in such discourse is rather like the stuff of deep normative deviation (material for sublation). But the relevant sublation is fractured by the simultaneous existence of the full-blown, "developed" human, the colonizer, and its offspring (i.e., beings clearly placed on a developmental trajectory), rendering invocation of the Infantile or the Primordial in representation of subject beings catachreses rather than theses.

32. Spivak, "From Haverstock Hill Flat to U.S. Classroom, What's Left of Theory?" in *What's Left of Theory,* ed. Judith Butler, John Guillory, and Kendall Thomas (New York: Routledge, 2000), p. 26.

33. See Spivak, "From Haverstock Hill Flat to U.S. Classroom," pp. 26–33. Spivak reads the aboriginal and the rural as catachreses with respect to the abstractions crucial to value in capital, the steam from the pot where value cooks and is cooked, the bit of the matter in the air, if you like. On my reading, what Poe does (inadvertently) is more like warning us that

the door of a tomb is insecure than it is like lifting the lid on a pot. In Poe, at least, the carnality of the material pressure is so powerful that it makes more sense to focus on revenants than on ghosts.

34. In a strange way, Cavell's treatment of what is in the air for Emerson underscores this point. In Cavell's reading of Emerson's work on fate and freedom, the crucial question in the air is the question of slavery. On words, breath, and what is in the air, see Cavell, "Emerson's Constitutional Amending," pp. 24–25.

35. The list of Freudian readings of Poe is very long. For a handful of these, see Jacques Lacan, "Seminar on 'The Purloined Letter,'" trans. Jeffrey Mehlman, in *French Freud: Structural Studies in Psychoanalysis, Yale French Studies* 48 (1972): 39–72; Dorothea von Mücke, "The Imaginary Materiality of Writing in Poe's 'Ligeia,'" *differences,* 11.2 (1999): 53–75; J. Gerald Kennedy, "Poe, 'Ligeia,' and the Problem of Dying Women," in *New Essays on Poe's Major Tales,* ed. Kenneth Silverman (Cambridge: Cambridge University Press, 1993), pp. 113–130; and the essays on psychoanalytically informed French readings of Poe anthologized in *The Purloined Poe,* ed. John P. Muller and William J. Richardson (Baltimore, MD: Johns Hopkins University Press, 1988). Roger Forclaz's critique of Marie Bonaparte's reading is somehow to the point here: "From this point of view, Poe's sexuality may take any possible form: sadonecrophilia, mother-fixation, erotic aggression, revolt against the father, passivity towards the father . . . the formulas presented to us are irreconcilable and cancel one another"; "Psychoanalysis and Edgar Poe," in *Critical Essays on Edgar Allan Poe,* ed. Eric W. Carlson (Boston: G. K. Hall & Co., 1987), p. 191. Poe is so rich a subject for psychoanalysis as to rather exceed the constraints of singular psychoanalytic reading.

36. Marginalia (June 1849), in *Edgar Allan Poe: Essays and Reviews,* p. 1465.

37. Poe's quarrels with his adopted father, John Allan, conducted by mail, are perhaps the clearest examples. The letter to Allan dated January 8, 1831, is a case in point; after insisting that he had written a letter Allan asked him to write, Poe continues: "The time in which I wrote it was within a half hour after you had embittered every feeling of my heart against you by your abuse of my *family,* and myself, under your own roof—and at a time when you knew that my heart was almost breaking." Quoted in Arthur Hobson Quinn *Edgar Allan Poe,* pp. 166–167.

38. Poe, "Al Araaf," in *Edgar Allan Poe: Poetry and Tales,* fn., p. 49.

39. All references to "Ligeia" in the body of the text are from *Edgar Allan Poe: Poetry and Tales,* pp. 262–277; hereafter 1984a.

40. For extended discussion of psychasthenia, see Pierre Janet, "On the Pathogenesis of Some Impulsions," *Journal of Abnormal Psychology* I, April 1906, pp. 1–17.

41. See John Owen King III, *The Iron of Melancholy* (Middletown, CT: Wesleyan University Press, 1983). Joan Dayan, *Fables of Mind* (Oxford: Oxford University Press, 1987) reads Poe as the intellectual heir of the Lockean strand in Jonathan Edwards's writings. She is expressly interested in stressing Poe's Americanism and his stature in the service of championing Poe in the face of Emersonian views on U.S. letters at the mid-nineteenth century.

42. *Acquisition* is not a bad way of marking any of Ligeia's features, since plain volition is her métier. I do not mean to suggest that she laid claim to her parts herself. They are the legacy of the nameless forefathers. One could say that she reclaims them; but, of course, you cannot reclaim them because their context is gone. I will read her as carrying them.
43. The best-known composite being in Poe is probably the titular hero of "The Man That Was Used Up." The story begins just like Ligeia's story, in forgetfulness and remarks about personal appearance: "I cannot just now remember when or where I first made the acquaintance of that truly fine-looking fellow, Brevet Brigadier General John A. B. C. Smith"; in *Edgar Allan Poe: Poetry and Tales*, p. 307. The general is all made of prosthetic replacement parts and alternately terrifies and fascinates the (probably psychasthenic) narrator as these are assembled with the aid of Pompey, "an old Negro valet." The general's original equipment was taken in various wars with indigenous peoples, and the black man helps him reassemble himself into the much-admired fellow that he is.

It would take me beyond the scope of this essay to read "The Man Who Was Used Up" here. Suffice to say that we get the links between composite bodies, forgetfulness, beauty, and even statuary (the narrator's first impression of the general is taken from viewing a commemorative bust) in both Ligeia's story and his, but that the parts of the victor/agent-of-conquest are designed for him whereas the female/colonized body parts are functionally indeterminate, that the woman's parts are relics of lost things whereas the victor's parts are manufactured for his use, that the victor is *used* up by wars of conquest whereas the woman is made up of things whose use is no longer their distinguishing feature. A teleological order disrupted by colonial enterprise can be remade after a (self-styled) fashion for the victor but not for the likes of Ligeia or her comparatively useless husband.
44. Dayan, "Amorous Bondage: Poe, Ladies, and Slaves," in *The American Face of Edgar Allan Poe,* p. 200.
45. Dayan, "Amorous Bondage: Poe, Ladies, and Slaves," in *The American Face of Edgar Allan Poe,* p. 201. Dayan's emphasis on ivory suggests the Orientalist tropes at the heart of representation of the tragic mulatta or octoroon mistress. The complexity of appropriation, distancing exoticism, domestication, and alterity at such junctures is considerable. The feminine figure emerges as made of trophies and shame all at once, without being entirely of the world that produced her, to its credit and its disgrace.
46. You can tell that the narrator is an American because of his method of furnishing a room. See Poe, "The Philosophy of Furniture," in *Edgar Allan Poe: Poetry and Tales*, pp. 382–387. I will take up the narrator's decorating scheme below. Here note that what secured the fortunes of psychasthenic Americans was usually their forefathers' and families' success in various colonizing enterprises. These ancestors are no part of Ligeia's story, the narrator assures us (and while it is hard to take him at his word, we can at least allow that whatever unites Ligeia and the narrator is not based in familial continuity). Whatever in Ligeia is made possible by the conditions that produced her is *not* the thing she threatens to set

in motion. This is partly why I am reading her as colonized rather than colonizing. Dayan's reading of race in Ligeia is another part. More reasons for the emphasis will, I hope, emerge in what follows.

47. For excellent discussion of this word, see Barbara Johnson's "Strange Fits: Poe and Wordsworth on the Nature of Poetic Language," in *The American Face of Edgar Allan Poe,* pp. 37–48.

48. In a strange way, this description fits Emerson's prose style, suggesting that his rhetorical practices intersect with Poe's. To whatever extent it makes sense to read the pair as producing differently inadequate responses to a similar ethical problem, this is unsurprising. Emerson is staging a starting place. Poe is staging the impossibility of moving forward from it in the terms set by focus on the individual.

49. Poe, "Edgar Allan Poe" (1848), in *Edgar Allan Poe: Poetry and Tales,* p. 868.

50. Kennedy, "'Ligeia' and the Problem of Dying Women," in *New Essays on Poe's Major Tales,* p. 121.

3

Calculating Compassion

KATHLEEN WOODWARD

Compassion, like so many of our other complex emotions, has a heady political life. Invoking compassion is an important means of trying to direct social, political, and economic resources in one's direction (indeed, compassion is one of those resources).

—————Elizabeth Spelman, *The Fruits of Sorrow* (88)

During the second presidential debate of the 1992 election, the three candidates—George Bush, Bill Clinton, and Ross Perot—were asked by a woman in the studio audience in Richmond, Virginia, how their own lives had been affected by the national debt. It was a moment that was to prove decisive. President George Bush, perplexed and nonplussed, literally did not understand the question. "I'm not sure I get it," he said. "Help me with the question and I'll try to answer."[1] Clinton, opening his arms, moved toward the audience and responded that he personally knew people in Arkansas who were suffering because they had lost their jobs. The clear implication was that he acutely felt their pain and Bush did not. What was at stake was the presidential politics of empathy. The rest is history.

Two weeks later, Bush, criticizing Clinton's plan to establish an office devoted to AIDS in Washington, insisted: "We need more compassion in our hometowns, more education, more caring."[2] If in fact there was a concerted effort on the part of the Bush campaign to establish compassion as a strong theme in 1992, it failed. But as we all know, eight years later the rhetoric of empathy uncannily returned, surfacing in George W. Bush's campaign against Al Gore. What the elder George Bush fumbled, the son repossessed. Under the well-calculated banner of compassionate conservatism, the Republicans successfully appropriated the rhetoric of feeling that had been so powerfully associated with the Democrats. Indeed, the presidential race of 2000 at times seemed marked by a competition between Al Gore and George W. Bush in terms of who could lay claim to being the most compassionate. Feeling someone else's pain. Compassionate conservatism. These presidential campaign slogans are testimony to the pivotal power of a national discourse of empathy, one on which, in great part, the political fortunes of George Bush, Bill Clinton, and George W. Bush turned.[3]

How do we understand the uses of compassion in the body politic today? How do appeals to sentiment—specifically to compassion—work? What are the limits of compassion? How do liberal and conservative narratives of compassion differ? In this essay I thread my way through some of the debates about the political efficacy of compassion, focussing on the work of scholars of sentiment—legal scholar Lynne Henderson, philosophers Martha Nussbaum and Elizabeth Spelman, and Lauren Berlant in literary and cultural studies. Taken together, the work of these scholars can be said to present the liberal narrative of compassion, albeit variously embraced and critiqued. I also consider some of the statements made about compassion by Republicans, including George W. Bush as well as Marvin Olasky, the author of *Compassionate Conservatism*, and Joseph Jacobs, the author of *The Compassionate Conservative*. Ultimately I conclude that the politically astute appropriation of the discourse of compassion by the George W. Bush presidential campaign in 2000 was made possible in part by the convergence of two distinct—and usually contradictory—trends in the way emotions are experienced and performed in contemporary culture: on the one hand, we are witnessing a flattening of the psychological emotions to intensities; on the other hand, we are witnessing the emergence of the sensitive man, the development of the man of feeling.

I have argued elsewhere that we are living in a cultural moment in which a new economy of the emotions is emerging.[4] Once relatively stable, discourses of the emotions are now circulating at a rapid rate. Even as the possibilities of an individual's emotional repertoire are expanding (hence the emergence of the man of feeling), our postmodern culture is increasingly characterized by what Fredric Jameson has called the waning of affect. I agree with Jameson's analysis. In a culture dominated by the media, much of our emotional experience, once understood in terms of a psychology of depth and interiority, has been reduced to intensities or sensations. Sensations such as the thrills spiked by good action films, or, as I explore in another essay, sensations such as the panic induced by the omnipresent discourse of statistical risks to one's health.[5] Or, given George W. Bush's rallying cry of compassionate conservatism, sensations such as the short-term intensity of self-satisfied sympathy. At the same time, if in the 1950s in the United States the emotions were distributed in the white middle class according to gender in conventional or stereotypical ways, this has radically changed. Generally speaking, we can say that in the 1950s the expression of grief was proscribed in men, the expression of anger in women. But today cultural scripts for the emotions are more flexible or mixed. The presidential campaigns of 1992 and 2000 are perfect cases in point. If conventional wisdom tells us that women are more empathetic than men, our cultural moment requires that our male leaders be both strong and sensitive, thus allowing them to play both conventional gender parts simultaneously; or, more accurately, that they display or perform sensitivity; or, in a further compression of story to slogan in our media-dominated culture, that they at least deploy the rhetoric of sensitivity. In the instance of Bush's compassionate conservatism, the two trends in the way the emotions are experienced and performed in contemporary culture coalesce: the performance of compassion by George W. Bush as a presidential candidate is paradoxically an instance of the flattening of feeling. The slogan "compassionate conservatism" trades on the rhetoric of feeling even as it is curiously empty of it. In this sense "compassionate conservatism" can be said to be an oxymoron.

It was widely remarked that President George W. Bush's inaugural speech of January 20, 2001, was long on the rhetoric of compassion and short on the principles of conservatism. But in terms of action, the converse has been the definite case in the Bush administration. The public masculinization of sentiment by Republicans serves as a screen for the privatization of the state, for the divestiture of the federal government of responsibility for many of our nation's citizens. The phrase "compassionate conservatism" is also code for the federal turn to faith-based organizations to undertake what could be called private spiritual and social work with public dollars.[6] There is a canny historical logic to this. In the United States there is a long tradition of the association of the private sphere with the feminine, with sentiment, and with religion. I am thinking here in particular of the nineteenth century, when what has been called the culture of sentiment stretched roughly from 1830 to 1870.[7] That this period saw the publication of the most famous—and effective—instance of the fictional sentimental narrative would seem to be no accident. Indeed, Harriet Beecher Stowe's *Uncle Tom's Cabin, or Life Among the Lowly* is the narrative to which scholars of sentiment in literary and cultural studies inevitably return. In the United States it is the ur-text of the liberal narrative of compassion.

Published in 1852, Harriet Beecher Stowe's *Uncle Tom's Cabin, or Life Among the Lowly* was the first book in the United States to sell over a million copies. Praised by literary critic Jane Tompkins in her own influential *Sensational Designs* as a potent cultural force in the abolition of slavery, *Uncle Tom's Cabin* has been widely credited with accomplishing, in Tompkins's phrase, important cultural work. In *Uncle Tom's Cabin*, the way of justice—I use the term, with its religious overtones, advisedly—is that of compassion. The reader is prompted to identify empathetically with a character that is suffering (generally through the medium of another character), and this response is read as an experience in moral pedagogy. A spontaneous burst of feeling leads to a change of heart; the emotions and morality are linked. Consider this small scene from *Uncle Tom's Cabin*. In a chapter entitled "The Little Evangelist," the tenderhearted little Eva, herself soon to die, takes pity on Topsy, the unruly, undisciplined slave girl who does not believe in God and who is driving everyone in the St. Clare household to distraction:

> "O, Topsy, poor child, *I* love you!" said Eva, with a sudden burst of feeling, and laying her little thin, white hand on Topsy's shoulder; "I love you, because you haven't had any father, or mother, or friends;—because you've been a poor, abused child! I love you and I want you to be good." (p. 409)

The tears in Eva's eyes beget tears in Topsy. Compassion inspires conversion. As Stowe writes, "The round, keen eyes of the black child were overcast with tears;—large, bright drops rolled heavily down, one by one, and fell on the little white hand. Yes, in that moment, a ray of real belief, a ray of heavenly love, had penetrated the darkness of her heathen soul" (p. 410). Salvation comes through love, here motherly love. Eva touches the abused Topsy, literally and emotionally. The drama has religious overtones; the laying on of hands has healing power. Topsy is granted faith. She also, as we would say today, acquires self-esteem. Hence key to the liberal narrative of compassion is a scene of personal suffering and pain. Topsy, portrayed partially as a comic figure, is a poor slave accustomed to being whipped, a motherless child. Also key to the liberal narrative of compassion is a witness—here the character of Eva and, further, the reader. Through the medium of Eva, the reader is called on to feel that pain, to understand Topsy's suffering, and to resolve to act like Eva and hence comprehend the injustice that is slavery.

I

Although they draw on texts that represent vastly different aesthetics, Lynne Henderson, Martha Nussbaum, Elizabeth Spelman, and Lauren Berlant can be seen as the heirs to this tradition. Their work attests to the high degree of interest in the emotion of compassion today, although it make its appearance under different names—empathy, pity, compassion, sympathy. Interested in the cultural politics of the emotions, coming from different disciplines, they variously stress the importance and ubiquity of personal narratives of suffering in eliciting compassion. For the most part they are not in dialogue with each other, and hence one of the purposes of this essay is to gather them together.

Both Henderson and Nussbaum make the case for compassion, or empathy, with conviction, if not passion, in ways that a scholar of cultural studies might well find pre-ideological and naïve. I am interested in their work, finding it preeminently reasonable, if not critical, and promising of practical consequences. Spelman and Berlant offer a more critical, if not severe, view of the uncertain relation between feeling and action or the limits of what I call liberal compassion. When is compassion translated into protest at injustice or transmuted into policy to alleviate suffering? When are these virtuous feelings fleeting, mere transient simulations of a passion for justice that by definition requires sustained commitment? In the space of this essay I will not be able to do justice to their arguments, strong and subtle as they are. I should note too that my primary intention is not so much to challenge their positions—indeed, it seems to me that they are each of them quite right in many respects—but rather to show the common ground among them even as they represent a wide spectrum of attitudes about the limits of compassion in the body politic, ranging from the brightly optimistic to the incisively pessimistic.

Lynne Henderson's purpose in her preeminently clear and wide-ranging essay "Legality and Empathy," published in 1987, is to persuade us that empathy should be cultivated as a moral capacity on the part of judges. For Henderson, empathy is a mode of understanding that includes both affect and cognition and "reveals moral problems" occluded by a reductionist legal rationality (p. 1576). She identifies three basic meanings associated with empathy: feeling the emotion of another; understanding the experience of that other person; and, perhaps most important for my purposes, the specific feeling of sympathy or compassion for a person, a feeling that "can lead to action in order to help or alleviate the pain of another" (p. 1582). "Empathy," she writes, "is the foundational phenomenon for intersubjectivity, which is *not* absorption by the other, but rather simply the relationship of self to other, individual to community" (p. 1584). She quotes the philosopher Bernard Williams, who believes that "sympathetic identification with others . . . [is] basic to ethical human experience" (p. 1585).[8] How does this identification take place? How is empathy fostered?

In the courtroom, what elicits empathy, Henderson believes, is a narrative that conveys the texture of emotional experience—specifically, the experience of suffering. Arguing that conventional legal discourse and the rule of law relentlessly refuse empathetic narratives,[9] she shows how the decisions of four important cases brought before the U.S. Supreme Court—*Brown v. Board of Education I* (1952), *Shapiro v. Thompson* (1969), *Roe v. Wade* (1973), and *Bowers v. Hardwick* (1986)—turned on the presence or absence of empathetic narratives in oral argument and on the understanding of these narratives or the lack of it on the part of the judges. "The argumentative steps taken to convey human situations to a judge might be described as creating affective understanding by use of a narrative that includes emotion and description ('thick' description, if you will) of a human situation created by, resulting from, or ignored by legal structures, and consciously placing that narrative within a legal framework," she concludes (p. 1592).

My principal point here is that these four cases are all characterized, albeit in different ways, by narratives of suffering: in *Brown v. Board of Education,* by the suffering of African Americans who were legally barred from attending schools with whites; in *Shapiro v. Thompson,* by the suffering of the poor, specifically people who moved to a new state and, on the basis of a one-year residency requirement, were denied welfare; in *Roe v. Wade,* by the suffering of pregnant women who had been denied access to abortion; and finally, in *Bowers v. Hardwick,* by gays in America who were persecuted for their sexual practices.

In her analysis of *Brown v. Board of Education,* for instance, Henderson concludes that it was the evocation of African-American suffering that ultimately convinced the hearts and minds of the majority on the U.S. Supreme Court to question the morality—and hence the legality—of segregation. The word "pain" rings throughout her discussion. *Brown v. Board of Education,* she writes, "was remarkable, and it remains so, in large part because it is a human opinion responding to the pain inflicted on outsiders by the law" (p. 1594). She regards the opinion of the Court as conveying the crucial "recognition of human experience and pain—of feeling" (p. 1594). Thurgood Marshall's arguments before the Court, she points out, relied repeatedly on "the narrative of the painful experience of being black in American society" (p. 1596). One of the dimensions of this pain, Marshall argued, is "humiliation," which is an "actual injury" (Argument 42). In the case of *Brown,* Henderson concludes that the three dimensions of empathy were present: "Feeling the distress of the blacks, understanding the painful situation created by segregation, and responding to the cry of pain by action" (p. 1607). Here the triumph is that, in her words, "legality in its many forms clashed with empathy, and empathy ultimately transformed legality" (p. 1594).

If scenes of personal pain are key to eliciting compassion, I want to stress that Henderson does not assume that a narrative of suffering will necessarily prompt understanding in those on the bench. She acknowledges that people are more likely to empathize with people who are like themselves. She understands the difficulty imposed by different cultural contexts. She is altogether aware of the power of racism, sexism, and other forms of prejudice. Indeed her examples also bear out the failure of empathetic narratives as tools of persuasion because the divide or difference between those judging and those being judged was too great to be bridged imaginatively. *Roe v. Wade* is one of them. "In *Brown*," she asserts, "the Court saw the pain and stigma of being black in America; in the abortion cases, the Court has arguably failed to see the pain, despair, and stigma of women with 'unwanted' pregnancies and 'unwanted' children" (p. 1620). Male justices could not fully understand the possible suffering caused for women by unwanted pregnancy. *Bowers v. Harwick* is another example, a case in which, Henderson concludes, there was a complete absence of empathetic understanding; indeed, instead of compassion, the dominant emotion seemed to be hate, a "perversion of empathy" (p. 1638). A man named Michael Hardwick, through a series of coincidences, was found by a police officer engaging in oral sex with another man in his own home. He was arrested under the Georgia law against sodomy and charged with a felony. The U.S. Supreme Court voted to uphold the sodomy law in Georgia. Henderson suggests that in this case the very absence of vivid empathetic narratives about the prejudice suffered by gays may have contributed to the unfeeling verdict. Hence if Henderson certainly questions any necessary connection between empathetic narratives—or narratives of compassion—and a compassionate judgment formed in part by responding to such a narrative, she is nevertheless decidedly optimistic about the possibility that such narratives *might* prompt action, which in her world would mean good judgments in our legal system.[10]

Here Henderson joins the philosopher Martha Nussbaum, who identifies compassion as the basic social emotion. In an excellent essay published in 1996 under the title "Compassion: The Basic Social Emotion," Nussbaum argues persuasively that compassion is a moral sentiment characterized by a certain mode of reason or of judgment; hence, like Henderson, she believes that emotion in general and compassion in particular can have a cognitive edge.[11] Like Henderson, Nussbaum sees compassion as an emotional bridge between the individual and the community, as, in a formulation that I think Henderson would admire, "a bridge to justice" (37).

For Nussbaum, compassion is also an instance of what she has elsewhere called the "narrative emotions," that is, emotions called up by literature, teaching us, in her view, about suffering. It is hence by design that she opens her essay by evoking the tragic suffering of Philoctetes in Sophocles' drama of the same name. Later in her essay she draws on what she calls the contemporary novel of realism—Richard Wright's *Native Son* is one of her examples—to think through the role of compassion. She concludes her essay with recommendations for putting compassion to use in public life today. Among her suggestions is the sensible call for a multicultural education in our schools, one of the primary bases of which would be the study of narratives of suffering. As she advises, "public education at every level should cultivate the ability to imagine the experiences of others and to participate in their sufferings" (p. 50).

One of Nussbaum's purposes is to recuperate under the rubric of compassion the original meaning of pity in the Aristotelian sense: pity entailed the spectator's sense that he or she could suffer similar misfortune. This was crucial, she argues, to a vision of social justice. Over time, however, pity acquired the injurious sense of the superiority of the spectator. This is clearly seen in the definition of compassion given in the *Oxford English Dictionary:* "The feeling or emotion, when a person is moved by the suffering or distress of another, and by the desire to relieve it; pity that inclines one to spare or to succour." Whereas compassion as "participation in suffering; fellow-feeling, sympathy" is obsolete, compassion is now understood as an emotion "shown towards a person in distress by one who is free from it, who is, in this respect, his superior." In Nussbaum's view, this negative connotation of condescension, which is implicit in the definition of pity today, works against a vision of social justice. I agree. Nonetheless Nussbaum does not so much concern herself with the dangers of appropriation of feeling as with the possibility of what she calls a "sense of commonness" (p. 35). This is a liberal position. But she is clearly sensitive to questions of difference. And this is also a liberal position. I quote her at some length:

> Pity does indeed involve empathetic identification as one component: for in estimating the seriousness of the suffering, it seems important, if not sufficient, to attempt to take its measure as the person herself measures it. But even then, in the temporary act of identification, one is always aware of one's own *separateness* from the sufferer—it is for *another*, and not oneself, that one feels; and one is aware both of the bad lot of the sufferer and of the fact that it is, right now, not one's own. . . . One must also be aware of one's own *qualitative difference* from the sufferer: aware, for example, that Philoctetes has no children and no friends, as one does oneself. For these recognitions are crucial in getting the right estimation of the meaning of the suffering. (p. 35)

As with Henderson, then, Nussbaum cautions that in responding to suffering, we must take care to take our own difference into account, to understand it. But there is a significant difference between them. As the cases she discusses attest, Henderson identifies, if you will, predominately with people who are suffering at the hands of social injustice, from the cruelties of a prejudiced society. Nussbaum, on the other hand, writes primarily from the point of view of the person who witnesses suffering, from the point of view of the reader or spectator, and her focus in the above passage is telling. Philoctetes is a tragic hero, a subject of tragedy. He is exemplary, not a common man.

Finally, Nussbaum argues convincingly that one may understand a situation with compassion even though one does not have the *feeling* itself. At base she understands compassion as "a certain sort of thought about the well-being of others," as "a certain sort of reasoning" (p. 28). How is this possible? If one has had the experience of the feeling of compassion, if one has learned to be sensitive to suffering, and if one feels passionately about social justice, and if this has become part and parcel of how one evaluates situations and is moved to action, then, Nussbaum concludes, one "has pity whether he experiences this or that tug in his stomach or not." "No such particular bodily feeling is necessary," she continues (p. 38). She joins Henderson here, who emphasizes the importance not just of feeling pain but of *understanding* the experience of suffering. Nussbaum makes a crucial theoretical distinction here, one that has significant aesthetic consequences: it allows her to distance herself from the aesthetic of the sentimental. One need not be, in Nussbaum's world, moved to tears in order to be moved to pity, her preferred term. In fact, given her taste in narrative (she is drawn to Beckett, not Stowe), she would no doubt agree with the poet Wallace Stevens that "[s]entimentality is a failure of feeling" (p. 162).

In her thoughtful book *Fruits of Sorrow: Framing Our Attention to Suffering*, the philosopher Elizabeth Spelman, unlike Henderson and Nussbaum, does not so much make the case for compassion as explore some of the complex contradictions that can be involved in the various ways our attention is focused on suffering. She draws on a wide spectrum of work—from Plato and Aristotle to Jean Fagin Yellin and Bill T. Jones. But in the context of my essay, it is her discussion of Harriet Jacobs's *Incidents in the Life of a Slave Girl*, written as a first-person narrative and published under the pseudonym of Linda Brent in 1861, that is most relevant. For Jacobs was herself, as Spelman shows, exquisitely attuned to the dangers as well as the promises posed by using compassion as a political tool in calling attention to the evils of slavery. Spelman in effect suggests that Jacobs rewrote *Uncle Tom's Cabin* by adding outrage to the emotional score of sentimentality, thereby emphasizing not just the importance of an individual's compassionate response to another's pain but also the importance of judging the institution of slavery. In such a case, compassion, in other words, must include the element of recognizing injustice, which is a political and social condition, not only an existential one.

Spelman quotes this passage from the book written by the former slave: "'Could you have seen that mother clinging to her child, when they fastened the irons upon his wrists; could you have heard her heart-rending groans, and seen her blood-shot eyes wander wildly from face to face, vainly pleading for mercy, could you have witnessed that scene as I saw it, you would exclaim, *Slavery is damnable*'" (pp. 78–79). Jacobs draws on the conventions of the sentimental but she stops short, surprising us by withholding the rhetoric of tears that is the stock in trade of sentimental literature, and inserting instead the rhetoric of outrage. A narrative scene of suffering is key. But the emotional response demanded of the reader is more complex than that in the scene I quoted earlier from *Uncle Tom's Cabin,* in which Eva sympathized with Topsy as a motherless child. The tender feeling of compassion, Spelman suggests, can be seductive, serving to seal a short circuit of feeling, confining it to the individual. Outrage, on the other hand, is here directed at the slave owners, which is just as it should be. Deserving of compassion, the slave is not reduced to a mere victim but retains moral agency, issuing a judgment call.

Not surprisingly, Spelman shrinks from the social structure of hierarchy and condescension implied by the contemporary understanding of pity; although she understands that compassion and pity are often used interchangeably, unlike Nussbaum she does not want to recuperate pity as a useful political emotion—and I agree that there is no reason to fight what would be, I think, a vain rhetorical battle. Yet for Spelman, as with Nussbaum, a person who experiences compassion for another is one who in fact imagines that they too could be the subject of suffering. All in all Spelman strikes a wise balance between the illicit appropriation of the pain of others and the possibilities of understanding others' pain. As she writes, "despite the ever-present possibility of such exploitative sentimentality—and here again is the tension, the paradox, in appropriation—it would be absurd to deny that in some important sense people can and should try to put on the experiences of other" (p. 119). I appreciate her common sense. At the same time, one of the continuing concerns throughout the pages of her book is the following question, and in her hands it is a both a philosophical and a political question: When does the feeling of compassion become an end in itself and thwart action? Ultimately, for Spelman, a cultural politics of compassion is understood as one that can have valuable effects and must be judged case by case.

The most trenchant indictment of the contradictions implicit in the sentimental narrative in relation to the politics of the American nation has been offered by Lauren Berlant.[12] In a brilliant essay entitled "Poor Eliza," she examines a rich archive of texts that draw on the strategies and tropes of *Uncle Tom's Cabin,* the ur-text of the American liberal narrative of compassion. Indeed, her title refers to *Uncle Tom's Cabin* through the textual relay—or what Berlant wonderfully calls an "emotional quotation or affective citation" (p. 647)—

of Rogers and Hammerstein's 1949 musical *The King and I,* which contains a memorable scene where a female slave in the king's court in Siam herself stages the scene from *Uncle Tom's Cabin* in which the slave Eliza runs for her life. In a complex reading of the musical, Berlant acknowledges the salutary aspects associated with the evocation of Stowe's novel, among them the impetus of a nation to be socially progressive at a critical historical juncture. But ultimately the scaffold of the sentimental, Berlant insists, collapses under the untenable weight of its contradictions:

> when sentimentality meets politics, it uses personal stories to tell of structural effects, but in so doing it risks thwarting its very attempt to perform rhetorically a scene of pain that must be soothed politically. Because the ideology of true feeling cannot admit the nonuniversality of pain, its cases become all jumbled together and the ethical imperative toward social transformation is replaced by a civic-minded but passive ideal of empathy. The political as a place of acts oriented toward publicness becomes replaced by a world of private thoughts, leanings, and gestures. (p. 641)

The sentimental framing of suffering, Berlant insists, is corrupt for many reasons, not least of which is that the sentimental narrative relies on scenes of pain that wrongly presume such suffering is universal. For the pain of slavery cannot be understood fully or assumed by a white middle-class reader; the politics of personal feeling cannot address the institutional (or what Berlant calls the structural) reasons for injustice. The narrative affords the pleasure of consuming the feeling of vicarious suffering—and its putative moral precipitate, the feeling of self-satisfaction that we wish to do the right thing and hence are virtuous. But the experience of being moved by these sentimental scenes of suffering, whose ostensible purpose is to awaken us to redress injustice, works instead to return us to a private world far removed from the public sphere. Hence, in a crippling contradiction, Berlant concludes, the result of such empathetic identification is not the impulse to action but rather a "passive" posture. Fundamentally, therefore, the sentimental narrative is deliciously consumable and cruelly ineffective. Berlant's critique of the sentimental narrative, or sentimental liberalism, is severe, even unforgiving. The genre of the sentimental narrative itself is morally bankrupt.[13]

But in "Poor Eliza," Berlant identifies as well what she calls the postsentimental text, offering James Baldwin's essay on *Uncle Tom's Cabin* entitled "Everyone's Protest Novel" (1949), Robert Waller's *The Bridges of Madison County* (1992), and Toni Morrison's *Beloved* (1987) as templates. What differentiates these texts from sentimental texts? Among other things, a clear-eyed if nonetheless ambivalent refusal of the fantastical optimism central to the sentimental narrative and more specifically, with "Everyone's Protest Novel," the "powerful language of rageful truth-telling" (p. 656). Like Harriet Jacobs, Baldwin adds outrage to the sentimental score, in effect understanding such a complex response to suffering as necessarily having a cognitive component. In "Little Eliza," Berlant's purpose is not only to critique the sentimental liberalism she abhors but also to explore the possibilities of a sentimental radicalism. Her own essay, concluding with an eloquent discussion of *Beloved,* itself rises to the condition of possibility beyond both cynical reason and an empty, commodified optimism based on falsely shared suffering.

The kinds of texts—literary, philosophical, cultural—that Henderson, Nussbaum, Spelman, and Berlant take up as paradigmatic are assuredly different, and hence their positions must necessarily be different as well. Henderson focuses on oral argument in the U.S. Supreme Court from the 1950s to the 1980s; Nussbaum, notwithstanding her references to contemporary multicultural texts, on Greek tragedy; Spellman and Berlant, on nineteenth- and twentieth-century literature and art that protest social injustice and are more complex and register ambivalence about the possibilities for social redress than does the optimistic sentimental narrative. In Nussbaum's world of liberal compassion, for example, we are far from Berlant's unrelenting critique of the aesthetic ideology of the sentimental. Nonetheless, all four emphasize scenes of suffering and of pain as basic to what I am calling the liberal narrative of compassion. All four as well are concerned, albeit to different degrees, with the potential corrupting relation of unequal power between the one who suffers and the one who witnesses that suffering, as well as with the related question of the ineffectiveness or effectiveness of the moral response evoked—whether empathy, pity, compassion, or sympathy—in achieving social justice.[14] Finally, all invest an appropriate emotional moral response, whatever it is called, with a cognitive component, arguing that a critical understanding of social injustice is crucial.

II

If sophisticated attention is being given today in the academy to the cultural politics of compassion, with serious concerns about its efficacy, the rhetoric of compassion, appropriated by George W. Bush, had a resounding success in the last presidential election. What calculus is involved in a conservatism that is labeled compassionate? What characterizes a conservative narrative of compassion?

In the liberal narrative of compassion, the word "compassion" is used primarily as a noun or a predicate adjective in relation to people. A person feels compassion or is compassionate. Compassion is a feeling, and it is embodied. In the conservative narrative, in contrast, compassion is deployed predominantly as an adjective, one that characterizes an ideological stance, policy, or program. Bush not only ran on a platform of compassionate conservatism, he has described his budget as compassionate. Detached from people, compassion is attached to policies and practices. Oddly, in the mouths of conservatives, the adjective "compassionate" seems to have no referent to a feeling at all—or at least not to the feeling of sympathy that is associated with compassion. It is merely a word that refers, through a sleight of rhetoric, to economic conservatism. Here is, I believe, an instance of the waning of affect that pervades postmodern culture.

Furthermore, even if sentiment, or sensitivity, is performed, it does not seem linked to sympathy for others. Consider, for example, the way in which Bush seemed moved during the delivery of his inaugural speech, affected by the rhetoric of his vision for America. At the same time a politics of gender is also at work. If compassion does not entail sympathy, it clearly does refer to a strict and stern paternalism, to the demand for discipline and responsibility. Under the screen of the feminine, compassion is masculinized in conventional tones. On July 22, 1999, in Indianapolis, for instance, in what is regarded as his first major policy address as a presidential candidate, George W. Bush pledged to "rally the armies of compassion in our communities to fight a very different war against poverty" and praised programs that practice "severe mercy" (Olasky 2000, 219). How far we are from the teary, sentimental rhetoric of *Uncle Tom's Cabin,* from Thurgood Marshall's passionate arguments in *Brown v. Board of Education,* from Harriet Jacobs's outrage, from Richard Wright's harrowing *Native Son,* and from Toni Morrison's *Beloved.*

What kinds of stories do compassionate conservatives tell? In our televisual political culture, a narrative of compassion is condensed into a visual sound bite. Hence, if Bill Clinton, in his January 20, 1999, State of the Union address, introduced Rosa Parks, calling up decades of struggle over civil rights and evoking her suffering as a profile in courage, to whom did George W. Bush gesture in his February 27, 2001, speech to Congress outlining his budget proposal? Appropriating the Democratic strategy of referring to people in the audience, Bush first pointed to John Street, Democratic mayor of Philadelphia, who has supported faith-based organizations in Philadelphia, and second, to Steven and Josefina Ramos:

> With us tonight, representing many American families, are Steven and Josefina Ramos. They are from Pennsylvania, but they could be from any one of your districts. Steven is a network administrator for a school district, Josefina is a Spanish teacher at a charter school, and they have a 2-year-old daughter. Steven and Josefina tell me they pay almost $8,000 a year in federal income taxes; my plan will save them more than $2,000. Let me tell you what Steven says: "Two thousand dollars a year means a lot to my family. If we had this money it would help us reach our goal of paying off our personal debt in two years time."[15]

Compassion is here referred to only through the implied relay to economic conservatism, which is in fact what compassionate conservatism is. Here is the calculus of compassionate conservatism laid bare. Note also that none of the members of this small nuclear family are suffering in the ways underlined in the cases brought before the U.S. Supreme Court that Henderson discusses. The *feeling* of compassion is not evoked. We are not told a story, which implies a past. Indeed there is no real *story* here. We are presented instead with the possibility of a bright economic future and the principle that people are to be rewarded for identifying goals and working hard to achieve them. Note also that there is only a gesture to difference—Steven and Josefina Ramos are presumably Hispanic—but the possible harsh realities of prejudice based on difference are not invoked. Instead these three people represent "many American families." Here we have a condensed version of the American Dream. As Lauren Berlant writes in *The Queen of America Goes to Washington City*, the American Dream "fuses private fortune with that of the nation: it promises that if you invest your energies in work and in family-making, the nation will secure the broader social and economic conditions in which your labor can gain value and your life can be lived with dignity. It is a story that addresses the fear of being stuck or reduced to a type, a redemptive story pinning its hope on class mobility" (p. 94).

What is the model for this condensed narrative of conservative compassion? Marvin Olasky's *Compassionate Conservatism: What It Is, What It Does, and How It Can Transform America*, published in 2000 and graced with a foreword by then-Governor George W. Bush, provides a template. A professor of journalism at the University of Texas at Austin and a born-again Christian, Marvin Olasky has been credited with the formulation of "compassionate conservatism," although ironically, as he himself points out, it appears that the phrase itself was first used by none other than Bill Clinton's good friend Vernon Jordan in 1981 (p. 9). *Compassionate Conservatism* is the triumphant sequel to Olasky's *The Tragedy of American Compassion*, a book published eight years earlier which traces the policies of compassionate conservatism to their roots in colonial America. If *Uncle Tom's Cabin* provides the reader with a sentimental education, enacting a moral pedagogy of the emotions, *Compassionate Conservatism* is a narrative of the political education of the younger generation, rehearsing the political—and spiritual—pedagogy of entrepreneurship, faith, and tough love. If *Uncle Tom's Cabin* and *Incidents in the Life of a Slave Girl* foreground scenes of feeling that are coded as feminine, Olasky's narrative is gendered male.

The father of four sons, Olasky recounts the journey he took in 1999 with his fourteen-year-old son Daniel to visit programs around the United States that embody the tenets of compassionate conservatism. A political travelogue of discovery, a field trip about government for a high school student, the narrative is, like *Uncle Tom's Cabin*, one of transformation. Transformation, however, is not a matter of enlightenment about the suffering of other people. Rather it is about what works. "The travel changed Daniel in several vital ways," Olasky writes, "but had also changed me. I became convinced that the best way to understand compassionate conservatism is not to go through a list of theoretical statements but to walk the streets of our large cities and talk with those whose faith is so strong that they refuse to give in" (p. 22).

In the course of the narrative, father and son, who live in Austin, travel to Houston and Dallas, Indianapolis and Camden, Philadelphia and Minneapolis, St. Louis and Washington, D.C. Consider Olasky's account of their visit to Indianapolis, the city where George W. Bush delivered his first major speech as a presidential candidate in July 1999. Olasky begins his chapter on Indianapolis by briefly sketching its business history and then taking us to the twenty-fifth floor office of the mayor, Steve Goldsmith, who, we are told, established the Front Porch Alliance, which throughout the nineties brought together "faith-based and other civic organizations to develop eight hundred partnerships for neighborhood action" (p. 62).

From the height of government, we descend into the streets of Indianapolis and are introduced to one person after another, all of whom have successfully developed a program or a center with support from city government, and virtually all of whom have a strong belief in Christianity. They are described. They are given names. The Reverend Jay Height, executive director of the Shepherd Community Center. Olgen Williams, a part-time pastor and "the long-married father of ten children" who was forced to quit his job as an oil refinery foreman when he fell and broke both wrists and now manages Christamore House, which provides food to the poor; in return for food, we are told, Williams insists on work (p. 73). Sixty-eight-year-old Ermil Thompson, a believer in Christ "who worked her fingers to the bone for several years cooking and selling lunches to raise thousands of dollars to buy and convert a dilapidated house" into what became the Lifeline Community Center (p. 76). And many others.

Who are the people for whom these programs are designed? They are identified only as drug dealers, killers, prostitutes, and gang members. If Olasky tells about the people who have established these programs, we do not hear the stories of people who have been helped by them. Not one such person is individualized or given the dignity of a name. It is clear that the reader's admiration is to be directed toward the organizers of these faith-based programs. They are the ones who have triumphed over the odds. If we are indeed to have sympathy for anyone, it is elicited primarily for them, a sympathy that is rapidly converted into respect for their achievement. Take Tim Streett, a minister who, when he was fifteen, witnessed his father's murder in a mugging by two inner-city young men and who now, at the age of thirty-six, married with a child of his own, has established an after-school sports program for inner-city youth. Even the evocation of abused children does not work so much to solicit our compassion for them as to engender our dismay at their parents. As we saw with *Uncle Tom's Cabin*, the suffering child is the stock in trade of sentimental literature. But here the focus is not so much on the child as it is on the parent as victimizer. Olasky quotes Judge James Payne, who has allowed faith-based organizations to work with the juvenile court system in Indianapolis, "'We see fetal alcohol abuse, mothers on drugs physically and emotionally aggressive with children'" (p. 81).

Overall the emphasis is on action, on getting things done, on what has been called *effective* compassion, with the stress on results and not on sentiment. The narrative is entrepreneurial, with tough love one of its major lessons. For example, one of the operating principles of Teen Challenge, a national program for drug treatment, is, as one of the members of its administration puts it, "We have a rule: If you don't work, you don't eat" (Olasky 2000, 219). As George Bush commented approvingly in his July 1999 speech, "This is demanding love—at times, a severe mercy" (p. 219).

This pragmatic stress on what works is also seen clearly in Joseph Jacobs's *The Compassionate Conservative: Assuming Responsibility and Respecting Human Dignity*, a book whose second edition was published in 2000 and blurbed enthusiastically by then-Governor George W. Bush on its red-white-and-blue cover. "Great Phrase! Great ideas!" In *The Compassionate Conservative*, Jacobs, a former businessman and now a philanthropist, adopts the American form of the jeremiad and lays out what he sees as the principles of compassionate conservatism. At its core is economic conservatism. As he writes, "compassion is an overarching moral value fundamental to all of us, no matter what our stand on specific moral issues. Wresting exclusive ownership of it from the liberal left will be easy if we say what conservative compassion will do. Elevating the debate to differences in how we make compassion work will attract the economic conservatives to our cause" (p. xxiii).

Pointing to some of the very problems identified by the scholars of sentiment I discussed in the previous section, Jacobs asserts that liberal compassion has failed but that conservative compassion will work. His attention is not focused on the suffering body. Rather, his concern is that liberalism creates dependency—emotional and economic dependency. He perceptively observes that the pleasures of compassion, identified by Spelman and Berlant, can create a "double dependency": those who find themselves uplifted by the feeling of compassion must maintain a constituency of people who require their compassion, a phenomenon he vividly calls "moral greed" (p. 44). Compassion is corrupting. It is an "emotional narcotic," a by-product of which is the toxic "feeling of superior moral strength" (p. 84).

But if in all of the texts I have chosen to discuss—from Stowe to Berlant—there has been sustained interest in the suffering of African Americans in particular in the United States, in *The Compassionate Conservative* we find instead the rhetorical transformation of the fact of this history of slavery and suffering into a brutal metaphor for dependency across the entire population of America that Jacobs believes is the responsibility of liberals. "The welfare state created by liberals in pursuit of their compassion has assumed the role of the benevolent slave owner of the twentieth century," he proclaims, crudely drawing on America's history of slavery to delegitimate Democratic policies (p. xxiv). What does Jacobs propose? His interest is not in faith-based charities—even if animated by tough love—but in the creation of jobs.

For him the creation of jobs is itself an act of compassion. What kinds of stories does he tell about compassion? Business stories. Early in his book he tells us about the difficult times he himself endured in 1984 when, as the head of his company, he was forced to restructure his workforce, including "reducing permanent staff by almost half" (p. 28). "The emotional toll on those of us who had to do this restructuring was debilitating," he writes. "We spent many sleepless nights as our compassion for those people who were being fired (I refuse to use softer words) was constantly being challenged by our compassion for the rest of the people who would lose their jobs if the company were allowed to fail. This is one more illustration that compassion is not an unalloyed virtue. Even with that noble virtue one needs to make choices—tough choices" (p. 28). It need hardly be noted that the focus is directed first to his wretched feelings, not those of the soon-to-be-unemployed.

But how, given the importance of the creation of jobs, does this narrative that begins with unemployment come to an end? On a note of enterprising optimism. In the business world, which Jacobs regards as a microcosm of America, his firing of people proved successful: some fifteen years later the company is four times larger, the result of tough love, among other factors. Thus calculation of compassion is at base quantitative, economic. As Jacobs recounts later in *The Compassionate Conservative,* telling another business story of compassionate conservatism, writing of the successful measures he put in place to reduce the number of injuries in his company, there was also an economic benefit, a brightening of the bottom line. The conclusion of this narrative? "Our insurance premiums are reduced," he notes. "Therefore, self-interest is served" (p. 154).

The liberal narrative of compassion asks us to have sympathy for those who are suffering unjustly; such suffering is understood as social suffering.[16] George W. Bush, in appropriating the rhetoric of compassion and drawing on the above two models of compassionate conservatism, has shrewdly excised the suffering body—one characterized by difference—from his national narrative of the future of the United States. Foregrounded are not the suffering bodies of African Americans and the poor, but ministers and businessmen. With Bush's plan for faith-based charities, calling on ministers who provide spiritual healing, we find ourselves in an uncanny return to the nineteenth century. Compassion is not only given a religious dimension, it is masculinized. With Bush's belief in economic conservatism, we return to the Reagan years under the banner of compassion.

Yet Bush does not ask us to focus on people in pain. He does not concern himself with the problem of the appropriation of feeling or of an unequal balance of power. If Nussbaum asks us to resurrect the emotion of pity in social and political life today, placing pity in an historical narrative and contending that we must recuperate its former sense of "fellow-feeling, sympathy," Marvin Olasky does not go to so much trouble; he simply insists on the obsolete definition of compassion given in the *Oxford English Dictionary:* "Suffering together with another, participation in suffering; fellow-feeling, sympathy." Compassion is, he declares in *Compassionate Conservatism,* "suffering with" (p. 2). In a politically brilliant move, by the sleight of hand of definition, the problem of an imbalance of power is eliminated. Hence in the conservative narrative of compassion—indeed, in a sense *there is no narrative,* merely citations, and hence virtually no emotion can be enkindled—the critique of the liberal narrative of compassion is converted into a strength for conservatives. If the liberal focus is on the uncertain connection between feeling and action, the calculated response of conservatives has been to sever incisively the link between feelings of compassion for people and action, eliminating the feeling of compassion altogether.

III

But I would be remiss if I concluded on the above note. As I did research for this essay, I was surprised by the ways in which I felt drawn to several of the pragmatic arguments advanced by conservatives and by the unexpected directions in which my reading took me. Jacobs ends his book not with his own words but with a confession on the part of two self-identified compassionate liberals—Jennifer Vanica and Ron Cummings. They have worked for five years as directors of the Jacobs Family Foundation and the Jacobs Center for Nonprofit Innovation and refer to themselves as having been converted by the experience. Having spent twenty years in the nonprofit world, they were more than skeptical of Jacobs's free-market strategies, including the tenet of accountability. But after some five years with the Family Foundation, they realized that grants that do not lead to self-sustainability simply do not work and hence pursued a bolder strategy of what they call venture philanthropy with the Jacobs Center for Nonprofit Innovation. And they have seen successes. They refer to his story of the 1984 restructuring of his company with respect, not cynicism. "Dr. Jacobs tells the story of coming out of retirement when Jacobs Engineering was floundering and having to fire middle management and restructure the company," they write. "He says it was the most painful experience of his professional life. But it saved the company and resurrected it to employ many more people" (p. 263).

I found their testimony sobering. I also found the idea that some action might *work* after all immensely hopeful. What was stirred in me was not compassion but hope, the feeling that something could be done. Perhaps I was only responding to being interpellated as a caring citizen, seduced by an empty promise. Certainly the workings of the Bush administration have not given me reason to increase my expectations. But I did find myself open to entertaining new possibilities, attracted to the meditations on compassion by the philosopher Simone Weil in great part because she asks us—in an unsentimental way—to take on the responsibility of doing good works. For her—although I simplify here—justice is a form of compassion, and justice is a social act. For her compassion is not so much a sentiment as it is a belief.[17]

I also turned to the challenging work of the German philosopher Agnes Heller, who argues that conscience is an emotion, an idea that is intriguing because she reverses the conventional understanding that feelings of caring are ethical, suggesting instead that an ethical sense is itself a feeling. Heller prefers to use the word "concern" to describe this moral orientation to the world. For Heller, concern includes helping those in need. Here she recalls Lynne Henderson's inclusion of the desire to alleviate the suffering of others in the meanings of empathy, but Heller's emphasis falls less on feeling and more on involvement. "Decent persons indeed feel empathy," she writes; "however their predominant emotional state of mind is one of concern rather than one of compassion (though it does not exclude the feeling of compassion). . . . Being concerned includes the readiness 'to do something about it'" (p. 130).

The legal scholar Martha Minow has recently spoken about the blurring of boundaries between the public and the private, the secular and the religious, and the nonprofit and profit worlds, closing her lecture with an invitation to join her in a "search for ways to turn rivals into partners in the service of fairness, skill, and compassion" (p. 1094). She suggests that we need new metaphors to help us build this world together—not the language of boundaries and lines but of commitments and values. I would further suggest that the boundaries are blurring, appropriately so, between the emotions and judgment or reason, and that we need to find a way to avoid accenting one term over the other.

The philosopher Annette Baier offers us one way; she theorizes trust as a value that mediates between what she sees in contemporary philosophical debates as a feminist emphasis on caring and compassion and a male emphasis on law, obligation, and contract, both of them ultimately inadequate positions for many reasons—for what we might without blushing or wincing call humane reasons. I like her singling out trust as a value. Trust does not belong to what Berlant would call a passive world of feeling, one that can be satisfied with the narcotic of feeling itself. Trust is a declaration of respect, an appraisal of the world—in the form of another person or an institution, for example—and is thus a judgment. Trust therefore has a cognitive dimension. It belongs not just to a world of solipsistic, self-regarding feeling, which is, as we have learned, one of the dangers of compassion. Trust assumes a world of interdependency. Trust confers agency on others. Trust can itself be a gift, in the hope that it is offered wisely.

Notes

1. Linda Diebel, "No Miracles for Bush in TV Debate," *Toronto Star,* October 16, 1992; p. A1; see also Nancy Mathis, Greg McDonald, Tony Freemantle, "Campaign '92," *Houston Chronicle,* October 16, 1992; p. A 16.
2. "On the Trail," *Atlanta Journal-Constitution,* October 1992; p. A6. While George Bush might not have won the election on the platform of compassion, he was nonetheless known as a man who was often moved to tears. See Mary Chapman and Glenn Hendler, "Introduction," *Sentimental Men,* p. 1.
3. This is clearly seen in five cartoons published in the *New Yorker* between November 1995 and June 2001. Mick Stevens, "We used to feel your pain, but that's no longer our policy," *New Yorker,* November 20, 1995; David Sipress, "Well, I guess this means we'll have to start feeling our own pain again," *New Yorker,* January 22, 2001; Mick Stevens, "Let me through. I'm a compassionate conservative," *New Yorker,* August 9, 1999; J. B. Handelsman, "I like that—'compassionate predators,'" *New Yorker,* November 1, 1999; and B. Smaller, "Maybe the compassionate part will kick in during the second half of the Administration," *New Yorker,* June 2001.
4. See my "Grief-Work in Contemporary American Cultural Criticism" and "Anger . . . and Anger: From Freud to Feminism."
5. See my "Statistical Panic."

6. What Lauren Berlant writes in *The Queen of America Goes to Washington City* about the right-wing Reagan revolution, continued in the George Bush years, applies here: "This brightly lit portrait of a civic arm of sanctified philanthropists was meant to replace an image of the United States as a Great Society with a state-funded social safety net" (p. 7).

7. Since the publication of Ann Douglas's *The Feminization of American Culture* in 1977 and Jane Tompkins's *Sensational Designs* in 1985, a fierce defense of the sentimental, the study of the sentimental in literary and cultural studies, including film studies, has emphasized the association of the sentimental with the feminine, notwithstanding much research that has sought to explore the intersections of the sentimental with race and ethnicity. But recent scholarship has shown that the man of feeling has in fact a long history. See Mary Chapman's and Glenn Hendler's *Sentimental Men,* a collection of essays that traces the antecedents of masculine displays of affect in various domains, including presidential politics. See also Julie Ellison's *Cato's Tears and the Making of Anglo-American Emotion,* where she brilliantly argues that we can understand in part the political attraction of today's sensitive men in terms of eighteenth-century male icons who, it is important to stress, displayed both sensibility and emotional reserve.

8. Williams p. 90.

9. See Martha Minow's and Elizabeth Spellman's "Passion for Justice." See also the collection of essays edited by Susan Brandes under the title *The Passions of Law.* If in 1987 Lynne Henderson argued for the introduction of empathetic narratives in the courtroom, there seems to be no need to make such an argument today. Indeed in the very first sentences of the first paragraph of her introduction, Brandes refers to compassion three times and to sorrow twice:

> Emotion pervades the law. This isn't an entirely surprising notion. We know that witnesses bring emotion into the courtroom, and that courtroom drama can be powerfully evocative. We've had many opportunities recently to watch the raw emotion of witnesses, barely suppressed by the legal filters designed to mute its force. We've heard the heartbreaking testimony of the victims, or families of victims, of the Oklahoma City bombing, which evoked widely shared sorrow and compassion. Louise Woodward's trial for killing a baby in her charge raised questions about Woodward's state of mind when baby Matthew was hurt, about whether the judge was properly detached or the prosecutor sufficiently compassionate, and about the role of national and international emotion—in this case a roller coaster of compassion, sadness, revulsion, and outrage at the act, the verdict, and the sentence. (p. 1)

10. Toni M. Massaro offers a sharp rebuttal to Henderson, arguing that the focus on empathy "represents a hope that certain specific, different and previously disenfranchised voices—such as those of blacks and women and poor people and homosexuals—will be heard, *and will prevail*" (p. 2113).

11. One of the major debates in studies of the emotions is whether the emotions have an epistemological dimension and, if so, under what conditions. In the past fifteen years in philosophy, convincing cases have been made that the opposition between reason and emotion is specious.

12. The scholarship in literary and cultural studies on sentimentality in American culture is vast; see Chapman and Hendler's *Masculinity and the Politics of Affect in American Culture* for a concise introduction. I single out two here—Elizabeth Barnes's *States of Sympathy* and *Cultures of Sentiment*, edited by Shirley Samuels. Generally speaking, studies of the sentimental and studies of trauma are not in dialogue with one another. Perhaps this is because, as Philip Fisher has pointed out, "one of the key sentimental assumptions [is] that suffering does not brutalize, nor does it silence its victims or lead them to save themselves by repressing what they have undergone" (p. 100). Trauma, on the other hand, is conceived of precisely as a pathology. As Cathy Caruth defines it, it exists "solely in the *structure of the experience* or reception: the event is not assimilated or experienced fully at the time, but only belatedly in its repeated *possession* of the one who experiences it" (p. 5). Berlant, however, makes an astute point about the similar grounds shared by the sentimental and traumatic narrative. "Currently," she writes, "as in traditional sentimentality, the authenticity of overwhelming pain that can be textually performed and shared"—she is referring to, among other things, to narratives of the Holocaust—"is disseminated as a prophylactic against the reproduction of a shocking and numbing mass violence" (p. 657).

13. How would Berlant respond, I wonder, to Jane Tompkins's claim that *Uncle Tom's Cabin* was in great part responsible for the abolition of slavery.

14. I have focused on texts by four women. I do not mean to imply, however, that men have not contributed to the exploration of the power of the narrative of social suffering in moving people to social justice. Consider, for example, Richard Rorty's essay "Human Rights, Rationality, and Sentimentality." His position is unequivocal. "We are now," he writes, "in a good position to put aside the last vestiges of the idea that human beings are distinguished by the capacity to know rather than by the capacities for friendship and intermarriage, distinguished by rigorous rationality rather than by flexible sentimentality" (p. 18). How do we convince someone to do the right thing for another person? The best way, he counsels, is to give a sort of long, sad, sentimental story which begins "'Because this is what it is like to be in her situation—to be far from home, among strangers,' or 'Because she might become your daughter-in-law,' or 'Because her mother would grieve for her'" (p. 19).

15. "Transcript of President Bush's Message to Congress on His Budget Proposal." *New York Times* February 28, 2001, A14.

16. "Social suffering" is a phrase used by the medical anthropologist Arthur Kleinman and colleagues in their book *Social Suffering*.

17. See, for example, Simone Weil's *The Need for Roots* and *First and Last Notebooks.*

Works Cited

Baier, Annette. *Moral Prejudices: Essays on Ethics.* Cambridge, MA: Harvard University Press, 1994.

Barnes, Elizabeth. *States of Sympathy: Seduction and Democracy in the American Novel.* New York: Cambridge University Press, 1997.

Berlant, Lauren. *The Queen of America Goes to Washington City.* Durham, NC: Duke University Press, 1997.

————. "Poor Eliza." *American Literature* 70.3 (September 1998): 635–668.

Brandes, Susan, ed. *The Passions of Law.* New York: New York University Press, 1999.

Caruth, Cathy, ed. *Trauma: Explorations in Memory.* Baltimore, MD: Johns Hopkins University Press, 1995.

Chapman, Mary, and Glenn Hendler, ed. *Sentimental Men: Masculinity and the Politics of Affect in American Culture.* Berkeley, CA: University of California Press, 1999.

Douglas, Ann. *The Feminization of American Culture.* New York: Knopf, 1977.

Ellison, Julie. *Cato's Tears and the Making of Anglo-American Emotion.* Chicago: University of Chicago Press, 1999.

Fisher, Philip. "Democratic Social Space: Whitman, Melville, and the Promise of American Transparency." *The New American Studies.* Ed. Philip Fisher. Berkeley, CA: University of California Press, 1992. 70–111.

Heller, Agnes. *A Philosophy of Morals.* Oxford, UK: Basil Blackwell, 1990.

Henderson, Lynne N. "Legality and Empathy." *Michigan Law Review* 85 (June 1987): 1574–1653.

Jacobs, Joseph J. *The Compassionate Conservative: Assuming Responsibility and Respecting Human Dignity.* Oakland, CA: ICS Press, 2000.

Jameson, Fredric. "Postmodernism, or the Cultural Logic of Late Capitalism," *New Left Review* 146 (1984): 53–92.

Kleinman, Arthur, Veena Das, and Margaret Lock, eds. *Social Suffering.* Berkeley, CA: University of California Press, 1997.

Massaro, Toni. "Empathy, Legal Storytelling, and the Rule of Law, New Words, Old Wounds." *Michigan Law Review* 87 (August 1989): 2099–2127.

Minow, Martha L. "Lecture: Partners, Not Rivals? Redrawing the Lines Between Public and Private, Non-Profit and Profit, and Secular and Religious." *Boston University Law Review* 80 (October 2000): 1061–1094.

Minow, Martha L. and Elizabeth V. Spellman. "Passion for Justice." *Cardoza Law Review* 10:37 (1988): 37–76.

Nussbaum, Martha C. "Compassion: The Basic Social Emotion." *Social Philosophy and Policy.* 13.1 (1996): 27–58.

————. "Narrative Emotions: Beckett's Genealogy of Love." *Love's Knowledge: Essays on Philosophy and Literature.* New York: Oxford University Press, 1990.

Olasky, Marvin. *Compassionate Conservatism: What It Is, What It Does, and How It Can Transform America.* New York: Free Press, 2000.

———. *The Tragedy of American Compassion.* Washington, DC: Regnery Gateway, 1992.

Rorty, Richard. "Human Rights, Rationality, and Sentimentality." *Yale Review* 81.4 (October 1993): 1–20.

Samuels, Shirley, ed. *The Culture of Sentiment: Race, Gender, and Sentimentality in Nineteenth-Century America.* New York: Oxford University Press, 1992.

Spelman, Elizabeth V. *Fruits of Sorrow: Framing Our Attention to Suffering.* Boston: Beacon Press, 1997.

Stevens, Wallace. "Adagia." *Opus Posthumous.* Ed. Samuel French Morse. New York: Alfred A. Knopf, 1957. 162.

Stowe, Harriet Beecher. *Uncle Tom's Cabin or, Life Among the Lowly.* Ed. Ann Douglas. New York: Penguin, 1981.

Weil, Simone. *First and Last Notebooks.* Trans. Richard Rees. London: Oxford University Press, 1970.

———. *The Need for Roots.* Trans. Arthur Wills. 2 vol. London: Routledge and Kegan Paul, 1956.

Williams, Bernard. *Ethics and the Limits of Philosophy.* London: Fontana Press, 1985.

Woodward, Kathleen. "Anger . . . and Anger: From Freud to Feminism." *Freud and the Passions.* Ed. John O'Neill. University Park, PA: Pennsylvania State University Press, 1996. 73–96.

———. "Grief-Work in Contemporary American Cultural Criticism." *Discourse* 15.2 (1992–93): 94–112.

———. "Statistical Panic." *differences* 11.2 (1999): 177–203.

4

Poor Hetty

NEIL HERTZ

Poor wandering Hetty, poor Mr Casaubon, poor Gwendolen: George Eliot's readers are familiar with that note in her narrator's voice, expressing no lightly assumed or casually dispensed sympathy, but rather a pity as attentive and informed as it is generous. Her readers are familiar, too, with the often harsh destinies assigned these characters, not by the compassionate narrator, but by whomever one holds responsible for the plotting of the novels—Gwendolen abandoned and all but crushed by Daniel's withdrawal, Casaubon dying, shrunken and unfulfilled, and Hetty, poor wandering Hetty, whom Raymond Williams has described as "the girl . . . the novelist abandons in a moral action more decisive than Hetty's own confused and desperate leaving of her child."[1] At such moments it may seem as though the best advice to give someone on the receiving end of George Eliot's narrator's sympathy would be: "Duck!"

Much has been written about these apparent scapegoatings. Hetty in particular seems to many critics to have been especially meanly dealt with, allowed, for the space of a few pages, the most intense inner experience recorded in *Adam Bede*, then dismissed from it not once but twice—first transported to the colonies, then killed off, it would seem gratuitously, in the Epilogue, while on her way home to England after serving out her sentence. In this paper I wish to look again at the question of Hetty's fate and, taking my cue from Raymond Williams's glancing but suggestive analogy, consider the ways George Eliot's investments in her work as a novelist may have shaped her dealings with Hetty.

If any particular warrant were needed for thus moving back and forth between events within and without a fiction, it may be found in three passages in Eliot's own writings. My claim is that these three passages are tightly interrelated and that, taken together, they provide access to an authorial dynamic characteristic of Eliot.

There is first her account of what she calls the "germ" of her novel. Eliot writes that her Methodist aunt, after whom Dinah was in part modelled, had told her stories of a prison visit to "an unhappy girl":

> Of the girl she knew nothing, I believe—or told me nothing—but that she was a common, coarse girl, convicted of child-murder. The incident lay in my mind for years on years as a dead germ, apparently—till time had made my mind a nidus in which it could fructify; it then turned out to be the germ of "Adam Bede."[2]

The echo of "child-murder" in "dead germ" suggests an equivalence out of which an implicit narrative of compensation and displaced guilt can be constructed: a child is buried; a seemingly dead germ comes to life. Something like a crime but maybe not exactly a crime—in the novel it is not certain that Hetty intended to kill her baby—figures the origin of *Adam Bede*. Eliot's novels frequently center around just such an equivocal criminal act, evoking what I have called a pathos of uncertain agency that can be read as implicating the novelist herself. (Why a *pathos* of uncertain agency? Because in the instances I was concerned with in Paul de Man's writings, it was not just that questions of agency were raised but also that the *feeling* of agency-in-question was evoked and undergone as a pathos.)[3]

In the case of *Adam Bede*, of course, the "crime" cannot be Hetty's alone; it takes two to make a baby, and, at the lowest point of poor pregnant Hetty's misery, at the end of the chapter entitled "The Journey in Despair," the (implicitly male) narrator turns to address his (implicitly male) reader directly and exclaims fervently: "God preserve you and me from being the beginners of such misery!"[4] Here is a second bit of analogizing: if a novelist may be like a woman, passively enduring the planting of the seed of a story, she may also be like a man, actively planting the seed and evading the consequences of his deed, if not entirely evading the guilt—another equivocation, but one we should not attempt to reduce too rapidly.

Let me add a third instance of such thematizing of the operations of the novelist within the story itself. This one concerns pools, the "dark pool" that Hetty twice seeks out in her suicidal despair (*AB* 411, 431), and the drop of ink out of which, in the novel's opening paragraph, Eliot proposes to draw the entire fiction. *Adam Bede* opens with its author disguised as a male narrator who figures himself at once as a magician and as someone entering into a contract or undertaking with his reader:

> With a single drop of ink for a mirror, the Egyptian sorcerer undertakes to reveal to any chance comer far-reaching visions of the past. This is what I undertake to do for you, reader. With this drop of ink at the end of my pen I will show you the roomy workshop of Mr Jonathan Burge, carpenter and builder in the village of Hayslope, as it appeared on the eighteenth of June in the year of our Lord 1799. (*AB* 49)

The conceit depends on the previous appearance of "a magic mirror of ink" in what was, for Eliot's readers, a widely known item of contemporary exotica. The identity of the Egyptian sorcerer would not have been a mystery in 1859. His name was 'Abd-El-Kadir El-Maghrabee and he had lived in Cairo earlier in the century. His powers had been attested to in a popular travel book of the 1830s, Edward Lane's *An Account of the Manners and Customs of the Modern Egyptians,* then questioned by other, more skeptical travelers. He had over the years become, in Lane's word, "notorious," an attraction, someone British tourists in the East made a point of visiting.[5] I mention all this because 'Abd-El-Kadir was to make at least one other appearance in fiction, in a brief text of J. L. Borges's written in the 1930s called "The Mirror of Ink."[6] And that text dramatizes, in Borges's characteristic rapid, teasing manner, the contract between author and reader—allegorized as the relation of a magician and his obsessed patron/victim—in a way that can serve as an illuminating contrast—and not just a contrast—to Eliot's practice.

Borges casts his story as a struggle for "command" between a wizard capable of conjuring up visions and a tyrant hungry for representations. The "cruelest of the rulers of the Sudan" discovers a plot against his life, kills the conspirators, and captures the brother of one of them. The brother pleads for mercy, offering to show the tyrant "shapes and appearances still more wonderful than those of the magic lantern," and, when his offer is accepted, returns daily, like Scheherezade, to the tyrant's chambers to continue his performance. As the sessions go on, the tyrant's desire to be shown "all the visible things of this world," is revealed to be laced with sadism, a scopic drive aiming at "the pleasures of the executioner and of the merciless."

At the heart of the story, acting as its fulcrum, is a verse from the Koran that Borges found in *Modern Egyptians*. Lane had there reproduced the Arabic script of his magician's invocation, including the lines "And we have removed from thee thy veil; and thy sight today is piercing." Borges repeats the formula, then builds his tale around a double unveiling—of the see-er and the seen. The tyrant's vision is unveiled as he looks into the drop of ink held in the palm of his hand, but what he finds there, after some preliminary images that whet his appetite, is a veiled figure who haunts the scenes of growing cruelty. At the tale's climax, the tyrant demands to be shown an execution, sees that the victim is the masked man, and orders that the veil be removed. The wizard's narration continues:

> At last Yacub's stricken eyes could see the face—it was his own. He was filled with fear and madness. I gripped his trembling hand in mine, which was steady, and I ordered him to go on witnessing the ceremony of his death. He was possessed by the mirror, so much so that he attempted neither to avert his eyes nor to spill the ink. When in the vision the sword fell on the guilty head, Yacub moaned with a sound that left my pity untouched, and he tumbled to the floor, dead.

Why does the tyrant not avert his eyes? Because, like many another reader, he would rather get his story straight than live. Borges allegorizes reading as a hungry habit, then construes hunger as a wish for absolute unveiling, for coincidence with one's image, a fatal specularity. But note that the movement from representing "all the things of this world"—one way of describing the realist project—to representing the see-er's self is possible only because of the built-in equivocation of mirroring in theories of representation: one can position the mirror to reflect the world or tilt it so that it returns one's image; it can be the mirror of mimesis, Stendhal's mirror, or the pool of Narcissus, in which a character, a reader, or an author may risk drowning.

Borges is a writer of tricksy modernist parables, and we need not expect to find his mode of legerdemain anticipated in Victorian fiction, although a glance at Eliot's own tricksy modernist parable, "The Lifted Veil," written a few months after the completion of *Adam Bede*, will considerably blur such distinctions of period and manner. (Eliot's use of the expression "the lifted veil," by the way, is usually traced back to a sonnet of Shelley's that begins "Lift not the painted veil which those who live/ call Life," but it seems to me likely that she also had the verses from the Koran in mind: "And we have removed from thee thy veil; and thy sight today is piercing.") In any case, unlike Borges, after the novel's opening paragraph, Eliot does not so explicitly or elaborately thematize its relation to its readers—unless you are willing to count the novelist herself among her readers—the first and most illuminating of them. Hence it is a structure of authorial mirroring that will engage us here, and its relation to pity or pitilessness; and we shall find Eliot occupying both of Borges's positions, that of the magician and that of the tyrant. That said, thus buffered, we may risk looking again at that dark pool, this time over the shoulder of George Eliot, herself looking over Hetty's shoulder.

We first learn of the pool in the chapter entitled "The Hidden Dread," when Hetty, as she becomes more visibly pregnant, first considers suicide. Walking off, ostensibly to buy some wedding clothes, she leaves the high road to avoid meeting anyone. Now, "behind the wide thick hedgerows," "her great dark eyes wander blankly over the fields," till she fixes on "an object" and heads toward "a dark shrouded pool," where she sits, unable to work up the courage to throw herself in (*AB* 409–411). If you ask why this rhyming of her dark eyes with that "dark cold water," you can find part of an answer in Ovid's more celebrated pool:

> There was a clear pool with silvery bright water, to which no shepherds ever came, or she-goats feeding on the mountainside, or any other cattle; whose smooth surface neither bird nor beast nor falling brush ever ruffled. Grass grew around all its edge, fed by water near, and a coppice that would never suffer the sun to warm the spot.[7]

That Hetty is narcissistic had already been established in the chapter called "The Two Bed-Chambers," and with a glancing reference to Ovidian mirroring; we have seen her elaborately—and secretly—engaged in what the narrator calls "her peculiar form of worship"

(*AB* 195), setting up candles in her bedroom and smiling at her reflection in a small looking glass, while Dinah, in the next room, is gazing out her window at a moonlit landscape, then shutting her eyes to feel herself "enclosed by the Divine Presence" (*AB* 202). But the scene is of interest less as a way of commenting on Hetty's character—her egotism, her dreamy fantasizing, and the narrowness of her views all have been made clear earlier—than as a placing of Hetty and Dinah within the particular contrastive structure that was to give shape to Eliot's writing from her earliest published sketches through *Deronda* years later.

In 1847, in a brief text she called "A Little Fable with a Great Moral," Eliot had imagined a time "when no maidens had looking glasses" and told the story of two Hamadryads who "loved better than anything to go down to the brink of the lake, and look into the mirror of waters; but not for the same reason." One, Hetty's mythical ancestor, sits "smiling at her own image all the day long"; the other "cared not to look at herself in the lake; she only cared about watching the heavens as they were reflected in its bosom" (*E* 21–22). The great moral is a simple one: the narcissist watches herself age with growing anger and despair and dies "lonely and sad"; her twin, unaware of her changing image, dies gently without ever "knowing she had become old." A chaste anticipation of *The Portrait of Dorian Gray*, its interest for us lies in its having clearly served as a template for Eliot's later use of the structure of double surrogation as a means of articulating her fictions, negotiating her investments in her characters and thereby willy-nilly allegorizing her own activity.

Like Dinah and Hetty, Gilfil and Tina (in *Scenes of Clerical Life*), Romola and Tito, Felix Holt and Esther Lyon, Dorothea and Casaubon or Dorothea and Rosamond, Daniel Deronda and Gwendolen Harleth or Daniel and his mother, are, among many other things, avatars of the two Hamadryads, paired emblematically to embody a series of telling binaries—as good or bad, idealistic or narcissistic, active or passive, outgoing or shrinking figures. In the case of Dinah and Hetty, we can add "voluble or silent" to that list of pairings, and even, as we shall see, "speaking or writing." In each case the valuing of the "good" surrogate is matched by the abjection or exile of her (or his) "bad" partner. To understand the harshness of Hetty's fate,

we need to look more closely at how this double surrogation plays itself out in *Adam Bede*.

To begin with, and before rejoining Hetty at the pool, I want to
note an odd turn of figuration that further links her to Dinah:

> What a strange contrast the two figures made! [the narrator comments
> when Hetty and Dinah are standing together in Hetty's bedroom]
> Hetty, her cheeks flushed and glistening . . . her beautiful neck and arms
> bare . . . Dinah, covered with her long white dress, her pale face full of
> subdued emotion, almost like a lovely corpse into which the soul has re-
> turned charged with sublimer secrets and a sublimer love. (*AB* 204)

The figure of Dinah as a corpse anticipates two later descriptions of
Hetty—first, when she faints at the end of her journey in search of
Arthur and, having "lost her miserable consciousness," looks "like a
beautiful corpse" (*AB* 423), then, more elaborately, when Adam sees
her for the first time after her arrest for child-murder:

> Why did they say she was so changed? In the corpse we love, it is the
> *likeness* we see—it is the likeness, which makes itself felt the more
> keenly because something else *was*, and *is not*. There they were—the
> sweet face and neck, with the dark tendrils of hair, the long dark lashes,
> the rounded cheek and the pouting lips: pale and thin—yes—but like
> Hetty, and only Hetty. Others thought she looked as if some demon
> had cast a blighting glance upon her, withered up the woman's soul in
> her, and left only a hard despairing obstinacy. But the mother's yearn-
> ing, that completest type of the life in another life which is the essence
> of real human love, feels the presence of the cherished child even in the
> debased, degraded man; and to Adam, this pale hard-looking culprit
> was the Hetty who had smiled at him in the garden under the apple-
> tree boughs—she was that Hetty's corpse, which he had trembled to
> look at the first time, and then was unwilling to turn away his eyes from.
> (*AB* 476–477)

The stressed words—"the *likeness* we see," "what *was*, and *is not*"—
give the passage an eerie tonality, like that of Roland Barthes's pages
on the pathos of early photographs or Maurice Blanchot's on the
corpse as likeness.[8] In a turn Barthes or Blanchot might envy—since
it would not work in French—Eliot is playing on the Anglo-Saxon

etymology that firmly links likenesses to corpses; in our language, it seems, representation is doomed to flirt with death. In keeping with that, it is worth noting that the beautiful corpse is here rendered as a vessel emptied of its contents, a vessel that can be filled with the return of consciousness or, more tellingly, with an influx of love, the "sublimer love" that animates Dinah's pale face or the "mother's yearning, that . . . essence of real human love" that allows Adam to recognize the Hetty he thought he knew in the degraded body he sees across the courtroom.

Indeed, animation—the giving of life or soul—is central to Eliot's understanding of love, of religion, of art, and of her own practice in creating characters, in enlivening representations. That is established early in the novel, and established in connection with the idea of surplus or overflow, of a content too ample for the chosen container, a love that "rushes beyond its object":

> [Seth] was but three-and-twenty, and had only just learned what it is to love—to love with that adoration which a young man gives to a woman whom he feels to be greater and better than himself. Love of this sort is hardly distinguishable from religious feeling. What deep and worthy love is so? whether of woman or child, or art or music. Our caresses, our tender words, our still rapture under the influence of autumn sunsets, or pillared vistas, or calm majestic statues, or Beethoven symphonies, all bring with them the consciousness that they are mere waves and ripples in an unfathomable ocean of love and beauty: our emotion in its keenest moment passes from expression into silence; our love in its highest flood rushes beyond its object, and loses itself in the sense of divine mystery. (*AB* 81)

But the generous overflow of feeling celebrated in passages like this one also invariably involves an incommensurability between container and would-be contents, a disproportion that can just as easily lead to fatal errors of estimation, as in this example: "It was one of those dangerous moments when speech is at once sincere and deceptive—when feeling, rising high above its average depth, leaves floodmarks which are never reached again." You may recognize the idiom as that of *The Mill on the Floss* (p. 437), but a similar point had been made in *Adam Bede*, also in terms that linked overflowing feeling to the possibility of deception, specifically of mistaking Hetty's beauty for a sign of soulfulness:

> Every man [in love] is conscious of being a great physiognomist. Nature, he knows, has a language of her own, which she uses with strict veracity, and he considers himself an adept in the language. Nature has written out his bride's character for him in those exquisite lines of cheek and lip and chin, in those eyelids delicate as petals, in those long lashes curled like the stamen of a flower, in the dark liquid depths of those wonderful eyes. . . .
>
> After all, I believe the wisest of us must be beguiled in this way sometimes, and must think both better and worse of people than they deserve. Nature has her language, and she is not unveracious; but we don't know all the intricacies of her syntax just yet, and in a hasty reading we may happen to extract the very opposite of her real meaning. (*AB* 197–198)

Yet it is not just the possibilities for misreading that George Eliot would have us take account of in Hetty's face. The generous, animating interpretation that Adam or Arthur may fondly, mistakenly put on Hetty's looks corresponds to something real, if not individualized, in her features:

> Hetty's face had a language that transcended her feelings. There are faces which nature charges with a meaning and pathos not belonging to the single human soul that flutters beneath them, but speaking the joys and sorrows of foregone generations—eyes that tell of deep love which doubtless has been and is somewhere, but not paired with those eyes—perhaps paired with pale eyes that can say nothing; just as a national language may be instinct with poetry unfelt by the lips that use it. (*AB* 330)

Like a national language, or—to recall Eliot's essay on "The Natural History of German Life" (1856)—like the faces of those contemporary Hessian peasants which so strikingly resemble the faces of saints carved by Marburg craftsmen in the thirteenth century (*E* 274), like European society itself, as Eliot contends in that essay, Hetty's face incarnates history: its lineaments are the traces of the experience of foregone generations. Hetty's beauty thus becomes the secular or esthetic equivalent of Dinah's transpersonal spirituality, which has its own (*super*natural) history, having descended to her, as she reminds the listeners at her preaching, from the Word of God through the mediation of Jesus's and "Mr Wesley's" words (*AB* 69). That is why Adam can be excused for having fallen in love with Hetty, for her beauty, the narrator tells us, is, like music, "impersonal," having "an expression beyond and far above the one woman's soul that it clothes, as the words of genius have a wider meaning than the thought that prompted them" (*AB* 400).

"The words of genius"—we are back, by way of Hetty's beauty and the beauty of music, to literature and to what must be read as George Eliot's own hope as a novelist: that her words may mean more than she intends. (George Eliot will engage the difference between meaning-as-signifying and meaning-as-intending in "The Lifted Veil" [1859]; I'll return to this later in the paper.) This is one function of the thematics of animation, surplus and overflow. Nor is this overflow limited to the spreading of the novelist's meaning; she figures as both a source of surplus and as its recipient, the vessel that cannot contain it all. This is particularly evident when George Eliot, after the publication of *Adam Bede,* writes of her dealings with her surrogates. Echoing Dinah ("words were given to me that came out as the tears come, because our hearts are full and we can't help it" [*AB* 135]), she remarks to a friend, "How curious it seems to me that people should think Dinah's sermons, prayers and speeches were *copied*—when they were written with hot tears, as they surged up in my own mind!" (*L* 3.176). And of the pages taking Hetty from the Midlands to Windsor across the English countryside, she reports a similarly urgent fluency: "the opening of the Third Volume—Hetty's journey—was, I think written more rapidly than the rest of the book, and left without the slightest alteration of the first draught" (*L* 2.504).

If superfluity is the condition of both spiritual communion and deception, it is also the condition of allegory. Morally, Dinah is to Hetty as generous speech is to sullen, self-involved silence; but the novel also renders this opposition allegorically, enlisting the difference between speech and writing. Hetty is no writer, but her silence is associated with writing—and with an allegory of authorship—at two critical points. When she is arrested for child-murder, we are told, Hetty "had a small red-leather pocket-book in her pocket, with two names written in it—one at the beginning, 'Hetty Sorel, Hayslope,' and the other near the end, 'Dinah Morris, Snowfield.' She will not say which is her own name—she denies everything, and will answer no questions" (*AB* 454). She will not say, for example, of which of those two fragments of writing she is the author, will not identify herself with either fragment. The conjunction of those two names anticipates the coming together of Eliot's two surrogates in prison, the scene Eliot described as "the climax towards which I worked" (*L* 2.503). It is the scene—we shall turn to it shortly—in which Dinah's prayerful volubility overcomes Hetty's silence, eliciting answering speech from her, exacting from her an equivocal confession (*AB* 493–500).

Still more telling is the oddly circumstantial account of Hetty's journey in search of Arthur, so scrupulously accurate in its real-world geography—place-name after place-name—that a reader can easily follow Hetty's path on a map of England as she traces a line from Derby south-southeast to Ashby de la Zouch, then southeast to Leicester, then—by mistake—instead of going south-southeast to Stony Stratford, where she had been directed, heads off to the southwest, passing through Hinkley and the Warwickshire countryside towards the other Stratford, Stratford-upon-Avon, then corrects her error by heading east again over to Stony Stratford and thence south-southeast to Windsor. Draw that crooked line on a map, connecting the dots, and you will see that the detour George Eliot has, as it were gratuitously, superfluously, plotted out for Hetty and her unborn baby has led them within only a few miles of Nuneaton—Mary Anne Evans's birthplace—on her way, still in error, to an even more famous literary birthplace, Stratford-upon-Avon. The general direction—south from the provinces to royal Windsor, so near London, from the periphery to the center—is in fact the path Eliot's literary ambitions had taken her ten years earlier; Hetty's journey reinscribes a writer's route to the big time, at one point veering off to trace a side journey past her own birthplace to a wished-for precursor's (*AB* 415–423). (In a first draft of this paragraph I had gilded the lily a bit, typing in—by mistake—Stratford-upon-Eden!)

It is time to return, with Hetty, to the dark pool. She reaches it by choosing—"strangely," as the narrator puts it, "by some fascination"

(*AB* 429), to retrace her earlier steps, going once more out of her way, through Stratford-upon-Avon toward "the grassy Warwickshire fields" among which she thought she might find just the sort of pool she had in mind (*AB* 429). What follows are a half-dozen of the most powerfully imagined pages George Eliot would write, pages that confer on Hetty an interior life of unexpected intensity and variety, an inner life that at first may strike a reader as disproportionate to its container: Hetty has never before seemed so *interesting*.

Eliot has constructed this account of Hetty's experience out of the most primitive materials, the antithetical claims of life and death, most immediately signified by Hetty's condition, her ongoing pregnancy, the growing, deadly shameful life within her, and played out in the vacillations of feeling and action with which she tries to deal with her predicament. It is the impossible-to-maintain innerness of this inner life that is stressed, the effort to keep contained what cannot be contained. ("It is necessary to me not simply to *be* but to *utter*," Eliot had written to one of her friends, in 1848. [*L* 1.255].)

In the chapters describing Hetty's journeys, the word "hidden" does triple duty, referring first to her pregnancy and her secret fear of exposure, her "Hidden Dread" (*AB* 408), then to girls like Hetty herself, "a human heart beating heavily with anguish . . . hidden among the sunny fields" (*AB* 410], finally to the "hidden pool" (*AB* 429) she imagines herself disappearing into. At moments that feels to Hetty like a solution: to have done with vacillation, to choose silence, to hide the child within the girl within the pool once and for all. But she can neither bring herself to drown herself nor give up the thought of doing so.

Because of the power and spareness of these pages, because of the initial difficulty of imagining Hetty as an adequate vessel for the experience attributed to her, and not least because of the mirroring, inky pool itself, "black under the darkening sky: no motion, no sound near" (*AB* 431), one can trace in this account of Hetty's night in the Warwickshire wood an allusive narrative of authorial reflection, what I call an end of the line.[9] What are its elements? To begin with, a verbal texture marked by antithesis, variations on the kernel opposition, the repeated words *life* and *death*.

Hetty's face is described as "the sadder for its beauty, like that wondrous Medusa-face, with the passionate, passionless lips" (*AB* 430). She feels "a strange contradictory wretchedness and exultation," she walks "backwards and forwards"; at one moment she experiences the "horror of this cold, and darkness, and solitude," at another—in a brilliant and affecting bit of invention—we are told that "the very consciousness of her own limbs was a delight to her: she turned up her sleeves, and kissed her arms with the passionate love of life." "Driven to and fro between two equal terrors," she is granted the relief of sleep, only to dream that her aunt is standing over her and, waking, to discover that it is not her aunt but a farm worker, "an elderly man." The startling flip-flop of gender—a woman's face dissolving into a man's as Hetty comes out of her dream—adds one more opposition to the series (*AB* 432–433).

Two more aspects of these pages are worth dwelling on. The first has to do with Hetty's veering between differently weighted recollections of her past life:

> O how long the time was in that darkness! The bright hearth and the warmth and the voices of home,—the secure uprising and lying down,—the familiar fields, the familiar people, the Sundays and holidays with their simple joys of dress and feasting,—all the sweets of her young life rushed before her now, and she seemed to be stretching her arms towards them across a great gulf. She set her teeth when she thought of Arthur: she cursed him, without knowing what her cursing would do. (*AB* 432)

Her cursing Arthur, the "beginner of her misery," is not surprising, but its antithesis is; this lengthy list of lovingly recalled details of the settings of Hetty's "young life" reads like a précis of Eliot's aim—and accomplishment—in all her early fiction, the affectionate representation of provincial life. In her rueful retrospect on the familiar, the lost familiar, Hetty is aligned with the narrators of *Scenes of Clerical Life*, of *Adam Bede*, of *The Mill on the Floss*, of "The Lifted Veil."

My second point concerns the thematization of agency in terms of the reaching of one's objective and its antithesis, a drifting or wandering. When Hetty first seeks out a pool near Hayslope, you may recall, we are told that "her great dark eyes wander blankly over the fields like the eyes of one who is desolate, homeless, unloved" (*AB* 410), she hesitates about which direction to move in, then chooses a path "as if she had suddenly thought of an object towards which it was worth while to hasten"—the object being the dark, shrouded pool. Suicide, the pool, *that* "object," is here set off against "the terror of wandering out into the world" (*AB* 411). And the pattern is repeated in the Warwickshire chapter, when Hetty, wandering across other fields, suddenly spots the pool she is hesitantly seeking:

> She walked through field after field, and no village, no house was in sight; but *there*, at the corner of this pasture, there was a break in the hedges; the land seemed to dip down a little, and two trees leaned towards each other across the opening. Hetty's heart gave a great beat as she thought there must be a pool there. She walked towards it heavily over the tufted grass, with pale lips and a sense of trembling: it was as if the thing were come in spite of herself, instead of being the object of her search.
>
> There it was, black under the darkening sky. (*AB* 431)

Is this thing an object, her willed objective, or is it "come in spite of herself?" This is Hetty's version of Dinah's account of her preaching: "sometimes it seemed as if speech came to me without any will of my own, and words were given to me that came out as the tears come" [*AB* 135], a description of uncertain agency I earlier aligned with Eliot's own discussion of the writing of Dinah's sermons. When Hetty, "poor wandering Hetty," leaves the side of the pool, frightened into resuming her journey, the narrator asks, in the closing lines of Chapter 37:

> What will be the end?—the end of her objectless wandering, apart from all love, caring for human beings only through her pride, clinging to life only as the hunted wounded brute clings to it?
>
> God preserve you and me from being the beginners of such misery! (*AB* 435)

There are another set of "two equal terrors" here—the terror of the object, the intended goal, when what is intended bears the mark of death and of the stasis of reflection, the mirror of ink; and the terror of the objectless, the aimless, what Eliot in *Felix Holt* would call wandering "in mere lawlessness" (*FH* 150).[10] But we have already heard the narrator saying, apropos of love "or art, or music," that "at its highest flood it rushes beyond its object" (*AB* 81). Chapter 37 offers a condensed reflection on novelistic wandering or flooding. Eliot collapses her surrogates into one—substituting the vacillations of Hetty's experience for the value-laden pairing of Hetty and Dinah— then reaches an impasse. Hetty is too fragile a vessel to bear this burden of consciousness for long. We sense the rising flood of the novelist's concerns over and above what could plausibly be called Hetty's own. Eliot's identification with this character cannot be sustained. As Hetty is dismissed to wander still further, one sign of the breaking of that identification is the narrator's reminding us of his (and our) unequivocally male status: "God preserve you and me from being the beginners of such misery."

Readers of *Adam Bede* have remarked on the ease with which several scenes, spaced at some distance from one another, can be confused— the two suicide attempts, obviously, with their seeking out of two geographically distinct but descriptively similar pools, but also the scene at the Warwickshire pool and Hetty's narration of the birth and death of her child near Stoniton, many miles and many pages later, when she finally breaks her silence and confesses to Dinah. One effect of these repetitions is to bring together two central and persistent characteristics of Eliot's fiction—the end-of-the-line sublimities we have been following in the diction and figuration of the suicide scenes, and the motif of speech under compulsion, the exacted, equivocal confession that had already been staged in "Mr Gilfil's Love Story" and would reappear in "The Lifted Veil," in *Middlemarch,* and in *Daniel Deronda.*

In each of these fictions a character—invariably a woman—is implicated in a murder, or what might be a murder, and maintains a sullen or terrified silence about the crime until she is brought, often in reaction to the sympathetic words of a generously voluble interlocutor—in a sort of reflux of energy—to feel that speaking out is possible. In each case the speaking-out is figured as the revealing of the truth—here, for example, before Hetty confesses, Dinah warns her that she is shutting her soul against God "by trying to hide the truth" (*AB* 495)—but in all but "The Lifted Veil," the truth that emerges, always a matter of intention or agency—did she or didn't

she do it?—is ambiguous. After Dinah's fervent prayer, Hetty sobs
out "I will speak . . . I will tell . . . I won't hide it any more . . . I did
do it, Dinah . . . I buried it in the wood . . . the little baby" but a moment later she adds "But I thought perhaps it wouldn't die—there
might be somebody find it. I didn't kill it—I didn't kill it myself" (*AB*
497). Hetty did and did not mean to kill her child. In "The Lifted
Veil," a bleaker account, meaning-as-signifying is collapsed into
"meaning-as-intending," and "meaning-as-intending" is unequivocally reduced to "meaning to kill."[11]

I should add that, in each case, the woman who speaks out—be it
Tina or Hetty or Mrs Archer or Lydgate's actress friend Laure, or
Gwendolen or Daniel Deronda's mother—that woman herself dies
or is dismissed—"pitilessly," we could say, in Borges's idiom—in
some other way from the novel. She is not punished for speaking
out—that is often made to seem like a hard-won *prise de parole* and
very much to her credit—she is punished for the unavoidable equivocation of her account of her "crime." We are left not with the pathos
of uncertain agency, but with its stigma.

Notes

1. Raymond Williams, *The Country and the City* (New York: Oxford University Press, 1973), p. 173.
2. Gordon S. Haight, *The George Eliot Letters*, 9 vols. (New Haven, CT:
   Yale University Press, 1954–74), 3.175–176; hereafter *L*.
3. See Hertz, "Lurid Figures" in *Reading de Man Reading*, eds. Lindsay
   Waters and Wlad Godzich (Minneapolis: University of Minnesota
   Press, 1989), pp. 82–104; and "More Lurid Figures," *Diacritics* 20:3
   (1990), pp. 2–27.
4. George Eliot, *Adam Bede* (1859) (London: Penguin, 1980), p. 435; here-
   after, *AB*. Henceforth, all page references to George Eliot's writings will
   appear in parentheses in the text. They are to the following editions: *The
   Lifted Veil* (1859; London: Virago, 1985), *LV*; *The Mill on the Floss* (1860;
   London: Penguin, 1979), *MF*; *Felix Holt: The Radical* (1866; London:
   Penguin, 1995), FH; *Daniel Deronda* (1876; London: Penguin, 1967),
   DD; *Essays of George Eliot* (London: Routledge and Kegan Paul, 1963),
   E; *Collected Poems* (London: Skoob, 1989), *P*.
5. See Edward William Lane, *An Account of the Manners and Customs of the
   Modern Egyptians* 2 vols. (London: Murray, 1871), pp. 409–422.
6. Borges, "The Mirror of Ink" in *A Universal History of Infamy* (New York:
   Dutton, 1972), pp. 125–129.
7. Ovid, *Metamorphoses* 2 vols. (Cambridge, MA: Harvard University
   Press, 1984) I, p. 153.

8. See Roland Barthes, *Camera Lucida: Reflections on Photography* (New York: Hill and Wang, 1981), pp. 92–97; and Maurice Blanchot, *The Gaze of Orpheus* (Barrytown, NY: Station Hill, 1981), pp. 79–89.

9. See the Afterword to Neil Hertz, *The End of the Line: Essays on Psychoanalysis and the Sublime* (New York: Columbia University Press, 1985), pp. 216–239. The melodramatic tableaux that Carolyn Williams examines in her essay in this volume, when their melodrama engages epistemological issues, qualify as end-of-the-line encounters, arresting moments in Diderot's sense, moments of paralysis in Freud's (see, for example, his account of his own fixation in front of the energetic stasis of Michelangelo's *Moses*). Another instance, from *Daniel Deronda,* may be useful here. When Gwendolen confesses to Daniel how badly she wants to kill her husband, how afraid she is that she might just do it, Daniel counsels her, in *Middlemarch* language, "Take your fears as a safeguard. It is like quickness of hearing. It makes consequences passionately present to you." The narrator goes on: "And so it was. In Gwendolen's consciousness Temptation and Dread met and stared like two pale phantoms, each seeing itself in the other—each obstructed by its own image and all the while her fuller self beheld the apparitions and sobbed for deliverance from them" (*DD* 738). The passage is unusual—and hence especially significant—in its substituting allegorical figures, Temptation and Dread, for human subjects, whether they be fictional characters, authors or readers. The effect is to embed affective ambivalence, the pull between opposite motives, the vacillation between attraction and repulsion characteristic of Kant's sublime, within a parable about the irreducible opacity that one's "own image" introduces into any attempt at seeing what is outside the self. Hence, in *Adam Bede,* Hetty's vacillations at Narcissus's pool emblematize Eliot's own vibratory impasse vis-à-vis Hetty.

10. In *Felix Holt,* this alignment of "wandering" with lawlessness—in a discussion of political freedom and political authority—occurs a page after a seemingly unrelated conversation about changes in ways of singing hymns: a choir, according to one parishoner, had "stretched short metre into long out of pure wilfulness and defiance, irreverently adapting the most sacred monosyllables to a multitude of wandering quavers [i.e., eighth-notes], arranged, it was to be feared, by some musician who was inspired by conceit rather than by the true spirit of psalmody" (*FH* 149). In Eliot's dramatic poem "Armgart" (1870), an opera singer is rebuked for adding "trills" to an aria of Gluck's, and, apologizing (ironically) for this "impudence," vows she will "do penance: sing a hundred trills/Into a deep-dug grave, then burying them/As one did Midas' secret, rid myself/Of naughty exultation" (*P* 118–119). I have discussed the relation between these buried trills, artistic exultation, and Hetty's buried child in "George Eliot's Pulse," in *differences: a journal of feminist cultural studies* 6.1, pp. 28–45.

11. I have discussed the means by which this reduction is accomplished in "George Eliot, Rousseau, and *The Lifted Veil*" in *Brief: Visions and Voices of Otherness* (Amsterdam: ASCA, 1996).

5

Moving Pictures

George Eliot and Melodrama

CAROLYN WILLIAMS

The phenomenon of fireworks is prototypical for artworks, though because of its fleetingness and status as an empty entertainment it has scarcely been acknowledged by theoretical consideration. . . . They appear empirically yet are liberated from the burden of the empirical, which is the obligation of duration; they are a sign from heaven yet artifactual, an ominous warning, a script that flashes up, vanishes, and indeed cannot be read for its meaning.

—————Adorno, *Aesthetic Theory*

This essay will dwell on several functions and effects of the melodramatic tableau within George Eliot's realism, and in so doing it will attempt to refocus our understanding both of realism and of melodrama. On the melodramatic stage the tableau interrupts and punctuates the ongoing action with its silent, composed stillness—calling for the audience to be likewise arrested yet all the while to be actively feeling and interpreting. So, too, the novelistic imitation of melodramatic tableaux represents and effects an invisible, silent activity of movement within and between subjects. The moments marked by tableaux appear unmediated and yet artifactual; they occur suddenly, with uncertain causal grounding, and they hang suspended as signs whose significance remains to be realized only retroactively, if at all; but in George Eliot's fiction, they are often posed within such an insistent blazon of aesthetic purposiveness that their momentous potential for future unfolding explodes with forward momentum.

All this, so far, may seem to describe a familiar dynamic within George Eliot's anthological realism, in which intertextual involvement

with other art forms and genres is continuously transformed and sublated within her "higher" and more comprehensive project. What
seems distinctive about her use of the melodramatic tableau is its capacity to turn both inward and outward—a visual, temporal, and
rhythmic dynamic suggestively homologous with the function of free
indirect discourse in novelistic narration. Within my argument, sympathy and compassion will be seen as affects produced through aesthetic effects, but it is important to keep in mind that they become not
less—but all the more—immediate and moving because of their suspension within an exquisitely dialectical, artifactual sequence. This
essay will return in the end to consider its epigraph from Adorno, but
meanwhile I hope to persuade my readers to imagine the melodramatic
tableau as a primary resource for an art form that purports to rise above
such lowbrow pyrotechnics of spectatorship and speculation.[1]

Writing to Barbara Bodichon on December 12, 1871, George Eliot
announced what seemed to her surprising news: "We are going
tonight to the theatre!! to see Erckmann Chatrian's play of 'The Bells.'
It is years since we went to an English house."[2] This sort of play was
decidedly not her usual theatrical fare. Characteristically, Eliot attributes the play to Erckmann-Chatrian, the composite name of two Al-
satian authors who specialized in sentimental fiction and who
collaboratively wrote *Le juif polonais* (The Polish Jew), the 1867 novel
from which *The Bells* was adapted.[3] She does not mention Leopold
Lewis, the English adaptor who reshaped the novel into a brilliant
melodramatic play text; nor does she mention the actor whose lead
performance in the play was currently the talk of the town. But despite her conventionally snobbish preference for the European page
over the English stage, she did go—less than a month after it
opened—to see the smash-hit melodrama at the Lyceum Theatre,
featuring Henry Irving in his very first star turn. At the time, George
Eliot was still in the midst of writing *Middlemarch*. Soon she would
begin collecting material for *Daniel Deronda*.

What did George Eliot and George Henry Lewes see that night?

The plot of *The Bells* turns on the hidden guilt of its central character, Mathias, who murdered a Polish Jew in order to steal his gold fifteen years before the opening of the play's action.[4] Mathias founded

his present, prosperous burgomaster's identity on this secret crime. After fifteen years of concealing his secret, Mathias imagines that he will be safe from the law's judgment forevermore. But of course, that is not to be.

While Mathias engages himself busily in the plans for his daughter's upcoming wedding, his past returns to haunt him more and more insistently. In order quickly to establish the principle of the return of the repressed, the play opens on a dark and stormy night, which several characters explicitly compare to the cold, snowy night during "the Polish Jew's winter" fifteen years before, when the Jew was murdered. Mathias enters from outside, bringing the feel of the cold and snowy night inside with him. At the end of Act I, Mathias is left alone on stage, and as he unlaces his boots, he begins to hear sleigh bells—just like the bells on the sledge of the murdered Jew. His increasing anxiety is expressed in the melodramatic "music with frequent Chords." But where is the sound of the bells coming from? The audience can see that Mathias is alone; no one else is onstage. What follows, then, in the famous "vision scene" that concludes Act I of *The Bells* is to be understood as a purely psychological effect, a projection of Mathias's memory and internal disquiet. At ten o'clock, the precise clock time marking the anniversary of the murder, the music swells as a tableau is disclosed at the back of the stage depicting the exact scene from the past: the Jew in his sledge being stalked by Mathias at the moment immediately before the murder.

Like the music of the bells, the tableau represents the persistence of the past in memory and Mathias's inescapable guilt; but we should pause to note the important point that all this is realized "outside" Mathias. (Since Mathias must watch himself within the vision scene, his self-division must be represented through the use of a body double.) In the depths of the stage's background, the tableau displays the distance of the past at the moment of its shocking return, while in the foreground the figure of Mathias guides the dynamics of audience response by suddenly becoming a spectator himself. He is traumatically divided against himself as he "realizes"—and as the scene "realizes"— what he has done. At first Mathias's back is turned away from the tableau; he faces the audience and does not see what the audience sees disclosed behind him. But then Mathias turns to face the tableau. At the very moment that he turns—and sees its externalized representation of his own interiority—the stillness of the tableau is suddenly broken. Suddenly the stage picture moves! The Jew suddenly turns his head and "fixes his eyes sternly" on Mathias, who recoils, arching balletically backward, "utters a prolonged cry of terror and falls senseless" to the floor (see Figure 1). At that point, the Act I curtain falls as well.

In Act II, a backstory involving mesmerism underscores Mathias's dawning and terrified awareness that his secrets perhaps cannot be dependably contained. The revelation of a secret is of course a stock melodramatic plot device; but I want to focus our attention on the fact that within the stage conventions of the melodramatic theater, this plot device takes on a generic or metatheatrical resonance. Mathias's fear that his interiority will be forcibly externalized is the content of melodrama's form, so to speak, just as the tableau and the music provide the form of its content. Both the tableau and the music concentrate our attention on the idea that invisible interiority can take

Fig. 5.1 Tableau: vision scene at the conclusion of Act I, *The Bells,* as illustrated by Alfred Concanen in *The Stage,* December 10, 1871. Harvard Theatre Collection, Houghton Library. Harvard College Library.

empirical form, bursting out in the music, for example, or flashing back in a sudden stage picture. In Act III the persistent music of the bells eventually drives Mathias into a mad dream sequence which precipitates the play's conclusion. That dream sequence is also projected externally: while a body double plays the role of Mathias sleeping, Mathias within the representation of his dream is arrested, put on trial, convicted of murdering the Polish Jew, sentenced to death, and prepared to be hanged. He awakes from this nightmare at the very end of the play, gasping for breath, struggling in his invisible bondage, and begging his family to "take the rope from [his] neck!" (see Figure 2). No one can take the imaginary rope from his neck, however. Mathias dies to the crescendo accompaniment of the music, and the final curtain falls.

Melodramatic effects achieved through expressive music or the sudden stasis (and sudden movement) of the tableau are so conventional now—in film especially—that it takes an act of historical and aesthetic imagination to fathom the lengthy process of their formulation as stage technologies. Melodramatic music subtends, expresses, and directs the play of the actors' balletic alternations between movement and stillness, speech and silence. When deployed within staged melodrama—which is by far their most important critical context in the nineteenth century—the tableaux interrupt and punctuate melodramatic action with their moments of static composure. The actors freeze suddenly into attitudes and pose like statues; and indeed, these tableaux often imitate familiar artworks (for an audience who, by the way, could be expected to recognize them).

Thus, within the melodramatic theater the term "realization" has a specific technical meaning, and it will be of great interest within the current argument that a melodramatic realization is a posed reenactment of a well-known work of art.[5] Melodramatic realizations often focus on domestic scenes, imitating genre paintings in current circulation. But scenes of psychic projection can also rely on the conventions of realization or they can be composed specifically for the stage, as in *The Bells*. In either case, however—whether domestic or otherworldly, whether realizing the world of art outside the theater or the psychic interior of one of the characters in the play—the tableau establishes a moment of hieratic silence and stillness within the ongoing action of

Fig. 5.2 "Take the rope from my neck." Photograph of Henry Irving posing as Mathias in the final scene of *The Bells*. London Stereoscopic Company. Harvard Theatre Collection, Houghton Library. Harvard College Library.

the play, a moment in which the representation is turned inside out. In general, melodramatic form should be understood as this oscillation between introversion and extroversion in the dramatic representation, between passages of movement accompanied by music and sudden moments of static, spatial composition.

Late in the history of stage melodrama, this 1871 production of *The Bells* metatheatrically condenses and illuminates the conventions of the genre. For within the conventions of melodrama, a dead face suddenly coming to life can be seen as a literalization or "realization" of the usual effect of the tableau: the suddenly frozen, then suddenly moving picture. By 1871, in other words, the spectacle of a frozen, dead face coming to life can be said metatheatrically to represent the technology of the melodramatic tableau itself, arresting the audience's attention and then delivering a shock when the still picture suddenly breaks into movement. Likewise the repetitive, insistent music of the bells, as a thematic or motival representation of Mathias's pressing secret, does but literalize the usual expressive role of the music in melodrama. But the music of *The Bells* is not only affective but also brilliantly *effective:* it conjures the visionary tableau, announcing but also bringing about the sudden flash of the past into present realization. And in the end, the music—the only empirical sign, in the end, of Mathias's persistent memory—in effect kills the guilty protagonist. In other words, the generic role of music in melodrama has also been forcibly realized here, not only as emotion externalized in the ambient space of the audience—and transferred to their susceptible feelings—but also as the principle of justice in the plot of the play, which penetrates now, haunting the interior and wreaking its vengeance there.

Denis Diderot, the first great theorist of the tableau, was concerned both with painting and with theatrical tableaux, especially with their compressed suggestion of dramatic action both before and after the moment depicted. As he put it, "there is only one moment for the artist to choose, but this moment may carry traces of the moment which preceded it and signs of the one which will follow. Iphigeneia is not yet being sacrificed, but I see the executioner's assistant approaching with the bowl which is to receive her blood, and this accessory makes me tremble."[6] Diderot's knowledge of the story is indispensable to the recognition of what will come and to the cultured suspense that makes him tremble. But unlike a painting, a tableau within the fabric of a play is entangled within action that is yet unfolding and not already known; in the theater, recognition goes hand in hand with suspensefully poised anxiety and premonition.

Diderot evaluated the success of any tableau according to its power to fixate an audience. The successful tableau must first appeal to, call out to, or attract the beholder's attention (*appeller*); then it must arrest the beholder, holding him or her in front of it for a time (*arrêter*); and finally it should enthrall or entrance (*attacher*) the beholder.[7] Thus, though these staged pictures are ostentatiously silent and still, for Diderot they are nevertheless eloquent and moving in several respects. They appeal to the audience to become both passive and active, to feel the shift in representational registers that invites detachment from the ongoing action and then to read the stage picture, scanning it for its form and possible suspended meanings. The tableau "appeals" to the audience by hailing and soliciting their interpretive engagement with the visual representation of psychic and social formation.[8] Thus the particular appeal of the tableau is at once aesthetic, hermeneutic, and social.

Melodramatic effects and sentimental domesticity are inextricably bound up together in Diderot's writings on both paintings and theatrical tableaux. He formulates a famous critical distinction between the *coup de théâtre* and the tableau, and he values the tableau much more highly than the *coup*, or sudden overturning in the plot or action of the play. "One is almost like a children's game," he says, and "the other is a stroke of genius." The example he gives of the "stroke of genius" happens to come from his own play, *Le fils naturel*, where he arranges a calm stage picture in which one character simply points out another character "on a sofa, in an attitude of despair."[9] It is precisely here that his critical distinction breaks down, however, for this absorbed, inward-turning, sentimental, and domestic scene is significant only because of the series of extremely melodramatic *coups de théâtre* leading up to it, *coups* involving—as the title of the play clearly indicates—all the trappings of melodramatic illegitimacy and the sudden revelation of identity. At the moment of its theoretical articulation, in other words, the tableau is already critically double: terrifying and sentimental, otherworldly and domestic, extravagant and realistic, outward and inward turning. Thus, paradoxically, the tableau represents—both within the action of the play and within the dynamics of spectatorship—absorption and theatricality bound up together.

Commenting on Diderot's distinction between the tableau and the *coup de théâtre*, Michael Fried points out that "a *coup de théâtre* took place as it were *within* the action and marked a sudden change in the consciousness of the characters involved; whereas the grouping of figures and stage properties that constituted a *tableau* stood *outside* the action, with the result that the characters themselves appeared unaware of its existence and hence of its effect on the audience."[10] Thus Diderot's "paradox of the actor" is forcibly highlighted in the tableau, for according to this principle of romantic dramaturgy, nothing breaks the illusion of "natural feeling" so surely as the awareness on the part of an audience that the actors themselves are aware of being watched.[11] During the tableau, in other words—while the audience pauses to remember that the actors are acting—the actors act as if their absorption in their acting has not been broken.

While audience members pause to look at the compositional syntax of the stage picture, they turn inward to contemplate an interpretation of its significance in relation to the suspended action. The configuration of bodies on stage will be legibly meaningful, but the pause itself solicits an additional sense of significance, breaking the action in order to suspend the potential of the future. Thus the sudden, even aggressive formalization of the tableau lends it an allegorical dimension; for the tableau rises out of the action, yet detaches from it to turn around and function as commentary on it, while at the same time heightening the mystery through its aloof removal from the ongoing action. It poses a mystery that is left over or left out of the action, and it is "excessive" in this precise respect.[12]

The stillness of the stage picture, then, is paradoxically moving. And in fact, soon the picture literally *will* move again, for each tableau—unless it marks the final curtain—gives way to another passage of movement set to music. On the level of generic form, then, it is the shift itself that is critically important. Melodramatic form may be understood as this musically accompanied representational oscillation, for the music underscores its alternations of motion and stillness, speech and silence, dispersive action and coalesced meaningfulness, extroversion and introversion, emptying and filling.

Eliot's reaction to *The Bells* is nowhere recorded. It is highly unlikely that she admired it, however.[13] Both George Eliot and George Henry Lewes are well-known to have shared an outspoken contempt for melodrama. For Lewes, "the aesthetic question" is decided by making a conventionally hierarchical distinction between "melodrama" and "Drama," not by supposing that melodrama has its own coherent aesthetic.[14] Eliot's own, similarly graphic (and punitive) critical distinctions have been analyzed with care—distinctions between "theater" and "drama," for example, or between "theater" and "poetry." To her credit, George Eliot undoes these critical oppositions in the novels themselves, tacitly incorporating what she elsewhere loudly disavows.[15] In fact, the strength of her very contempt is a strong sign of the importance of melodrama to the oppositional and sublationary formation of her own aesthetic.[16] For as we all know, despite Eliot's contempt for melodramatic characterization, plotting, and "mechanical" effects, she practiced them with a gusto sometimes hardly mediated—and certainly not hidden—by the surface texture of her realistic narration.

While she was collecting material for *Daniel Deronda*, George Eliot and George Henry Lewes read several novels aloud together. One of them was *Le juif polonais*, the novel by Erckmann and Chatrian from which *The Bells* was adapted for the English stage.[17] Thus we must certainly recognize both *Le juif polonais* and *The Bells* as crucial in the planning of her final, most overtly and unapologetically melodramatic novel. (The sentimental fiction of Erckmann-Chatrian will appear in a cameo role in Chapter 17 of *Daniel Deronda*, as we shall soon see.) But this essay will not pursue an argument about the relation of Eliot's novel to *Le juif polonais* or *The Bells* in particular; instead it will be concerned with the larger issue of Eliot's engagement with melodramatic form in general. My introductory discussion of *The Bells*, then, should now be seen to have been just that: a way of introducing the crucial features of melodramatic form, a way of showing conclusively that Eliot was familiar with them. We can now turn to see how she puts them to work within her novel.

I doubt that I need to belabor the point that Eliot specialized in melodramatic plotting; all readers will recall Hetty Sorrel's fall at the hands of Arthur Donnithorne, her secret pregnancy, her murder of the newborn child, its haunting cries, her hard, frozen, and inexpressive face during the trial, and her last-minute rescue from the scaffold. George Eliot usually domesticates melodramatic plots like these, thereby turning them toward the representational register we call realism (whose mysteries this essay will continue to explore). Think of how Daniel Deronda's extensive meditations on illegitimacy span the entire novel and are seen to be the fountainhead of his wide sympathies, especially for women. Or think of how Eliot's famous scenes of grandiose sympathy and "confession"—Dinah with Hetty, Dorothea with Rosamond, Daniel with Gwendolen, Mordecai with Daniel—may be read as scenes of melodramatic *anagnorisis*, domesticating and sentimentalizing tragedy while secularizing confession, with a greater person and a lesser one gazing into one another's eyes with hard-won recognition.[18] Domesticated plots of melodrama, in other words, provide George Eliot's novels with their tragedies as well as their drive toward compassion, as if domestication were itself a form of sublimation—in this particular case, the sublimation of a popular form of the sublime.

In the crafting of plot, then, melodrama, negatively and dialectically engaged, makes for realism. From another angle of analysis, however, it is clear that melodrama is itself already pressing toward realism in several respects. A postrevolutionary form of prose rather than poetic drama, melodrama insistently concentrates on the implacable force of social relations and the consequences of deviating from their conventions of normalization. Famously said to be written for people who could not read, melodrama is one of the most important cultural forms—and the novel is the other—mediating the development both of class and of class consciousness in the late eighteenth and early nineteenth centuries.[19] Indeed, both melodrama and the novel mediate the development of other forms of group consciousness as well: especially gender and nationality, but also ethnicity and sexuality. Melodramatic characterization is poised on the cusp of this modern development of sociological thinking about groups and types.

Still usually lampooned for the stock stereotypicality of its characters, melodrama is in fact full of deviants and radicals. The characters *are* stereotyped, yes, but they are also novel figures, implicitly displayed against the background of more traditional, heroic, and tragic types. Melodramatic characterizations are like diagrams of social relation, operatically coded to a restricted repertory of social registers. They are meant to insist upon new potentialities registered by the particular postrevolutionary deviances of certain new social actors: servants whose wit exceeds that of their masters; rustic artisans with radical propensities; dashing rescuers and innocent escaped prisoners; honest sailors combating the injustices of the Royal Navy; women seduced, betrayed, violated, or abandoned who might or might not be restored to their domestic roles in the end; and, of course, illegitimate children inheriting through the machinery of the plot despite the degeneracy of their aristocratic fathers.

In melodrama, the type is foregrounded as a way of emphasizing the character's determinate social role, whereas in novelistic realism, the character's individuality is foregrounded but is always set against the aura of the social type. It is the form of typification alone that differs, for both work on the same modern, sociological notion that individuated forms of social life can be understood only in relation to generalized group formations.[20]

In *Daniel Deronda*, George Eliot was obviously writing against the type of the "melodramatic Jew" depicted in *The Bells*, where the avenging, otherworldly retribution for Mathias's crime crystallizes anti-Semitically around the stereotypical image of the rich, itinerant Jew, his money belt hanging conspicuously around his waist. Needless to say, this was not the kind of representation George Eliot was aiming for. The "Polish Jew" highlighted in *Daniel Deronda* is another sort altogether: Salomon Maimon, the eighteenth-century philosopher whose autobiography Daniel buys from the shop attendant who later turns out to be Mordecai (pp. 436–438). That scene is only the first in a series of descriptive and dramatized assurances that Mordecai does not fulfill the stereotype of popular anti-Semitic prejudice; entering Ezra Cohen's shop, Daniel "saw, on the dark background of books . . . a figure that was somewhat startling in its unusualness." Though the figure Daniel saw had "a finely typical Jewish face," he is evidently not "the ordinary tradesman," for though he knows the "worth" of Salomon Maimon's work, he does not know the "market-price" of the book. Like the philo-Semitic stereotype of sentimental drama, the character of Mordecai seems most immediately meant to overturn the punitively anti-Semitic stereotype.[21]

But George Eliot's experiments with stereotypes are more subtle in *Daniel Deronda*, where the signification of "the Jew" drives toward the invisible through the visible and through the force of sociological representation toward other logics. She attempts the risky strategy of posing her novel figures against the stereotypes of popular prejudice not only to overturn those stereotypes but also to complicate them. In Chapter 33, for example, as the narration follows Daniel in his rambles around "those parts of London which are most inhabited by common Jews," his reactions form a studied representation of class prejudice only intermittently resisted. The poverty-stricken and shopkeeping Jews of Holborn provoke "cringing" responses in Daniel which his growing attachments to Mordecai and Mirah—not to mention his later embrace of his discovered parentage—will eventually overturn. But Eliot's strategy of arguing for the diversity that exists within every religious type leaves most Jews unconverted from the stereotypical manners implied by "shopkeeping." In the argument of the novel, there are good Jews and bad Jews just as there are good Christians and bad Christians; but shopkeepers are always shopkeepers.[22] Thus class stereotypes reign as the price of Eliot's investment in exceptionalism. The stereotype is not exactly overturned, in other words; it is shifted to another register of representation—the register of class and social environment.

The grand example of this tangle, of course, involves Mordecai and Daniel. Mordecai seeks a classy vehicle to embody his visionary alter ego; the figure he seeks must "glorify the possibilities of the Jew" (p. 529). But after all, Daniel could never have fulfilled Mordecai's vision if he had not been raised in Sir Hugo's household and *not* as a Jew. This is one of the many reasons why Daniel is both believable and unbelievable; and it is also a reason why the politics of representation in this novel are bound to seem ambivalent and perhaps finally undecidable, both passionately philo-Semitic and yet disingenuously anti-Semitic by turns, engaged in preparing to overturn the sordid stereotypes of worldly prejudice with the glorious vision of something that eludes visualization in the terms of "what actually was."

Daniel Deronda's search for what it might or might not mean to be "a Jew" is a version of this conventionally novelistic—and conventionally melodramatic—meditation on the difficulties of reading within the competing claims of multiple social types and stereotypes. To the stranger who accosts him in the synagogue at Frankfort, implying that he might be a Jew, Daniel's cold reply is "I am an Englishman," a defensive disavowal which is an amusing *non sequitur* from the larger viewpoint of the novel's utopian, transnational logic (p. 417). Hans Meyrick imagines that these determinate social roles might be merely superficial and a bit unreal, like theatrical typecasting. "We must not make you a *rôle* of the poor Jewess," he says to Mirah, who replies quite simply, "But it is what I am really." "People don't think of me as a British Christian," Hans protests in turn—and of course we immediately do think of Hans as a representative of just that particular version of religious nationalism (pp. 545–546). The Princess Halm-Eberstein's protest against being cast in life as both "Jew" and "woman" is a version of this struggle as well, as Eliot makes brutally clear in her first interview with Daniel. Her oedipal fury at the father who desired her to fit the type of "what he called 'the Jewish woman'" impels her to make a career of resisting the role of "makeshift link" in the patriarchal chain of inheritance, yet by the time she meets Daniel, she has receded into the domestic background and bitterly acknowledges that she has become precisely that link (pp. 694, 692). Like Daniel's prejudiced gaze as he ambivalently searches through Holborn for Mirah's family, the mother's negativity is posited in order that it might eventually be overturned in Daniel's embrace of his Jewish identity.

Eliot searches in *Daniel Deronda* for ways to figure the Jew as a type of transnational ethnicity that can serve as an emblem of the novel's own transnational vision. In crafting this vision, she employs yet another sort of type. Not only, then, does Eliot overturn the stereotypes of popular prejudice and complicate each sociological type by showing that it is inevitably riven by the others, but she also attempts the conjunction of typological with sociological purposes. Nineteenth-century novels frequently draw on typological models for their plotting, and this is one residual marker of their romantic and only partially secularized vision of historical time.[23] At first nothing might seem further from the melodramatic stereotypes than these typological figures, yet they are made to play with and against each other in *Daniel Deronda*.

Notably Eliot distributes both poles of this theory to the Jews, for Mirah and Mordecai variously personify the typological commitment to historicity on the one hand and to its visionary promise of an eschatological future on the other. Mirah holds fast to the significance of "what really was," while Mordecai takes what "actually was" as an assurance of what is yet to be (pp. 419, 550, 564). I think it must be admitted that the novel suffers from its confusion among all these various types of typification, though the majesty of Eliot's aim is clear enough: the typological dynamics of prefiguration and fulfillment are meant to provide extra suspense and momentum, pointing beyond even the novel's end. Thus Mordecai's visionary sense of the possible future is wont to triumph over the novel's visual, sensory grasp of the present. But time also runs backward in this novel, and it sometimes stands absolutely still.[24]

Meanwhile, the coincidences of prefiguration and fulfillment are sometimes so blatant as to seem "melodramatic" in even the most colloquial sense of that word. Their melodrama reaches deeper, however, as we will see in the next section of this essay, when we examine the famous scene of mutual recognition between Mordecai and Daniel on Blackfriars Bridge. In that scene, the coincidental structure of the plot is fully entwined with the visual representation of types and figures and the sudden melodramatic extroversion of interiority. When the novelistic and particularized figure rising within and against the prefigured type is set off in a melodramatic tableau, the tableau itself becomes a metanovelistic figure for the novel's appropriation of melodrama. Of course the mood is reverent rather than terrifying, dignified rather than garish; but despite all the difference, by now we should also be able to see the similarity between the realization of Mordecai's vision and the vision scene in *The Bells*.

Let us now look closely at three sequences from *Daniel Deronda*: the sequence from chapters 38 and 40 of Mordecai and Daniel's mutual recognition at Blackfriars Bridge; the sequence from Chapter 17 of Daniel's rescue of Mirah during her preparation for suicide by drowning; and the sequence from Chapter 6 of Gwendolen's *tableau vivant* of Hermione from *The Winter's Tale*. We will move backward through the novel for reasons that will soon become clear. In each sequence Eliot draws on the resources of the melodramatic tableau. Each sequence contains the momentary realization in visual terms of a scene of visual recognition in the plot. Further, the characters' visual experience in each case includes the shock of melodramatic anagnorisis, realized through the mutual gaze between two faces: Mordecai and Daniel, Daniel and Mirah, Gwendolen and the dead face in the wainscot carving.

These scenes of recognition are also scenes of self-reflection, with the other face uncannily figuring the self as something seen outside itself.[25] Thus these sequences also critically explore the mutually constitutive relations between insides and outsides, subjective and objective views. While the free indirect discourse manages these exchanges by moving from the omniscient perspective of the narrator to the subjectivity of first one character and then another, the plot explores the consequences of psychic projection. In each sequence, interiority is suddenly extroverted and objectified as representation. Will it—or how will it—become effective in the plot? At the moment of the tableau, the answer to that question remains to be seen.

The narrative sequence leading up to Daniel's and Mordecai's scene of mutual recognition on Blackfriars Bridge is blatantly structured as a sequence of prefiguration and fulfillment. Furthermore, we are first told about Mordecai's expectations in Chapter 38, and the fulfillment of those expectations occurs in Chapter 40, so in the duration of reading time, Mordecai's expectations seem to be fulfilled almost magically or immediately. Chapter 39 serves to suspend the prefigurative momentum briefly while Herr Klesmer calls on Mirah to hear her sing; in Chapter 39, then, the novel tacitly knits Mirah's story to Mordecai's even though their sibling relation has not yet been revealed.

The narrator's introduction of "some facts about Mordecai" begins with an "apology for inevitable kinship" within the "type." Eliot's by-now-routine argument that every type includes both great and abject members is applied in this instance to "the visionary," for she would like us to believe in Mordecai's visionary power while also dissociating him from the stereotype of the crazy fanatic. The series of distinctions meant precisely to specify Mordecai's exact visionary power is surrounded by emphatic statements of his vast difference from Daniel. Great differences, in other words, must be spanned in the upcoming scene, set symbolically at London's newest bridge. The novel's inculcation of a refined commitment to social tolerance and its project of making us believe in prophetic vision are oddly associated here, as we have seen; and while the narrator admits that "second-sight is a flag over disputed ground," the logic of the plot attempts to ground its credibility through the interlocking of Morde-

cai's prefigurative vision with Daniel's gradually corrected view of the
Jews. Through their mutual identification, Daniel's already elastic
sympathies will be stretched far beyond their current scope, while
Mordecai's vision will be grounded in the real.

The narrative leading up to the recognition scene emphasizes the
visual component of visionary power. Mordecai had attempted to envision the particularity of his desire by looking at pictures in the National Gallery, hoping to find an example in the nation's collection of
images for the man who would extend his life into the future (p.
529). A capitalized and faintly personified "Art" is explicitly said to
have been inadequate to this task of training Mordecai's vision toward what it seeks, for "the instances are scattered but thinly over
the galleries of Europe" of a face that perfectly combines youth,
grandeur, beauty, melancholy, force, and the potential for heroism.

But despite its relative lack of sustenance from the outside world of
Art, Mordecai's vision grows inexorably within him. His visionary
power is depicted precisely as romantic *imagination* in the strict sense
of the word, a force at once growing naturally from within, attempting
to match its inward forms to the forms of the visual world, and in the
process becoming itself a partially secularized supernatural power.
The narrator tells us that "there are persons whose yearnings . . . continually take the form of images which have a foreshadowing power";
for those persons a visual image "starts up before them in complete
shape, making a coercive type" (p. 527). Mordecai's fantasy, we are
told, has gone through several stages of visualization, and by the present time of narration, his envisioned figure has turned his face toward
Mordecai, has begun to advance, and at last has been identified specifically as Daniel Deronda:

> Thus, for a long while, he habitually thought of the Being answering to
> his need as one distantly approaching or turning his back toward him,
> darkly painted against a golden sky. The reason of the golden sky lay in
> one of Mordecai's habits. He was keenly alive to some poetic aspects of
> London; and a favourite resort of his . . . was to some one of the bridges,
> especially about sunrise or sunset. . . . Thus it happened that the figure
> representative of Mordecai's longing was mentally seen darkened by the
> excess of light in the aerial background. (pp. 530–531)

(If this passage falls a bit flat, it might be because "the reason of the golden sky" lies not so much "in" one of Mordecai's habits as in the conjoined conventions of medieval illumination and theatrical back-lighting, but we will come to that in a moment.) The "coercive" or "foreshadowing power" of Mordecai's "type" must find its way outward to be realized in the plot; this shift in representational registers will be accomplished in a tableau, as Mordecai recognizes his vision outside himself. The scene begins with the narration following Daniel's point of view and soon switching to Mordecai's:

> As he lifted up his head . . . his eyes caught a well-remembered face looking towards him over the parapet of the bridge—brought out by the western light into startling distinctness and brilliancy—an illuminated type of bodily emaciation and spiritual eagerness. It was the face of Mordecai, who also, in his watch towards the west, had caught sight of the advancing boat, and had kept it fast within his gaze, at first simply because it was advancing, then with a recovery of impressions that made him quiver as with a presentiment, till at last the nearing figure lifted up its face towards him—the face of his visions—and then immediately, with white uplifted hand, beckoned again and again.
>
> For Daniel, anxious that Mordecai should recognise and await him, had lost no time before signalling, and the answer came straightaway. Mordecai lifted his cap and waved it—feeling in that moment that his inward prophecy was fulfilled. Obstacles, incongruities, all melted into the sense of completion with which his soul was flooded by this outward satisfaction of his longing. His exultation was not widely different from that of the experimenter, bending over the first stirrings of change that correspond to what in the fervour of concentrated prevision his thought has foreshadowed. The prefigured friend had come from the golden background and had signalled to him: this actually was: the rest was to be. (pp. 549–550)

Pivoting around "the face of Mordecai, who also . . . had caught sight" of his object, the point of view shifts from Daniel's gaze to Mordecai's. And once the narration begins to follow Mordecai's feelings, we see the melodramatic extroversion of his interior "pre-visions" realized in this current "vision." No one is actually seeing anything, of course; we are not in a theater. But Eliot's highly modulated, free indirect discourse can accomplish something that cannot be done in the theater, as the viewpoint switches rapidly back and forth around the figure of Mordecai's face and then of Daniel's beckoning hand.

As the sun sets in the west behind Daniel, its light casts Mordecai's face into sharp resolution, while Daniel emerges as a dark figure against "the golden background." This figure of backgrounds and foregrounds always establishes the illusion of visualization, laying out the spatial planes of a scene and establishing the parameters of its points of view. In the nineteenth century, however, the figure of a figure posed against or emerging from within a background is often used to suggest the dynamics of historical emergence: the present emerging within and against the background of the past, for example, or a novel, particularized character emerging within and against its type.[26] And indeed, in natural, aesthetic, and historical terms, Mordecai stands to Daniel as type to figure, as past to present and future. Mordecai's concentration, his asceticism, his emaciated body, his poetic fervor, and his palpable expectation of death are here made to suggest the "illumination" of a medieval manuscript, while Daniel's haloed aura is provided by the sunset—the supposedly natural, though actually slightly garish and theatrical backlighting of typological fulfillment.

A more wonderful—and more realistic—prefiguration of Daniel's meeting with Mordecai has already happened in the novel, in Chapter 17 before and during Daniel's rescue of Mirah. That earlier sequence of Daniel rowing on the river near another bridge clearly prefigures his later rowing toward Mordecai. But this relation is allowed to remain tacit in the novel, and its prefigurative significance is therefore more realistic than overtly typological. But the narrator gives a clue to the connection between these two sequences when Eliot offers what Mordecai could not find: an image from the history of art that conveys Daniel's perfect embodiment of "refinement with force."[27] Titian painted the portrait of Daniel's type, which shows him as "not seraphic any longer [but] thoroughly terrestrial and manly" (p. 226). We are told, too, that Daniel angrily and habitually rejected any notion that his face was particular or remarkable, for "his own face in the glass had during many years been associated for him with thoughts of some one whom he must be like." This sense of his unknown mother's face within his own will soon be activated as he passes under Kew Bridge "with no thought of an adventure in which his appearance was likely to play any part." For soon he will see another whose face and figure suggest a kinship with the mother—and therefore tacitly reflect his own face as well.

Daniel's rescue of Mirah on the banks of the Thames is patently melodramatic throughout—in its patterns of recurrence, its coincidences, its agitated hurry, and its plotting as a series of tableaux. Considered as a sequence, the rescue takes place in three scenes: two on the river and a third at the Meyricks' house, the domestic setting to which Daniel takes Mirah after the rescue. The scenes are arranged as a sequence of double takes, and this structure is important both to the retention of melodramatic effect and to its negation within the protocols of realism.

Like so many of Eliot's most dramatic chapters, this one opens with a dense framework of visual, textual, and musical citations, all of which help to establish the hypothesis of voice and gaze that will be needed in the rescue sequence. Voice and gaze are George Eliot's favorite figures for pure presence, and Daniel's limpid, penetrating eyes and his thrilling voice have been much insisted upon before this point in the novel. During the chapter's introductory web of citations, we are told of Daniel's facial type and vocal register: he looks like the Titian portrait, and he is "a high barytone." What words will be set to the music of this voice? The chapter's epigraph begins to let us know, offering Tennyson's translation—from "Locksley Hall"—of a famous passage from Dante's *Inferno*. Daniel will soon be singing the very same passage within the action of the chapter.

In another nineteenth-century setting, Dante's words appear as the gondolier's aria from Rossini's *Otello: Nessun maggior dolore / Che ricordarsi del tempo felice / Nella miseria* (There is no greater pain than to recall the happy time in misery).[28] In other words, this ekphrastic representation of music *within* the action of the chapter also stands epigraphically *outside* the action and comments on it. The words function as mood or key signature—but also as motto or caption— for the series of tableaux that will follow. These intertexts cluster at the beginning of the chapter and then recede, leaving a residue of feeling and a suspension of disbelief behind them.

As he sings the Rossini aria, Daniel suddenly becomes fixated before a tableau on the riverbank. In a representation of the expressive function of music in melodrama, here a visual figure seems to express the music as Deronda's feelings are suddenly extroverted in a picture:

> Deronda . . . now turned his head to the river-side, and saw at a few yards' distance from him a figure which might have been an impersonation of the misery he was unconsciously giving voice to: a girl hardly more than eighteen. . . . Her hands were hanging down clasped before her, and her eyes were fixed on the river with a look of immovable, statue-like despair. This strong arrest of his attention made him cease singing: apparently his voice had entered her inner world without her having taken any note of whence it came, for when it suddenly ceased she changed her attitude slightly, and looking round with a frightened glance, met Deronda's face. It was but a couple of moments, but that seems a long while for people to look straight at each other. . . . He felt an outleap of interest and compassion toward her. (pp. 227–228)

After he sees the figure who seems to impersonate his song, Daniel falls silent, as if to signify the complete transfer of his feelings outward into the figure before him. Her fixated stillness arrests him in turn. When Daniel grows silent, the figure moves: "she changed her attitude slightly, and looking round with a frightened glance, met Deronda's face." Their long mutual gaze suspends the moment while Daniel tries to penetrate her look, and the free indirect discourse follows his attempt: "was she hungry, or was there some other cause of bewilderment?" This baffled attempt on Daniel's part to interpret the figure leads immediately to his "outleap of interest and compassion toward her." And then she turns away. He drifts passively away with the tide, now literally detached and daydreaming about this example of the "probable romance" or the unheeded "girl-traged[y]" he has just witnessed; but the river's tide naturally brings him back. His drifting—or lack of vocation—has been an impending trouble, as this chapter emphatically begins by telling us; this drifting is the negative side of the same character trait that produces his capacity for sympathy and compassion, and both are seen to derive psychologically from his lack of mooring, his unknown origins, his uncertainty about his parentage.

Now comes the formative scene of identification, attachment, and futurity. Daniel pulls ashore and finds a secluded vantage point "so that he could see all around him, but could not be seen by anyone." As he gazes across the river, engaging in a thought experiment to see "how far it might be possible for him to shift his centre till his own personality would be no less outside him than the landscape," the scene is set for the retake of the tableau:

> He was forgetting everything else in a half-speculative, half-involuntary identification of himself with the objects he was looking at . . . when the sense of something moving on the bank opposite him . . . made him turn his glance thitherward. In the first moment he had a darting presentiment about the moving figure; and now he could see the small face with the strange dying sunlight upon it. He . . . watched her with motionless attention. She . . . took off her woolen cloak. Presently she seated herself and deliberately dipped the cloak in the water. . . . By this time Deronda felt sure that she meant to wrap the wet cloak round her as a drowning-shroud; there was no longer time to hesitate about frightening her. He rose and seized his oar to ply across; happily her position lay a little below him. The poor thing, overcome with terror at this sign of discovery from the opposite bank, sank down on the brink again. . . . She crouched and covered her face as if she kept a faint hope that she had not been seen. . . . She raised her head and looked up at him. His face now was towards the light, and she knew it again. But she did not speak for a few moments which were a renewal of their former gaze at each other. . . . Her eyes were fixed on him. . . . She rose from her sitting posture, first dragging the saturated cloak and then letting it fall on the ground. . . . Her little woman's figure as she laid her delicate chilled hands together one over the other against her waist . . . was unspeakably touching. . . . The agitating impression this forsaken girl was making on him stirred a fibre that lay close to his deepest interest in the fates of women—"perhaps my mother was like this one." (pp. 229–231)

Again he is "arrested," watching with "motionless attention." Seeing Daniel approach from across the river, Mirah freezes again into a second tableau of catatonic, terrified suffering: she "sank down . . . crouched and covered her face as if she kept a faint hope that she had not been seen."[29] During this "renewal of their former gaze at each other," while "her eyes were fixed on him," the narrative follows her every movement with balletic, pantomimic precision as she forms yet a third tableau of female suffering. Dropping her sodden cloak, she puts "her chilled hands together one over the other against her waist," presenting a figure that to Daniel is "unspeakably touching."

He speculatively identifies this tableau of female suffering with his unknown mother: " 'perhaps my mother was like this one.' " In this moment lies a deeper fixation than the arrested gaze, for in this moment he identifies himself and his unknown origins with the figure he sees before him. In seeing a type of "Mother," Daniel also uncannily sees himself outside himself; but he does not know the implications of what he sees. In this respect, Daniel's imagination of his mother at this point in the novel bears a striking resemblance to Gwendolen's blank terror in Chapter 6, to which we will turn next. Since Daniel does not know who his mother is, the sense of "Mother," figured as the inaccessibly archaic past, can be retrieved only through this fleeting sensory recognition, especially the recognition of voice and gaze.[30] The displaced and metaphorical substitution through which "Mother" returns in these tableaux of course prefigures Daniel's future commitments to Mirah and to Mordecai; but it is his "habitual" search to fill in this blank that elicits his compassion and provokes his openness to being taken up by the realities outside himself. Later in the plot, this type of "Mother" will be rationalized—and in turn displaced—in the figure of a specific mother. But for now, "Mother" is a blank mystery, the floating signification for Daniel of any and every tableau of "unspeakable calamity."

This mystery is soon broken by action, for it must be accommodated within the fiction of an ongoing real world—an accommodation which the next scenes perform by absorbing it within a series of domestic tableaux. Again we see the dialectical operation of the double take, for not only do the domestic scenes of Chapter 18 absorb the melodramatic rescue into their sentimental realism, but the domestic sequence itself involves a first scene loaded with aesthetic citation whose conversion through dialectical negation in the second scene asserts the sense of disenchanted reality. When Daniel enters the Meyricks' house, the four Meyrick women have just been reading aloud together from none other than a novel by Erckmann-Chatrian, *L'Histoire d'un conscrit* (The History of a Conscript). They are bantering with serious purpose about how the Erckmann-Chatrian novel might fit into a taxonomy of the literary genres: "'[I]t is hardly to be called a story,' said Kate. 'It is a bit of history brought near us with a strong telescope.'" Thus Kate stands up for its representational correspondence to forms of life unknown to them and less fortunate than theirs, while Mab counters with an argument about its ethical force in their own lives: "'I don't care what you call it,' said Mab, . . . 'Call it a chapter in Revelations. It makes me want to do something good, something grand. It makes me so sorry for everybody. It makes me like Schiller—I want to take the world in my arms and kiss it'" (p. 239).

Certainly George Eliot is arguing here that lower art forms can be a force for good in the world, inducing compassion as an aesthetic effect. Within this context—a discussion of sentimental affects and aesthetic effects—it is hilarious to hear Mab pursue her argument through an effusion of condescension toward Schiller. These literary-historical debates are about to be subsumed in the striking realization of yet another tableau, however, as Daniel's entrance with Mirah is depicted as an answer to their aesthetically induced compassion: "'Here is somebody to take care of instead of your wounded conscripts, Mab,'" Mrs. Meyrick announces, for Mirah's appearance seems to be an eerie fulfillment of Mab's wish.

Then, fixated on the sight of Mirah backgrounded by the light in the doorway, the three Meyrick sisters form a tableau of spectatorship, standing "near each other in mute confidence that they were all feeling alike under this appeal to their compassion. Mab looked rather awe-stricken, as if this answer to her wish were something preternatural" (p. 240). And of course it *is* "preternatural"—or at least it *was* preternatural—before the impact of coincidence and psychic projection is rationalized by the explicit act of narrative detachment exerted by the words "*as if.*" Thus George Eliot makes a respectful point about the salutary use of sentimental fiction—artificial as it may be, devoted to sentimental stereotypes as it may be, it *can* influence its readers to extend their compassion into the real world—

while at the same time she subordinates it within the grander, "higher," and more comprehensive claims of her own novel to accomplish this same effect.

The last sequence we shall consider comes first in the novel, in Chapter 6. It is, perhaps, the passage most likely to leap to mind when thinking of *Daniel Deronda* in light of the melodramatic tableau. Preparing to consider it, we need simply recall that when Gwendolen and her family first arrive at Offendene (in reduced circumstances as family dependents), they discover an odd hinged panel in the wainscotting at the far end of the drawing room. Inside is a frightening scene suddenly revealed: "The opened panel had disclosed the picture of an upturned dead face, from which an obscure figure seemed to be fleeing with outstretched arms" (p. 56). Gwendolen shudders silently with horror at the shocking sight and, in her characteristic tone of girlishly imperious self-defense, gives an order that the suddenly disclosed tableau should be shut up and never opened again. "Let the key be brought to me," commands Gwendolen. No stronger novelistic hint could be given that whatever is being shut up will eventually be opened again (with a "key" that will also return, transformed).

Soon daily life is humming along at Offendene, and Chapter 6 focuses on the holiday performance of charades. The rector reasons that charades are more decorous than the "private theatricals" which he will not allow in his home—for after all, charades are a mere "imitation of acting," and presumably the act of acting as if one is acting denatures and domesticates the acting (pp. 89–90). Reminding us that these family tableaux are melodrama's respectable kin, Herr Klesmer provides the musical accompaniment to Gwendolen's tableau charade of Hermione from *The Winter's Tale*. With a game good humor at his own descent to the low register of these home theatricals, he strikes up a melodramatic chord on the organ:

> Herr Klesmer struck up a thunderous chord—but in the same instant, and before Hermione had put forth her foot, the movable panel, which was on a line with the piano, flew open on the right opposite the stage and disclosed the picture of the dead face and the fleeing figure, brought out in pale definiteness by the position of the waxlights. Everyone was

startled, but all eyes in the act of turning towards the panel were recalled by a piercing cry from Gwendolen, who stood without change of
attitude, but with a change of expression that was terrifying in its terror.
She looked like a statue into which a soul of Fear had entered: her pallid
lips were parted; her eyes, usually narrowed under their long lashes,
were dilated and fixed. Her mother . . . and Rex too could not help
going to her side. But the touch of her mother's arm had the effect of an
electric charge; Gwendolen fell on her knees and put her hands before
her face. She was still trembling, but mute. (pp. 91–92)

The narrative point of view, following "all eyes" of the audience, rico-
chets quickly between the opened panel and Gwendolen, whose expression, "terrifying in its terror," presents the conventionally fixated
gaze of the tableau: "She looked like a statue into which a soul of
Fear had entered: her pallid lips were parted; her eyes . . . were dilated and fixed." When her mother and Rex Gascoigne rush to her
aid, she breaks down into the still and silent posture of female suffering; she "fell on her knees and put her hands before her face. She was
still trembling, but mute."

This double tableau is structured as a double take for both Gwendolen and her audience—and hence calls attention to itself as an inten-
sively aesthetic meditation. Of course everyone expects Hermione to
come to life, just as she does in *The Winter's Tale*, but instead Gwendolen is frozen into a deeper and more deathlike stillness, with the
blank eyes of a statue and muteness that signify "absence" just as surely
as voice and gaze signify presence. Thus an overtly mimetic (and therefore "false" or merely theatrical) tableau gives way to a sincere, un-
feigned (and therefore "real") tableau, "outside" the action of the
theatrical performance. We are meant to believe that art gives way to
real life—for no matter how low and narrow the bourgeois amusement
of charades may be, the performance of Shakespeare does lend a whiff of
higher art to it, and national high art at that. Eliot mixes the flavors of
her broadest culture in this scene, offering us a stew of high and low
aesthetic signs, with classical sculpture, the now nationalistically en-
coded Renaissance drama, and a form of contemporary popular entertainment (*tableaux vivants*) all stirred up together. But again, these
aesthetic citations are posited only to be displaced and replaced—with

the turn toward Gwendolen's blank terror. The sudden motion of the picture signals the shift in registers of representation and the appropriation of melodramatic convention to the purposes of narrative realism, whose rapid movements of absorption and negation aim to move us "outside" the mode of representation altogether.

This sudden shift in representational registers implies a distance or detachment in the second instance, which makes the unintended tableau of real terror "doubly striking." The terrified and ungrounded anagnorisis is privileged over the cluster of aesthetic citations comprising the showy, stagy form of the charade. Let me be clear: again, I am not primarily concerned with unpacking the significances of the intertext here, though that endeavor has had extremely productive critical results.[31] Instead I am concerned with the rhythmic sequence of these tableaux and with my related argument that the periodic representation and negation of overtly aesthetic objects serves to guarantee the realism of the scene. A work of art flashes by and disappears in order to make us believe that we are now seeing something other than art, something real. "These things are a parable," in other words—in this case, a parable of George Eliot's production of realism.[32]

But the flickering sequence of moving pictures is stubbornly opaque: What is it that we have seen, or imagined that we have seen? Gwendolen's unintended tableau is the sign of *something* real—but what? The narrator has loudly reminded us, early in this same chapter, that epistemological and hermeneutic doubt are very much the rule in the real world, where "all meanings, we know, depend on the key of interpretation" (p. 88). Certainly George Eliot's entire corpus is full of this warning that the *theatrum mundi* is rather unfortunately not *enough* like a real theater: for in the real world, the signs that are given may—or may not—be sufficient to ensure an accurate reading.[33] Gwendolen thinks she holds the "key" (to the panel), but she does not understand herself—and neither do we—for something has been opened here that defies rationalization or even interpretation.

To remind us of this uncertainty, this sequence returns us from Gwendolen's tableau of terror to a babble of interpretive queries from her audience: "'Was it part of the play?'" (p. 92) Was it inside or outside the representation? As we follow the various possible interpretations offered by dramatized voices from the audience and by the free indirect discourse following several characters in their feelings, we might be fooled temporarily into thinking we can interpret Gwendolen's terror. But in fact we do not actually know anything much about what her terror really means. Like her audience in the scene, we too are placed "outside" Gwendolen's tableau and must remain conscious of our enforced distance. We are told that this event is representative (as we would expect), but that helps us only to the tautological point of understanding that these moments of blank terror are a given trait of Gwendolen's character: her "susceptibility to terror" erupts "in these occasional experiences, which seemed like a brief remembered madness, an unexplained exception from her normal life" (p. 94). The moments are "unexplained" because, as we are told, this "liability of hers to fits of spiritual dread . . . had not yet found its way into connection" with anything else. Her estranged and unpsychologized blankness—like the melodramatic tableau itself—is sheer datum, *donnée*, the suddenly given thing. Our "identification" can operate for now only at the distance of (hypothetical) visuality; we "see" but do not yet understand. The tableau of the real, in other words, serves as an empty placeholder here, "excessive" in the strict sense that it will not be cognitively limited until later and then, of course, retroactively.

In other words, it is the work of the novel to "connect" her "spiritual dread" to real-life causes and effects.[34] All along, Gwendolen's dreadful sense of metaphysical exile is recruited to explain her attraction to Deronda. Alas, Gwendolen's susceptibility to dread will eventually be all too "connected" to her life story, for this early tableau of her habitual, blank terror will later in the novel be recognizably reduced to a prefiguration of Grandcourt's drowned face. Gwendolen will then react with terror at her sudden awareness that she had witnessed a tableau of her own guilty wish: "I saw my wish outside me," she confesses, with a sense of despair that her life had closed around this meaning: "a dead face—I shall never get away from it" (pp. 761, 753).[35] But this eventual processing in the mill of realistic narration happens much later in the durational time of reading—perhaps even casting a spell of amnesia over our earlier, anxious moments of epistemological uncertainty in the face of the frozen image of terror. If this scene in Chapter 6 is melodramatic, then, it is also a demonstration of the voracious, anthological appetite of realism—especially George Eliot's realism—which takes up into itself all other genres and dialectically sublates them. If the effect of the return of the repressed in melodrama is to fill reality with psychic terror, the effect of novelistic realism is to premise psychic terror and gradually to cover it over with real-life sociologized and psychologized connectedness. Yet it should be remembered that in either case a crucial mystery remains.

The very structure of Gwendolen's character, in other words, posits or institutes the melodramatic oscillation between durational, quotidian reality and graphically foregrounded, static moments of uncertain meaningfulness. If George Eliot shows us that "character, too, is a process and an unfolding" (*Middlemarch*, Chapter 15), each character unfolds from a premised (and in this case pictorialized) and mysteriously *given* form of implication. The novel's epigraph announces this postulate melodramatically: "Let thy chief terror be of thine own soul: / There . . . Lurks vengeance, footless, [and] irresistible." Unfolding Gwendolen's character over the duration of realistic narrative time, George Eliot rationalizes—and "realizes"—the narrative form of melodrama.

In conclusion, let us look again at Adorno's suggestion—itself momentarily and mysteriously *en passant* within the long duration of dialectical unfolding that is his *Aesthetic Theory*—that the spectacular display of fireworks might be seen as "prototypical for artworks" in general: "[Fireworks] appear empirically yet are liberated from the burden of the empirical, which is the obligation of duration; they are a sign from heaven yet artifactual, an ominous warning, a script that flashes up, vanishes, and indeed cannot be read for its meaning." I have focused in this essay on George Eliot's use of the melodramatic tableau as a strategy for exempting certain scenes from what Adorno calls the novel's "obligation of duration," a way to emphasize the uncertain significance of appearances and to endow them momentarily with the sense of mystery that is born of their uncertain status as both providentially given and artifactually crafted. This momentary mystery is itself entirely artifactual, generated in a sequential narrative process of theatricalized realization—visualized take and double take—as we have seen.

Thus Eliot bundles together questions of perception, epistemology, and attention to art (and the history of art). And thus, her particular brand of realism is "aesthetic" in several senses: it is concerned, of course, with producing the illusion of empirical experience; but it also emphasizes its distance or detachment, displaying the artifactual production of its illusion. That double aim—to produce the sense of reality together with the awareness that it is artificially produced—is frequently unfolded in the novel's time as a sequential dynamic, with one scene, established as a tableau, giving way to another's supposedly more immediate realism. This dialectical dynamic is often pursued through reference to artworks "outside" the action; the subsequent gesture (in the double take) of turning away from art-historical citation back toward the scene of action is meant to secure the realistic immediacy of the action. But the intensified realism of these later scenes is itself artifactual, as we have seen, and they, too, often imitate the melodramatic tableau.

I have wanted, then, to stress Eliot's disavowal, assimilation, and sublimation of popular art within the formation of what we still—and with good reason—call her "high" realism. Melodrama does, finally, have to be seen as popular art, though it has been one purpose of this essay to suggest that its particular aesthetic form should be given due critical consideration nonetheless. During Adorno's discussion of genre categories and the modern erosion of their traditional hierarchy, he argues quite strongly for the role of "low" art forms within bourgeois and modernist aesthetics.[36] The anthological and sublationary form of Eliot's novelistic discourse should be seen as one monumental result of this historical process.

In stressing the aesthetic induction of a residual, empty sense of revelation—"a sign from heaven yet artifactual"—Adorno offers an apt characterization of the secularizing aims of nineteenth-century realism, which internalizes the memory of an earlier providentialism. George Eliot's tangle of "Jewish" and "Christian" narrative forms displays this ongoing project as yet in process. Her version of the novel's generic skepticism about appearances keeps her providentialism in "the aerial background," as it were; the meaning of appearances is uncertain now that they are understood to be unhinged from supernatural revelation, and the sky is instead filled with the pyrotechnics of the urban sun, setting in the west. Because it is so incompletely secularized—and therefore predicts too blatantly its narrative fulfillment—the tableau of Mordecai's vision is not as successful as the tableaux of rescue, female suffering, and domestication in Chapter 17 or the tableau of terror in Chapter 6. But even in the most successful cases, the eruptive, interruptive, punctual, and momentous form of these realistic sequences contains a faint nostalgia residual in the form of revelation itself. Visual revelation, in other words, still partakes of its romantic attachment to visionary revelation. These secularized, melodramatic moments of revelation seem meaningful and yet uncertain partly *because* they "flash up" and so quickly vanish. They present us with a novelistic form of "second sight."

In fact this pattern—in which continuous duration is periodically interrupted by a "script that flashes up [and] vanishes"—describes a particularly nineteenth-century narrative form, discernible across several genres. In English, this narrative form is most often associated with Wordsworth, whose "spots of time," those temporarily unconnected lyrical moments of "visionary dreariness" or "visionary splendour," rise out of and interrupt the depressed background of ongoing experience. Martin Meisel, in his great exploration of the relations between narrative, theatrical, and pictorial art in the English nineteenth century, calls this shared narrative form "serial discontinuity," a term whose theoretical and historical potential can hardly be overemphasized. Throughout his work, he highlights the period's concentration on the function of pictures to provide the highlighted moments that must then be connected by narrative or dramatic sequencing, whether the logic of causation remains implicit or is rendered explicit.[37] Like Meisel, I have been urging us to see this narrative form operating in melodrama, where the interart *mélange* that also became a grand aspiration of the period may be clearly seen as well, and where the suddenly exempted moments are literally visualized (and not only figuratively or metaphorically so, as they must be in novelistic narration). And so, I have also wanted to stress the necessity of seeing theatrical melodrama and novelistic realism as two sides of the same epistemological and representational coin, developing in mutual implication over the course of the nineteenth century.[38] The implications of this cluster of issues are complex and far-reaching, and I can only begin to unfold them here.

Even recently it has been suggested that narrative realism brings about its effects because it imitates and refers us to the supposed transparency of the photograph, or because its multiple perspectives converge in the illusion of truthful representation.[39] Instead, I think we should focus on free indirect discourse as the crucial technology of novelistic realism. It is this groundbreaking technique that mobilizes narrative exchanges between interior and exterior, subjective and objective views. In realistic narration, free indirect discourse stabilizes and mediates the melodramatic oscillation between representations "inside" and "outside" the action, replacing the melodramatic oscillation with an oscillation of its own between subjective and objective representations. As we have seen, the melodramatic tableau (like novelistic narration) can also express the sudden extroversion of interiority; and novelistic narration can of course (like melodrama) also step outside the action, turn around, and comment on it. The critical switch point can be so modulated in Eliot's narration that the moment is often unperceived when the narration switches out of free indirect discourse to reassume an objective or omniscient stance.

But the important point for now is my focus on this dynamic mobilization of positions, whether situated in novel or in melodrama. It is the modulation or oscillation itself that is critically important—and the access each set of techniques lends to exterior and interior views, the different yet mutually implicated epistemological stances set in motion by free indirect discourse and by the music and moving pictures of melodrama.[40] The novelistic imitation of the melodramatic tableau becomes fully significant only within an understanding that the nineteenth-century history of these two quintessentially modern, bourgeois genres might be seen, in this respect, to be working on the same set of problems.

Like the switch points operated by the melodramatic tableaux, the technology of free indirect discourse inculcates in its readers an internal mobility, the skill of following as the representation turns inside out, over and over again. Once the technique becomes conventional, it seems invisible—and even inevitable—but like the development of the melodramatic tableau, the development of free indirect discourse took time, and when accomplished, it marked an epoch in the history of the novel.[41] Both melodrama and the nineteenth-century novel, then, participate in the post-Lockean and post-Kantian project of developing technologies for reading the mutual metamorphoses of "inside" and "outside" views. Both melodrama and novelistic realism must by the same token be seen as significantly prepsychoanalytic, for in their investigations of psychic projection, both nineteenth-century melodrama and the novel consider the notion that inside and outside views are not only mutually implicated and not easily distinguished but above all mutually *formative*. In *Daniel Deronda*, for example, George Eliot's meditation on wish fulfillment and her uses of the melodramatic tableau can be seen as one spectacular culmination of a long history of romantic, "Gothic," and melodramatic concern with the potentially "real" effects of psychic phenomena. This is, of course, a scientific issue as well as an aesthetic one.

Therefore I have meant to indicate that the melodramatic tableau should be seen as one solution to a complex and long-term aesthetic and technological problem. Simon Shepherd and Peter Womack, exceptionally witty cultural historians of the theater, have characterized nineteenth-century melodrama as "the work of mechanical reproduction in an age of art."[42] And truly, in a sense, one great "work of mechanical reproduction" in the nineteenth century—one question that occupied a great deal of attention in just about every field of endeavor—was the question of how to get the picture moving. Hence, of course, film history takes up the technical and aesthetic problems I have been discussing—the exchange of inside and outside views, the role of pictures in constituting this relation, the goal of mobilizing the relation—where melodrama leaves off.

The early cinema is so fully indebted to melodrama as to seem from one point of view continuous with it—in its use of live music to accompany the silent film and in its wholesale adaptation of melodramatic plots, stock characterizations, and acting styles. But historians of film have also drawn our attention to the alternation, in silent film, between passages of action and screens empty of moving pictures, bearing only written captions.[43] In this model, the place of the still and silent tableau is replaced by a blank screen with words on it, demanding to be read and directing the viewer's interpretation with its "outside" commentary on the dramatic action.

The technology of cinematic moving pictures represents the apotheosis of "serial discontinuity," since the illusion of motion is created by a sequence of discrete still shots serially juxtaposed and set in motion so rapidly that the spectator's persistence of vision elides the discontinuity altogether. Thus does the aesthetic of serial discontinuity transcend and negate itself, especially after the talkies eliminate the captions and after the audience becomes skilled in reading the visual syntax that distinguishes cinematic realism. Like the development of free indirect discourse, these technologies took time to develop; like free indirect discourse, they modulate the exchange between inside and outside views. Eisenstein famously claimed that D. W. Griffith learned the techniques of crosscutting and montage from Dickens,[44] but of course it has been one purpose of this essay to imply that Dickens himself learned them from the melodramatic theater that he frequented and loved. George Eliot saw them there, too.

A long history of technological innovation in the production of images—both still and moving—may be traced throughout the nineteenth century, and here my essay points outward toward other vast and related topics. In the exploration of those topics, however, as Adorno might caution, the flash points of aesthetic determination must also be taken into account, certainly not to displace the determinations of technology but to aid in resisting the temptation to make technological determinism the only story. The nineteenth-century anthology of moving-picture technologies includes panoramas and dioramas, optical toys of all sorts, the magic lantern with its serially "dissolving views," and of course, photography, whose formalities of instantaneous composure suggest it to Adorno and Benjamin as the model for a dialectical and material history, written as the past flashes up in the present moment.[45] The photograph is not the opposite of the "moving picture," but—as we now can see—its apparent stillness is merely one side of its potential suddenly to move. Finally, then, it has been the aim of this essay to suggest that behind the photograph, where perhaps we have not clearly seen it yet, lies the melodramatic tableau.

Acknowledgments

Thanks especially to readers of the first draft of this essay, who offered invaluable suggestions: Rosemarie Bodenheimer, Barry Qualls, and Michael McKeon. Other friends and colleagues responded generously after listening or reading, and their comments have provoked important revisions: Mary Baine Campbell, Jay Clayton, Nancy Henry, Neil Hertz, Rachel Jacoff, John Kucich, George Levine, Joe Litvak, Jonathan Loesberg, Jack Matthews, Peggy Phelan, Adela Pinch, Yopie Prins, Eve Kosofsky Sedgwick, Jeffrey Wallen, and Tina Zwarg.

Notes

1. The epigraph appears in Theodor W. Adorno, *Aesthetic Theory*, trans. and ed. by Robert Hullot-Kentor (Minneapolis: University of Minnesota Press, 1997), p. 81. Adorno's subsequent discussion of Benjamin's "dialectical image" and Lessing's "pregnant moment" is particularly relevant to the present essay (pp. 84–86). Thanks to Peter Osborne, whose leadership of the Kant and Adorno reading group significantly altered my thinking about aesthetics (Center for the Critical Analysis of Contemporary Culture, Rutgers University, 1997–1998); and to Ankhi Mukherjee, whose work on the aesthetics of hysteria made me aware of the importance of this particular passage.
2. Gordon S. Haight, ed., *The George Eliot Letters*, 9 vols. (New Haven, CT: Yale University Press, 1954–1974), vol. V, p. 225.
3. Émile Erckmann and Pierre Alexandre Chatrian, *Le Juif polonais* series/vol. 8 of *Contes et romans populaires* (Paris: J. Hetzel, 1866–1867). The French adaptation had been performed at the Théâtre Cluny in 1869, with music by Etienne Singla.
4. Leopold Lewis, *The Bells*, in *Nineteenth-Century Plays*, ed. George Rowell (Oxford: Oxford University Press, 1972), pp. 467–502. See also *Henry Irving and "The Bells": Irving's Personal Script of the Play*, ed. David Mayer (Manchester, UK: Manchester University Press, 1980), pp. 31–99. Nigel Gardner (in Mayer, ed.) discusses Singla's music for *The Bells* and gives several musical examples from the score (pp. 108–131).
5. Martin Meisel's study takes this technical term and extends its significance greatly; *Realizations: Narrative, Pictorial, and Theatrical Arts in Nineteenth-Century England* (Princeton, NJ: Princeton University Press, 1983); see esp. pp. 91–96. The example of a melodramatic realization most widely remembered today is Douglas Jerrold's use of David Wilkie's *The Rent Day* as the opening tableau of his play by the same name, and his realization of Wilkie's *Distraining for Rent* in the tableau ending Act I (see Meisel, *Realizations*, pp. 148–157). See also Martin Meisel, "Scattered Chiaroscuro: Melodrama as a Matter of Seeing," in Jacky Bratton, Jim Cook, and Christine Gledhill, eds., *Melodrama: Stage, Picture, Screen* (London: British Film Institute, 1994), pp. 65–81. There, amid larger issues of visualization and time, Meisel discusses the use (in post-1860 productions) of Jean-Léon Gérôme's *Duel after a Masked Ball* to realize the psychic projection in the duel scene of Boucicault's *The Corsican Brothers* (pp. 73–74).
6. Denis Diderot, "Isolated Thoughts on Painting," in *Selected Writings on Art and Literature*, trans. and ed. Geoffrey Bremner (London: Penguin, 1994), p. 333.

7. Michael Fried, *Absorption and Theatricality: Painting and Beholder in the Age of Diderot* (Chicago: University of Chicago Press, 1980), p. 92: "that is, a painting had to call to someone, bring him to a halt in front of itself, and hold him there as if spellbound and unable to move."

8. In the tacit theoretical overlay of Althusser on Diderot here, I am admittedly recruiting Althusser for an aesthetic argument. But the truly salient point is rather that the aesthetic formation of the tableau not only "contains" but also makes possible critique of and resistance to social solicitation and ideological interpellation. This argument will have to be bracketed here, but I will return in forthcoming work on melodrama to the function of the tableau as a moment both of interpellation *and* of critical class consciousness.

9. Denis Diderot, "Conversations on 'The Natural Son,'" in *Selected Writings on Art and Literature,* p. 15. The "conversations" in this critical dialogue feature Dorval, the main character from the play, who is speaking here. Diderot's reflexivity in this piece is both humorous and critical, as for example when Dorval is given the lines: "I speak without partiality. I invented neither of them. The *coup de théâtre* is a fact; the tableau, a happy circumstance created by chance which I was able to take advantage of."

10. Michael Fried, *Absorption and Theatricality,* p. 95.

11. Diderot, "The Paradox of the Actor," in *Selected Writings on Art and Literature,* pp. 98–158. Fried's work has been underappreciated for the way it suggests the interrelations of "absorption" and "theatricality" as well as their opposition in theory.

12. In other words, I want to specify an understanding of the tableau within the "mode of excess," "the aesthetics of astonishment," "the text of muteness" that Peter Brooks explores in his landmark study, *The Melodramatic Imagination: Balzac, Henry James, Melodrama and the Mode of Excess* (New Haven, CT: Yale University Press, 1976, new preface 1995).

13. There is concrete evidence elsewhere in her letters and in the reminiscences of friends that she did not admire Irving's acting in other plays. For example, see Haight, ed., *George Eliot Letters,* vol. VI, p. 242; vol. VII, p. 289; and vol. IX, p. 175. For a rare, positive comment on Irving, see *Letters,* vol. VII, p. 23.

14. Even when Lewes admires a specific production, he turns with disgust against the genre; see George Henry Lewes, "Déjazet—*The Corsican Brothers,*" review from *The Leader,* February 28, 1852, in *Dramatic Essays by John Forster and George Henry Lewes,* ed. William Archer and Robert W. Lowe (London: Walter Scott Ltd., 1896), pp. 183–189.

15. The best studies of Eliot's vexed appropriation of theatricality take up these critical oppositions (and include fine readings of *Daniel Deronda*). See "Poetry and Theatricality in *Daniel Deronda,*" in Joseph Litvak, *Caught in the Act: Theatricality in the Nineteenth-Century English Novel* (Berkeley, CA: University of California Press, 1992), pp. 147–194; and "Daniel Deronda and the Wisest Beholder," in David Marshall, *The Figure of Theater: Shaftesbury, Defoe, Adam Smith, and George Eliot* (New York: Columbia University Press, 1986), pp. 193–240.

16. On what I'm calling the "oppositional and sublationary form of her aesthetic," see, for example, Jonathan Arac, "Rhetoric and Realism in Nineteenth-Century Fiction: Hyperbole in *The Mill on the Floss*," *ELH* 46 (1979), pp. 673–692. Arac uses the figure of hyperbole to demonstrate realism's self-consciousness or reflexivity.

17. Gordon Haight, *George Eliot: A Biography* (Oxford: Oxford University Press, 1968), p. 472.

18. In "Notes on Form in Art" (1886), George Eliot may be taken to suggest that a modern form of *anagnorisis* ("in . . . later . . . fable") is literalized in character recognition. See *Essays of George Eliot*, ed. Thomas Pinney (New York: Columbia University Press, 1963), p. 436.

19. That melodrama was intended for illiterate audiences was the famous claim of Guilbert de Pixerécourt, the master of postrevolutionary French melodrama.

20. Frankfurt Institute for Social Research, *Aspects of Sociology*, preface by Max Horkheimer and Theodor W. Adorno (Boston: Beacon Press, 1972).

21. George Eliot, *Daniel Deronda*, ed. Barbara Hardy (Harmondsworth: Penguin, 1967). All references to the novel will be cited from this edition. Edgar Rosenberg's "The Jew in Western Drama: An Essay" (added in 1968 to *The Jew in English Drama: An Annotated Bibliography*, compiled by Edward D. Coleman [New York: New York Public Library and Ktav Publishing House, Inc., 1943]) is particularly helpful in its treatment of the historical doubleness discernible in dramatic stereotypes of the Jew (see pp. 43–45). He argues that the effort to play against anti-Semitic stereotypes issued in the creation of a philo-Semitic stereotype in late-eighteenth-century sentimental drama (e.g., Cumberland, Dibdin, Inchbald, Kotzebue, and Iffland). This antistereotypical stereotype produced the novel character he calls "the Jew as Christian." In these plays, "the crisis on which the play hinges reveals [the Jew] to be a paragon of generosity and samaritan self-sacrifice" (p. 44).

22. Joseph Litvak argues that Eliot's distinction in *Daniel Deronda* between "good" Jewishness and "bad" Jewishness is aligned with her distinction between great art and bad art (and that neither distinction will hold); *Caught in the Act*, pp. 171–172 and ff.

23. On typology as narrative form in George Eliot's fiction, see Barry Qualls, "Speaking Through Parable: George Eliot," in *The Secular Pilgrims of Victorian Fiction: The Novel as Book of Life* (Cambridge, UK: Cambridge University press, 1982), pp. 139–188; and Mary Wilson Carpenter, "The Apocalypse of the Old Testament," in *George Eliot and the Landscape of Time: Narrative Form and Protestant Apocalyptic History* (Chapel Hill, NC: University of North Carolina Press, 1986), pp. 131–153.

24. For the argument that cause and effect are reversed in the novel, see Cynthia Chase, "The Decomposition of the Elephants: Double-Reading *Daniel Deronda*," in *Decomposing Figures: Rhetorical Readings in the Romantic Tradition* (Baltimore, MD: Johns Hopkins University Press, 1986), pp. 157–174. As Chase points out, the "rhetorical principles by

which the text is constructed" are "at odds with the meanings indicated" by [the] narrator and dissimulated by the novel's narrative mode" (p. 157). For a strong critique of the novel's Christian Hegelianism, see Christina Crosby, "George Eliot's Apocalypse of History," in *The Ends of History: Victorians and "The Woman Question"* (New York: Routledge, 1991), pp. 12–43.

25. This is the figure of self-reflection "at the end of the line" that Neil Hertz has identified and explored in *The End of the Line: Essays on Psychoanalysis and the Sublime* (New York: Columbia University Press, 1985). See in particular his "Afterword," which discusses *Daniel Deronda* among other examples. With thanks to Neil Hertz for making this connection between our arguments during his presentation at the English Institute ("Fatal Compassion," September 17, 2000, included in this volume as "Poor Hetty").

26. See my *Transfigured World: Walter Pater's Aesthetic Historicism* for more on this metafigural figure (Ithaca, NY: Cornell University Press, 1989).

27. The particular Titian portrait, *The Young Man with a Glove* (Louvre) is reproduced and discussed by Hugh Witemeyer, *George Eliot and the Visual Arts* (New Haven, CT: Yale University press, 1979), fig. 21, following p. 173 and pp. 101–104. Witemeyer points out that after Daniel is identified by Mordecai on the bridge, Eliot turns to *The Tribute Money*, also by Titian, to illustrate Mordecai's appearance and Daniel's acceptance of his vocation.

28. *Inferno* V. *The Divine Comedy of Dante Alighieri: Inferno*, trans. John D. Sinclair (New York and Oxford: Oxford University Press, 1939), p. 79.

29. Andrew Thompson finds in this tableau a visual and literary citation of Leopardi's statuesque poetic portrait of Italy sitting "like a disconsolate mother in chains, hiding her face on her knees and weeping." I think he is right. But it is important that this resemblance cannot be felt at this time in the novel and may only be discerned retroactively (in Chapter 39), when Mirah sings the words of Leopardi, set to music by the fictional "Joseph Leo." Andrew Thompson, *George Eliot and Italy: Literary, Cultural and Political Influences from Dante to the Risorgimento* (London: Macmillan, 1998), pp. 161–166.

30. Only one vague memory of "Mother" remains to Daniel: "Daniel then straining to discern something in that early twilight, had a dim sense of having been kissed very much, and surrounded by thin, cloudy, scented drapery, till his fingers caught in something hard, which hurt him, and he began to cry" (p. 203).

31. The best reading of the Shakespearean intertext is by David Marshall, *The Figure of Theater*, pp. 230–231.

32. The pointed reminder that "these things are a parable," is pronounced by Eliot's narrator in both *Felix Holt* and *Middlemarch* (Chapter 27, concluding the famous pier glass passage). See Qualls, "Speaking Through Parable" pp. 160–161.

33. As David Marshall has pointed out, the Shakespearean intertext itself raises the issue of epistemological skepticism in visual interpretation with an allusion to dumb show, an important precursor to the pantomimic conventions of melodrama. The scene that precedes Hermione's

tableau (Act V, *The Winter's Tale*) contains this commentary on the king and Camillo: "There was speech in their dumbness, language in their very gesture. . . . But the wisest beholder, that knew no more but seeing, could not say if the importance were joy or sorrow." David Marshall, *The Figure of Theater*, pp. 230–231.

34. Though, as Cynthia Chase has shown us, "causes" sometimes masquerade as "effects" ("The Decomposition of the Elephants: Double-Reading *Daniel Deronda*").

35. Neil Hertz has made this point powerfully: "It is not just her wish but her dread that she sees outside herself, and, as her interior life is turned inside out, she appears 'within' it as a passive victim as well as a projecting agent." "Some Words in George Eliot: Nullify, Neutral, Numb, Number," in *Languages of the Unsayable: The Play of Negativity in Literature and Literary Theory*, ed. Sanford Budick and Wolfgang Iser (New York: Columbia University press, 1989), pp. 291.

36. Adorno, *Aesthetic Theory*, see especially pp. 199–225.

37. Meisel, *Realizations*, esp. pp. 38, 247–281.

38. Jeffrey Franklin's recent book also argues for the mutual implication of novel and melodrama; *Serious Play: The Cultural Form of the Nineteenth-Century Realist Novel* (Philadelphia: University of Pennsylvania Press, 1999). See esp. the sections on "the novelization of the theatrical," "the novel versus melodrama," and "sympathy/theatricality," pp. 83–87, 87–92, and 120–123.

39. Nancy Armstrong, *Fiction in the Age of Photography: The Legacy of British Realism* (Cambridge, MA: Harvard University Press, 1999); Elizabeth Ermarth, *Realism and Consensus in the English Novel* (Princeton, NJ: Princeton University Press, 1983).

40. In discussing the "exclusively literary" style of free indirect discourse as a method of internalization, Michael McKeon argues that "the effect of greater interiority is achieved by the oscillation or differential *between* the perspectives of narrator and character, by the process of moving back and forth between 'outside' and 'inside,' a movement that seems palpably to carve out a space of subjective interiority precisely through its narrative objectification." *Theory of the Novel: A Historical Approach* (Baltimore, MD: Johns Hopkins University Press, 2000), p. 485.

41. On the significance of free indirect discourse for the history of the novel, see McKeon, "Subjectivity, Character, Development," in *Theory of the Novel* (pp. 485–491) and the selections by Dorrit Cohn and Ann Banfield in that volume (pp. 493–536); John Bender, *Imagining the Penitentiary: Fiction and the Architecture of Mind in Eighteenth-Century England* (Chicago: University of Chicago Press, 1987), esp. pp. 203, 210–213, and 226–228; and Margaret Anne Doody, "George Eliot and the Eighteenth-Century Novel," *Nineteenth-Century Fiction*, (1980), pp. 269–291. Bender argues that free indirect discourse and the penitentiary "present collateral images of one another." Doody stresses the experimental nature of free indirect discourse to represent feminine projective affiliation in the work of female novelists earlier than Jane Austen. Bender as well as David Marshall discuss free indirect discourse as a legacy of Adam Smith's meditations on sympathy as a triangulated, theatrical

production of the impartial spectator. See Bender, pp. 226–228 and Marshall, *The Figure of Theater,* pp. 167–192.

42. Simon Shepherd and Peter Womack, *English Drama: A Cultural History* (Oxford: Blackwell, 1996), pp. 211–218.

43. See, for example, A. Nicholas Vardac, *Stage to Screen: Theatrical Method from Garrick to Griffith* (Cambridge, MA: Harvard University Press, 1949), p. 75. Vardac's work (outdated in particular because of its naïvely progressivist assumption that melodrama was striving but failing to achieve full realism) has been superceded by several recent studies, including Ben Brewster and Lea Jacobs, *Theatre to Cinema* (Oxford: Oxford University Press, 1997); and Michael T. Gilmore, *Differences in the Dark: American Movies and English Theater* (New York: Columbia University Press, 1998).

44. Sergei Eisenstein, "Dickens, Griffith, and the Film Today" (1944), in *Film Form* (New York: Harcourt, Brace, 1949).

45. Hence, for example, Walter Benjamin, "Theses on the Philosophy of History," in *Illuminations,* ed. Hannah Arendt (New York: Harcourt, Brace & World, Inc., 1955), from thesis V, p. 257: "The past can be seized only as an image which flashes up at the instant when it can be recognized and is never seen again." On Benjamin's photographic conception of history, see Eduardo Cadava, *Words of Light: Theses on the Photography of History* (Princeton, NJ: Princeton University Press, 1997); on the historical ontology of the photograph, especially with reference to Benjamin's conception of historical mediation, see Peter Osborne, *Philosophy in Cultural Theory* (London and New York: Routledge, 2000), chap. 2. And for a detailed account of the historical *timing* of the origins of photography and an explicit argument that a "desire to photograph" preceded the technology, see Geoffrey Batchen, *Burning with Desire: The Conception of Photography* (Cambridge, MA: MIT Press, 1997), esp. chaps. 2 and 3.

6

Provoking George Eliot

MARY ANN O'FARRELL

I

When, in 1867, Nina (Mrs. Frederick) Lehmann writes to her husband of her visits to George Eliot that "It is impossible to be with that noble creature without feeling *better*,"[1] she seems to be thinking not only of the comfort Eliot's often unhappy women visitors are said to have sought and sometimes found in their visits to Eliot's home, the Priory; Lehmann's letter more clearly invokes instead the sense of titillated elevation that pilgrims might be imagined to have experienced in the presence of the Priory's alleged saint of ethical feeling. Feeling (comparatively) "better," Lehmann understands herself ennobled by a desire to be (absolutely) good. No Lehmann in temporal access to the Priory's "noble creature," I know Eliot best in the form of what criticism and culture have taught me I am to see, reductively, as her noble creations: her novels. And, no Lehmann in contingencies less temporal than temperamental, I find that this George Eliot makes me want to be bad.

Not evil, mind, the bad self formulated in response to Eliot, but—provoking and gossipacious, undermining of dignities, excessive of decorous and budgetary limitations, fractious and infractionary, distracted rather than directed—it is instead that particular cultural formulation, the *bad girl*, whose celebration of her pinprick violations is the working consolation she has taken in Opposite World for her failures to suit the arbiters of good-girl standards. Though the news of the bad girl's assumption of a particular posture as a specific defense against her good-girl desires comes as no surprise at all, it is perhaps still both surprising and surprisingly difficult to catch the good girl in her more convincing act of self-defense—in the act, that

145

is, of making herself up. Biographers have tended to decide that when, invited to pay calls, George Eliot would let it be known that she would much prefer to be called upon, she did this in order not to leave herself open to rejection.[2] However often in signature she took his last name or however publicly in print she took his first, the Marian Evans who was nevertheless not married to George Henry Lewes might still be solicited by trickster invitations into soliciting in turn the attentions of those who might at the last refuse to admit to the vulnerable Victorian home a threat to susceptible wives and daughters. The saint of the Priory, "at home" for the attendance of what biographer Kathryn Hughes insistently calls "acolytes,"[3] is a resulting formation; the saint who is visited is the abject product of an anxiety about being the person not to be received. Earlier and later, the persistently ethical George Eliot of novelistic construction and of cultural memory screens the scandalous Eliot from view and obscures the desires and susceptibilities (less particular and more pervasive than the details of a romantic attachment) that produce the need for her. Removed by distanciations narrative and temporal from sex and from a scandal that seems no longer scandalous but the domestic exception that reinforces domesticity's rule, the remnant figure of the ethical George Eliot obscures something that might be more interesting than a marriage exemplary if also faux: the cast-off materials of that figure's own production.

In talking of Eliot's novels while working on this essay, I found myself on frustrated days using a language of admission (as to a parlor) or of penetration (as of a body); unlike Jane Austen and Charles Dickens, friends will tell you I have whined, she will not let you in. If Eliot's social and communal encyclopedism would seem to invite everyone, it nevertheless keeps everyone at bay. Describing the celebratory rituals of the spectacularly diverse partakers in "The Harvest Supper" that she stages late in *Adam Bede,* Eliot lingers over the farm laborer Thom Tholer, known as "Tom Saft," "a great favourite on the farm," who—though saft (soft) in the head—"played the part of the old jester, and made up for his practical deficiencies by his success in repartee." Eliot continues:

> His hits, I imagine, were those of the flail, which falls quite at random, but nevertheless smashes an insect now and then. They were much-

quoted at sheep-shearing and haymaking times; but I refrain from recording them here, lest Tom's wit should prove to be like that of many
other bygone jesters eminent in their day—rather of a temporary nature, not dealing with the deeper and more lasting relations of things.[4]

Eliot's expansive pleasure in the jester—in the fact of his flailings, in
the frenzy of his seasonal renown—is the pleasure exercised by a narrative condescension that will bend so far and no farther: George Eliot
will not tell a joke. Though it would seem to be the very aim of Eliot's
novels—her harvest suppers—to show that they will and ought admit
anyone (that they are able to serve and to contain all), this supper refuses to admit either the jester's provocations or his fallings flat. The
plenitude of the supper as occasion proves itself a repletion, even a
crowding, in which the human plenty makes impossible the movements of the joke in circulation; there is no room for laughter's disruptive vibrations and none for their collapse. In refusing the chronospatial
risk of the joke (you had to be there), Eliot refuses to understand that it
is the joke telling (and not the telling that there was a joke) that constitutes, demonstrates, and determines the "deeper and more lasting relation of things" that she would claim her harvest suppers have invited.

The imagined relation between the "will not" and "cannot" of harvest jesting incites the speculations of George Eliot's responsive bad
girl. The protective and authoritative "will not" of the narrative's mild,
benevolent, and seasonal act of "refraining"—we would tell no joke
that's past its prime—strains in screening tightly and too well the sadder, unsociable, and enduring characteristic: George Eliot cannot tell a
joke. This Eliot—the one whose compelling admissions and refusals
seem sometimes like the elaborations of the linguistic hedge against the
joke—provokes me to provocation. Wanting something from the good
girl, the good-girl-gone-bad pokes and prods and opens, enjoying those
transitive pleasures for their own faux-wicked sakes, but also because
she wants the good girl to be more fun, to have more fun, to know—as
daily she still learns them—the angry joys of being loosened up.

After the success of *Middlemarch* and of John Cross's investment
of her funds and those of Lewes, biography reports, George Eliot
came to love shopping. Diverting the acolytes from simple worship,
Eliot exploits their interest and their desire for their fortuitous exper-
tise in fashion and in ornament. Kathryn Hughes writes: "Emilia

Pattison and Jane Senior took her round the shops and guided her towards the best fabric and design, while Lady Castletown and Alice Helps helped her choose furs—a subject with which both Leweses were obsessed. . . . It was now that Marian adopted a lace mantilla as her signature indoor wear."[5]

The comments of Edmund Gosse about "the frivolity of [her] headgear" tell something about Eliot's taste, which was for flouncy hats that are, as he puts it, "always in the height of the Paris fashion," and if his shock about the disparity between those flounces and what he records as Eliot's "massive features, somewhat grim" serves to make the ornaments more prominent even than perhaps they were, their prominence in fantasy makes it possible to imagine what frippery invites: the tuggings and untyings, the unbuttonings and unlacings of an Eliot who wanted the unloosing wrought by a repressed for once admitted.

But Gosse's account of Eliot's appearance repeats and represents for a literary posterity worldly lessons that might drive a girl good. "The contrast between the solemnity of the face and the frivolity of the headgear," said Gosse, "had something pathetic and provincial about it."[6] If in this biographical account it is possible to see in Eliot for a moment both a desire and that which has made it a desire to be denied, the self-mastering Eliotian narrative more often condenses and obscures the relation between the two. This essay, then, addresses something about my reading experience of George Eliot by wanting to find in her novels traces of the susceptibilities and resistances that both underlie and produce the culturally figural good-girl saint and the textually compelling authority that (and not exactly "who") models and espouses ethical feeling. But these are sometimes hard to see: the susceptibilities and resistances of the Eliot corpus are visible only in the presence of the structures that exist to manage and contain them.

II

Early in *Felix Holt: The Radical*, upon looking into the face of her employer, Mrs. Transome, soon after Mrs. Transome's awaited and anticipated reunion with her desperately beloved son, Mrs. Transome's loyal and aptly described "waiting woman," Denner, sees in

Mrs. Transome's face, as Eliot says, "that the meeting with the son had been a disappointment in some way." Denner tries to denegate the mother's disappointment by praising the returned son for the comfort of the mother, commenting on his grown handsomeness and reminding Mrs. Transome of her own past satisfactions in him. Denner comments: "There's a fine presence about Mr. Harold. I remember you used to say, madam, there were some people you would always know were in the room though they stood round a corner, and others you might never see till you ran against them. That's as true as truth."[7]

Though truth may indeed be true, as Denner's wisdom of self-evidence would have it, it may yet be fairly odd. Mrs. Transome's assertion of the power of personal presence and of personal affiliation seems as wishful and supplementary as it is descriptive and worldly, naming and announcing as fantastic a relation that its very inadequacies would render unspeakable; readers of the novel may suspect that Denner offers up a recalled observation first made by Mrs. Transome not to account for the specific lure for a mother of her golden son, but rather to explain her long-past hyperconsciousness, as a straying wife, of her unacknowledgeable lover.

Still, the logic that operates the fantasy of a presence felt round the corner needs an explanation that proves unexpectedly if tenuously available by means of a recurrent figure in Eliot's text: the stirring vibration. Throughout *Felix Holt*, alternations of mobility and immobility create a figural oscillation of their own, as characters are caught repeatedly in stillness and in motion; sometimes they are found "motionless" (p. 252), for example; found eerily reoccupying positions assumed hours before and from which one imagines they must have moved (p. 467), or found with a "marble look of immobility" (p. 440); and sometimes they are in motion—trembling (p. 53) and tremorous (p. 441), "fitful" (p. 431), vibrant (that is, "vibrating," p. 306) and concussive (p. 463).

Mrs. Transome's articulation of her connection to son and lover aligns itself with a textual, figurative logic that understands and renders mobility as the physicalization of responsiveness to another person, often (though not always) to another's needs. When the novel's quasi-heroine, Esther Lyon, for example, is told in outline, by the man she has always known as a father, the previously withheld facts of her parentage,

Eliot indexes the effects of the story on Esther by a series of startings from scrupulously noted positions of stillness. Elsewhere described as sitting "like an embodied patience" (p. 432), Esther in the scene of revelation is first "motionless but mentally stirred," having "taken a place opposite to her father," in which place she "had not moved even her clasped hands" (p. 252). "Rising" and gliding (p. 252), Esther sits again "still," "looking fixedly," and (with her father) "enclasped in silence" (p. 253) until (again) "suddenly rising" to speak to her father "with a flush across her paleness, and standing with her head thrown a little backward" (p. 253), only to sit "down [yet] again" (p. 253).

Vibrating, concussing, trembling, tremulous, Eliot's characters and Eliot's language in *Felix Holt* register the disruptive shatterings of emotion and literalize them; in this novel, being moved is imagined physically as an agitation, an incitement to move one's body. The novel values such movements differently. The "fitfulness" (p. 431), "restlessness" (p. 468), and pacing (p. 466) of the troubled Mrs. Transome seem quite different from the startings out of lingering stillness of Esther Lyon; the prior condition of immobility seems to give a priority in value to Esther's excitements.

A bookend scene near the end of the novel seems written to explain Mrs. Transome's fantasy of perceptible presence by enacting it. Anguished by complications in her relation to her son, Mrs. Transome waits up in vain hope that he will come to her with comfort. Thinking of Esther as an alternative source of solace, she approaches Esther's room but stops herself before arriving there, unable to ask for what she wants: as Eliot writes, she "had never yet thrown herself in faith on an unproffered love"; "[s]he had never yet in her life asked for compassion" (p. 469). Though—in her room and mulling over matters of her own—Esther seems clearly not to have heard Mrs. Transome, she nevertheless seems fantastically aware of the presence outside the door, around the corner: Mrs. Transome, Eliot writes, "might have gone on pacing the corridor like an uneasy spirit without a goal, if Esther's thought, leaping towards her, had not saved her from the need to ask admission" (p. 469). Opening her door to a Mrs. Transome she has no reason to know is there, Esther responds to Mrs. Transome's barometric presence and acts on the basis of a motif taken to its logical extreme; her physical leapings are apotheosized as leaps of responsive and compassionate thought, and her action corrects Mrs. Transome's obsessive logic. Where Mrs. Transome understands the magic of perceptible presence to inhere in the presence felt (the "some people" whose presences are felt round the corner are distinguishable from those, like Denner, unfelt even in concussion),[8] the scene suggests the inverse, that it is Esther's preparatory stillness that makes possible the leaping forward.

The argument made by this figuration suggests that a certain ethical responsiveness depends upon a readiness to be distracted by the felt needs of another person. The result of this ethical distraction is another aspect of the scene in which Esther's thought-leap towards Mrs. Transome is an emotive leap as well. An Eliotian construction of the relation between passion and compassion elides the differences between the two; if it is *compassion* that Mrs. Transome's hesitation to ask for it indicates her need of, it is *passion* with which Esther responds. Eliot writes of Esther that "[a] passionate desire to soothe this suffering woman came over her" (p. 469). Eliot's fantasy that compassion can move with the overtaking force of a passion explains the erotic charge of the leapings (the risings, vibratings, fervors, and tremors) with which characters in *Felix Holt* are jolted from a state of still readiness by the perceptible presence of need.

What makes Eliot's elision of passion and compassion necessary for her is the liability of compassion, in the most colloquial of senses, to be produced quite differently and only with difficulty. As easily as she might be understood to feel with the force of passionate vibration a passionate response to Mrs. Transome, Esther might be imagined to experience Mrs. Transome in the hall as the very thing Mrs. Transome would not want her desire for compassion and comfort to make her: with a sensational twist, Eliot's fantasy of presence felt round the corner becomes Mrs. Transome as lurking, hulking need, her presence a monstrosity, a voracity, at least a demand perceptible even through oaken doors. The admissions that facilitate compassion may be as much the product of argument as of feeling, and thinking compassion as a passion achieves a work of condensation by which the necessity and the fact of argument may be obscured.

Elsewhere, with respect to Dorothea Brooke's famous realization, in *Middlemarch*, that Casaubon must have "an equivalent centre of self," Eliot seems more ready to acknowledge with the language of difficulty the argumentative nature of the process that formulates compassion: the distinct conception of Casaubon's difference, equivalence, and centrality by means of a process that is "no longer reflection but feeling" is more difficult to fantasize and to achieve, she indicates, than the "easier" fantasy of a devotion to Mr. Casaubon.[9] But here, in *Felix Holt*, Eliot chooses the fantasy (or perhaps the lie) of the elision that disguises argument and work through its elaborate construction of compassion as a passion. Doing so, she values (as precedent and prior to a passionate compassion) a stillness readable—in the way the leaps and risings are readable finally as a thought-leap—as a state of ethical readiness. I choose from the Eliot lexicon as a name for that state of ethical readiness the word "susceptibility" in part because of susceptibility's ability, as a word, to gesture in more than one direction. If it can name a preparedness and receptivity (and can do so invoking the physicality that Eliot herself invokes through the vibrations of passionate compassion), susceptibility can name as well a vulnerability—a state of endangerment—that reflects the difficulties, ambivalences, and resistances that Eliot herself experiences in the novelistic working out of her own compassionate and inclusive project.

This essay turns now to *Adam Bede*'s Hetty Sorrel, not only because she serves it as an instance and a product of this ambivalence on George Eliot's part, but also because she makes for Eliot a place to work out something about her own relation to susceptibility and to what Hetty teaches and permits us to define as its opposite: a certain indifferent impenetrability. If sometimes compassion is a product of argument, the traces of George Eliot's argument with herself are evident in the characterization of Hetty. A part of *Adam Bede*'s project as a novel would seem to involve taking as its heroes those who are able to enact a compassion for Hetty, and the novel uses Hetty to measure the extent of heroisms grounded in compassion. But while Eliot's project involves the production of compassion for Hetty, it seems also to be a project invested with and inflected by Eliot's hostile fascination with Hetty's apparent insusceptibility and indifference.

More than halfway through the novel, as Hetty talks with Adam, the carpenter to whom she is to be married, Adam asks her how she will feel if his mother lives with them, and he is "delighted" with Hetty's reply: "Yes; I'd as soon she lived with us as not" (*AB* 408). Adam's inattentive delight means he has not heard Hetty, whose "as soon as not"—in this or in any other of their interactions—is indication of the much-noted indifference and impenetrability that leads

Hetty's uncle, Mr. Poyser, to find her "aggrivatin'": "there's no knowin' what she's got a likin' to," Mr. Poyser remarks, "for things take no more hold on her than if she was a dried pea" (p. 384). If there is something transfixing and even distantly enviable in Hetty's "self-engrossed loveliness" (p. 186), there is nothing enviable in Eliot's removal of her from the plenitude of Eliotian community. And if the chapter Eliot entitles "Hetty's World" (Chapter 9) acknowledges that Hetty works in different ways, it does not do so by according her the equivalent center of self that Casaubon has earned in *Middlemarch*. In reflecting Hetty's milkmaid-from-another-planet quality of absent presence ("Hetty answered with a smile, as if she did not quite know what had been said" [p. 186]), it justifies Hetty's complex linguistic exclusion from set-up domestic and communal intimacies where, although she is included, she is included only by what marks her exclusion as "even Hetty."

Thus articulated—as the self-engrossed product of an "as soon as not" indifference—Hetty might seem well removed from the stirrings of susceptibility. And yet, alongside Eliot's pervasive diction of impenetrability, the novel employs a metaphorics that makes Hetty a figure of susceptibility as well. The dual character of Hetty's susceptibility is best introduced by way of Eliot's discussion of susceptibility in Adam. Writing late in the novel of Adam and not of Hetty, Eliot describes the nature of susceptibility in itself by considering it in different manifestations. Frustrated in himself by his reluctance to know about Hetty's trial for infanticide, Adam feels himself "powerless to contemplate irremediable evil and suffering" (p. 471). Eliot writes, "The susceptibility which would have been an impelling force where there was any possibility of action, became helpless anguish when he was obliged to be passive." Determined by conditions and contingencies, susceptibility is revealed here as a set of formal properties having to do with responsiveness, whose uses are themselves responsive to circumstance and agency.

Susceptible in a way I fantasize Hetty's folksy aunt, Mrs. Poyser, fashioning into a warning or a prophecy ("she's too susceptible, that girl"), Hetty is most obviously susceptible in being a girl who will meet a boy alone in the forest and, once there, she is susceptible to romance, to sex, to the sex in class, to the clothes in class, to the negative allure of "as soon as not" preferences. But something of the responsive susceptibility that, I have argued, Eliot comes to value in

Esther Lyon is abstracted and promised in Hetty, and it is most visible in her tastes.

Hetty's often-noted "love for finery" is particularized in the novel as a longing for "Nottingham lace" and "white stockings," for "something to make her handkerchief smell nice" (p. 144) and for "the time when she would have a silk gown and a great many clothes all at once" (p. 381); her possessive joys are catalogued as gold and pearl and garnet earrings in a "pretty little box lined with white satin" (p. 294), a locket and a scent bottle (p. 296), a string of brown berries—"her neck would look so unfinished without it" (p. 296)—green stays, and an old scarf of black lace. The novel is most clearly interested in Hetty's tastes insofar as they are set as vanities against the tastes of the preacher Dinah, whose "absence of self-consciousness" goes along with "no blush, no tremulousness" (p. 66), and "no keenness in the eyes" (p. 67) to delineate a negative femininity unsupported by finery and refined by pleasures disallowed.

But Hetty's itemized treasures also counter the perception that she is wholly indifferent and point toward a Hetty whose delight in the flash of great googly glass earrings like those of Bessy Cranage, or whose pleasure in her own boxed baubles, indicates a responsiveness to the aesthetic—a susceptibility in form. A refined aesthetic might account for the appeal of glass earrings in the way Dorothea Brooke famously accounts (in *Middlemarch*) for her response to emeralds that vulgar fantasy makes just as great and googly—as the synaesthetic penetration of the body by a color behaving like a scent. But a vulgar aesthetic might enjoy understanding Hetty's pleasure in her earrings as indexical of a capacity for near-ethical Eliotian distraction.

Writing of the way Dinah's negative femininity is set off by the vulgarity of conventional young womanhood, Eliot invokes the language of gratuitous headgear to make her point. Appreciating Dinah even in her absence—she is for him a presence felt round the corner—Seth Bede (Adam's brother, unlucky in love) contemplates the time he has spent at Arthur Donnithorne's birthday feast. Eliot writes that:

> It had been a rather melancholy day to Seth: Dinah had never been more constantly with him than in this scene, where everything was so unlike her. He saw her all the more vividly after looking at the thoughtless faces and gay-coloured dresses of the young women—just as one

feels the beauty and the greatness of a pictured Madonna the more, when it has been for a moment screened from us by a vulgar head in a bonnet. (p. 326)

Wrapped up tight, Eliot's analogy operates by the logic of the foil (the good girl Madonna is set off by being seen against, or after, the bad hat) and depends upon an apparent self-evidence of preference. But I wonder about the attractions of that distracting hat. And I wonder what it means to understand a head as vulgar. Eliot's metonymic characterization of the head in the terms of what sits upon it makes a figure a chastisement and suggests an uncomfortable sense of the suitability for one another of a love of finery and a taste in art; the contrast between the solemnity of one's Madonna, as an Eliot or Gosse might put it, and the frivolity of one's headgear might not be so easily resolvable and could leave a head feeling vulgar, provincial, and pathetic.

Rejecting the vulgar head to choose a Dinah, say, or a pictured Madonna, or to choose a wrapped-tight narrative authority that in its inclusiveness *contains*, one exploits the fungibility of the aesthetic to choose the perfection of form over those things that glitter and dangle (like Hetty's finery or Bessy's glittering glass) in a way that invites a tugging or an opening or a hanging on. It is the brilliance of Hetty as a novelistic creation that she lets George Eliot do so much disciplinary work while still and despite this facilitating the admission of inadmissible tastes. It is probably clear enough that, in writing susceptible Hetty, Eliot chastens susceptibilities while itemizing and indulging them. But in writing impenetrable Hetty, she chastens as well, with the angry chastening of those who have been chastened, the refusals that constitute a mastered plenitude.

III

One morning some weeks after her arrival at Lowick, Dorothea—but why always Dorothea?

The well-known beginning to *Middlemarch*'s twenty-ninth chapter goes on from its abruption to examine questions of point of view in the novel and to "protest," as Eliot puts it, "against all our interest, all our effort at understanding being given to the young skins that look blooming in spite of trouble; for these too will get faded, and will know the older and more eating griefs which we are helping to neglect" (*M*, 228–229). And our interest *chez* Eliot indeed often *is* directed to such places; the girl and the formation of her habits amidst her susceptibilities is no less a subject really for Eliot than it is so more notoriously for James. But the startling first lines solicit attention for themselves and not just for the direction in which they point. "One morning some weeks after her arrival at Lowick, Dorothea—but why always Dorothea?" Presenting themselves as a susceptible bit of text, these first (and broken) lines of Eliot's announce by enacting it their readiness to be distracted from a characteristic intent by the felt needs of a person round the corner, and they stage the self-critical work of revision, even if in the form only of diversion; some paragraphs later the direction and focus of the narrative is reestablished and the broken-off piece of sentence is apparently completed: "Thus Mr. Casaubon was in one of his busiest epochs, and as I began to say a little while ago, Dorothea joined him in the library where he had breakfasted alone" (*M*, 231).

In its inclusion of the anxiogenic dissatisfaction of what might as well be a reader's question (why always Dorothea?), the short opening passage is self-critical, making space—as if for a reader—but then inevitably asking a reader's questions for her and writing that reader in itself. It is the self-mastery in self-criticism that is most to be demonstrated in the chapter opening's broken bit and in the artifice that—by means of the minor fanfare of a sentence that never means to end—produces distraction as a textual event.

For George Eliot this may fulfill the promise of the harvest supper's restraint; the interruption of the supercontrolled text for purposes of self-examination is the dignified version of what it might look like for a bending Eliot to tell the worst and oldest of harvest-supper jokes, and what that looks like is too elaborately powerful (if only Browning's Ferrara had known) a choosing to stoop, the better to demonstrate one's graciousness in stooping. Still, in the very obviousness of its operations, this bit of text exhibits, too, a more pleasingly vulgar susceptibility. The dark-night-of-the-soul effect of a guardedness relieved in self-examining confession is in perhaps too sharp a contrast with the inviting breeziness and cheer of that "one morning"; the reproduction in written narration of a set of speech effects is too obvious a mimicry; the spontaneity of the interruption—persistent through drafts and printings—is too apparently the end of deliberation and rehearsal; and in its stooping dignity, the self-qualification makes far too steep a bend. In its dignity, then, is the written gesture's ridiculousness. And precisely in the ridiculousness of its execution is the dignity of Eliot's risking and loss of, well, dignity.

I catch myself tending toward a humanist conclusion I'm suspicious of. You know how the argument goes: George Eliot's inclusive community and textual plenitude make me feel excluded; but in some slip or in some moment, I see that she's having a need; O, look—it's for me! She wants me to help her pick out a hat: I *am* included. Oops. (And, by the way, why always hats?)

Let Edmund Gosse help me out of this. His comments about Eliot's fashion sense (about the disjunction between her face and her late style) are readable as evincing a certain disappointment and bookend my response to disjunctions in the texts. Though his response is disappointed and mine is pleased, the two alike depend upon and in the end reinforce a version of Nina Lehmann's elevated Eliot, too good for us all. And this, in some way, is the achievement of Eliotian self-command and its production of the cultural Eliot: that she makes us want it of her despite ourselves.

Acknowledgments

For the stimulations of their company in thinking about George Eliot, I would like to thank Joseph Litvak, Neil Hertz, and Carolyn Williams, and, for their appreciation of vulgarity, D. A. Miller, Melanie Hawthorne, Pamela Matthews, and David McWhirter.

Notes

1. Quoted in Marghanita Laski, *George Eliot and Her World* (London: Thames and Hudson, 1973), p. 100.
2. See, for example, Kathryn Hughes, *George Eliot: The Last Victorian* (London: Fourth Estate, 1998), p. 252.
3. Hughes follows this practice throughout her biography, in which Eliot's women followers (perhaps friends) are indexed under Eliot's name, subhead "life," as "female acolytes." See *George Eliot*, p. 378.

4. George Eliot, *Adam Bede* (Harmondsworth, UK: Penguin, 1985), p. 561. Subsequent references will appear in the text.

5. Though Hughes speculates that Eliot and Lewes may have been interested in furs "because they felt the cold," Eliot's interest, at least, may have been less practical if no less comforting, given her attraction to fabrics and laces. See Hughes, *George Eliot*, p. 306.

6. Edmund Gosse, "George Eliot," in *Aspects and Impressions* (New York: Charles Scribner's Sons, 1922), p. 1. Also quoted in Hughes, p. 306.

7. George Eliot, *Felix Holt, The Radical* (Harmondsworth, UK: Penguin, 1995), p. 27. Subsequent references will appear in the text.

8. Bruce Robbins notes, of Denner's comment on Mrs. Transome's assignment of relative value by way of her relative acknowledgments of presence, that "We do not need to be told, much later, that 'the sensations produced by Denner's presence were as little disturbing as those of a favorite cat' . . . in order to feel the weight of comparison carried in her praise of her mistress' son." See Robbins's *The Servant's Hand: English Fiction from Below* (New York: Columbia University Press, 1986), p. 212. Mrs. Transome's failures with respect to the devoted Denner echo what may have been Eliot's failures as apostle to her acolytes; in their attentions to Eliot, responsive, perhaps, to their own aspirations to lives of intellect and accomplishment such as might be lived in the compelling presence of George Eliot, they serve as attendants on her desires for fabric and fashion, assistants to her experiments in style.

9. George Eliot, *Middlemarch* (Oxford and New York: Oxford University Press, 1988), p. 173. Subsequent references will appear in the text.

7

Compassion's Compulsion

LEE EDELMAN

Compassion can be a touchy subject, touching, as it does, on what touches the heart by seeming to put us in touch with something other than ourselves while leaving us open, in the process, to being read as an easy touch. Not that some anti-compassionate lobby takes arms against the emotion, mounting a campaign of aversion therapy meant to bring out the latent "ouch" in compassion's electric "touch"; what makes compassion so touchy is, rather, the *absence* of such a lobby, the fact that every hardening of the heart against compassion's knock presents itself as hardheaded reason resisting *false* compassion the better to keep the way clear for the true. For just as compassion confuses our own emotions with another's, making it kissing cousin to its morbid obverse, paranoia, so it allows no social space that is not already its own, no ground on which to stand outside its all-encompassing reach. From ruthlessness to *Schadenfreude,* its antonyms proliferate, but who would make his home in the sterile landscape they call forth? What future could one build upon their unforgiving slopes when social relations, collectivity, the very weave of communal life, all seem to hang on compassion's logic, though that logic may, as Kant insists, demand a dispassionate, mathematical abstraction of compassion's tender touch until it becomes the vise-like grip of duty's iron fist. That fist may then curl back inside compassion's velvet glove, but only the better to pack the punch that, even when stopping us dead in our tracks, always stops us in the name of love.

If compassion in this takes love's name in vain, it's vain to think compassion *outside* the register of love. One could, for example, cite Augustine, who observes, in *De doctrina Christiana,* that the fifth of the seven steps to wisdom—he calls it the "resolve of compassion"—

involves, along with a cleansing of the soul, diligence in "the love of [one's] neighbor."[1] I prefer, however, to cite Ronald Reagan, a traditionalist of compassion himself, by way of introducing a text that considers compassion and its politics in order to engage the figure called forth to embody its negation. "We shall reflect the compassion that is so much a part of your makeup," President Reagan declared in his first inaugural address. "How can we love our country and not love our countrymen," he asked rhetorically, "and loving them," he continued, "reach out a hand when they fall."[2] Let me freeze-frame that figure of compassion—its defining feature, its distinctive touch—so that you focus on the outstretched hand evoked by the president whose image some have suggested be added to those on Mount Rushmore. And now, with that image firmly in mind, let us cut to Mount Rushmore itself, where this figure of speech will be literalized and its emotional claim—to which Reagan presupposed the impossibility of resistance—will receive an unexpected response from one who refuses compassion's compulsion as if he had taken to heart in advance the doctrine of "just say no."

I refer, of course, to Leonard (Martin Landau), the sadistic (and fashion-conscious) agent of America's unspecified Cold War enemies in Alfred Hitchcock's *North by Northwest* (1959). Dedicated "secretary" and loyal right arm to his superior, Phillip Vandamm (James Mason), Leonard—with self-evident pleasure—performs the various acts of violence for which the plans of his boss may call. As pitiless and persistent as the crop-dusting plane that attacks Roger Thornhill (Cary Grant) in the film's most famous sequence, Leonard himself—bereft of sympathy, immune to reason, and unmoved by any appeal to so-called natural bonds of kinship—embodies a machinery of destruction. The climactic scene on Mount Rushmore, where he pursues the film's protagonists across the indifferent faces that protrude from the stony cliff, thus brings to a head in more ways than one Hitchcock's concern throughout the film with the humanizing traits to which Leonard stands immovably opposed: compassion, identification, philanthropic feelings for one's neighbor. It plays out, that is, against the lifeless rock made to take on human form, the tension between the appeal of form, the formal identity by means in which the social subject knows itself, and the rock of the Real that resists whatever identity the subject knows—a tension Hitchcock makes vivid by staging this final chase on Mount Rushmore, a site whose carvings literalize, as if in order to make proper, the catachresis by which, through linguistic convention, we refer to a mountain's "face": a site that thus brings us face to face with the similar catachresis that produces but also disfigures—returns to its status *as* a figure—the human face as the face of everything we recognize as human.[3]

So when Roger Thornhill extends his hand in an effort to rescue Eve Kendall (Eva Marie Saint) from the craggy outcrop to which she holds after Leonard has callously pushed her to what seems her certain death, his act of compassion on the stony cliff redeems the stony-heartedness—or so the film wants us to think—that she, like the American intelligence officials for whom she is working, displayed in conspiring with Leonard to arrange for Thornhill's death in Prairie Stop's fields. But hardness of heart is hardly a charge to which the government's top cops cop. Even when he is fully informed about Thornhill's thorny situation, when he learns, that is, that their opposite numbers had mistaken this smooth-talking advertising man for George Kaplan—a fictional agent invented to "divert suspicion" from their "real Number One," this very same Eve Kendall, engaged in acts of espionage "right under [the enemy's] nose"—the head of American intelligence, known as the Professor (Leo G. Carroll), announces to his colleagues that Roger Thornhill will have to fend for himself.[4] Questioned about the morality of such a refusal to save Thornhill's life—"Aren't we being just a wee bit callous?" an agency official asks—the Professor rejects that charge out of hand: "No, my dear woman, we are *not* being callous. . . . We created George Kaplan . . . for a *desperately important reason*. If we make the slightest move to suggest that there *is* no such agent as George Kaplan . . . then Number One . . . will immediately face suspicion, exposure, assassination, like the two others who went before" (p. 46).

With so calculated a lesson in compassion—that it commits us to a calculus, a quantification of the good—the Professor attempts to plant his feet securely on moral high ground while he justifies pulling the rug out from under Thornhill's in the process. On the literal high ground of Mount Rushmore, though, when Leonard—once again, literally—plants his foot to the same effect, similarly targeting

Thornhill to take the necessary fall by crushing beneath the sole of his shoe the fingers with which the advertising man tries to cling to the monument's face, the callousness the Professor shrugged off attaches to Leonard with a vengeance, so that he, with the crack of a bullet fired by a marksman from above, can take the fall for Thornhill, the Professor, the audience, and the film all at once.

But shed no tears for Leonard. A victim of compassion's compulsory disavowal of its callousness—a sacrifice to its fantasy of holding the other in love's embrace—Leonard refuses compassion, refuses, at any rate, its fantasy, insofar as he embodies what I have been calling *sinthom*-osexuality, the positioning of the queer as figure for the subject's unthinkable implication in the Real as evinced by the meaningless *jouissance* of what Lacan calls the *sinthome*.[5] In *sinthom*-osexuality the structuring fantasy undergirding and sustaining the subject's desire, and with it the subject's reality, encounters its beyond in the drive that undoes it, derealizing the collective logic of fantasy by means of which subjects mean, and insisting instead on the *jouissance*—particularized and irreducible—that registers the absolute contingency of every subject's being.

All sexuality, I have argued, is *sinthom*-osexuality, but the burden of figuring that condition, the task of instantiating the force of the drive (which is always necessarily a partial drive, incapable of totalization) that tears apart both the subject's desire and the subject *of* desire, falls only to certain subjects who, like Leonard, serve as fall guys for the failure of sexual relation and the intolerable reduction of the subject to the status of *sinthome*. Such *sinthom*-osexuals fall because they fail to fall in love, where love names the totalizing fantasy, which is also a fantasy of totalization, through which the subject would shelter itself against the disintegrative force of the drive.[6] As Jacques-Alain Miller observes, "perversion is the norm of the drive. Thus, what is problematic is the existence of a sexual drive toward the opposite sex. Lacan's thesis here is that there is no drive toward the opposite sex; there is only a drive toward the libido object, toward partial satisfaction qua object. To take a person, a whole person as an object, is not the role of the drive, it leads us to introduce love."[7]

But love, Lacan argues, with its orientation toward the wholeness of a person, only reproduces, and in more ways than one, the subject's fundamentally narcissistic fantasy in the face of the initiating wound inflicted by the fact of "sexed reproduction"—a fact that sexes the subject at the cost of repudiated libidinal possibilities and therefore of sufficiency unto itself. Love expresses the subject's pursuit "not of the sexual complement," according to Lacan, "but of the part of himself, lost forever, that is constituted by the fact that he is only a sexed living being, and that he is no longer immortal."[8] Love, therefore, like fantasy, seeks to regain that lost immortality and to do so, fantasmatically, within a heterosexualizing Symbolic order, by translating sexed reproduction, through which immortality was lost, into the very mode and guarantee of its future restoration. The future assured by, in order to assure, the continuity of sexed reproduction establishes the horizon of fantasy within which the subject aspires to the meaning that is always, like the object of desire, out of reach.

Sinthom-osexuality, by contrast, affirms a constant, eruptive *jouissance* that responds to the inarticulable Real—to the impossibility, that is, of any sexual rapport or of signifying the relation between the sexes. It stands in the place of the drive that is, Lacan writes, "profoundly a death drive and represents in itself the portion of death in the sexed living being."[9] *Sinthom*-osexuality, like the death drive, engages, by refusing, the immobility, the murderous stasis, of normative sexuation, to which the mandate of Symbolic law, with its pairing of male and female, delivers us. Refusing the fixity of forms that make the sexed subject into a monolith, a petrified identity, *sinthom*-osexuality breaks down those mortifying structures, the alienated signfiers within which we know ourselves *as* selves, with all the insistent force of the Real such forms must fail to signify.[10]

With no sympathy for the subject's desires and no compassion for the ego's integrity, with no love insofar as love names the subject's defense against dissolution, *sinthom*-osexuals, like the death drive they are produced to represent—and produced to represent insofar as the drive undoes all representation—endanger the fantasy of survival by endangering the survival of love's fantasy, insisting instead on the machinelike working of the partial, dehumanizing drives and ceaselessly offering access to their surplus of *jouissance*. As such they deserve to be characterized by the words of François Abadie, formerly mayor of Lourdes and a senator aligned with France's radical Left before being ousted from the party when he expressed in the pages of *Le Nouvel Observateur* his repugnance for "those I call the gravediggers of society, those who care nothing [for] the future: homosexuals."[11]

Conflations like this of homosexuality with the negativity of *sinthom*-osexuality continue to shape our social reality despite the well-intentioned efforts of many, gay and straight alike, to normalize queer sexualities within a logic of meaning that can only be realized *in* and *as* the future. When the *New York Times Magazine*, for example, published an issue devoted to the status items pursued by various demographic groups in 1998, Dan Savage found in a baby's gurgle the music to soothe the gay male beast: "Gay parents," he wrote, "are not only making a commitment to our political future, but to the future, period. . . . And many of us have decided that we want to fill our time with something more meaningful than sit-ups, circuit parties and designer drugs. For me and my boyfriend, bringing up a child is a commitment to having a future. And considering what the last 15 years were like, perhaps that future is the ultimate status item for gay men."[12]

The messenger here may be a gay man, but the message is that of compulsory reproduction: choose life, for life and the baby and meaning are hanging in the balance, confronting the lethal counterweight of narcissism, AIDS, and death, all of which spring from commitment to the meaningless eruptions of *jouissance* encouraged by the "circuit parties" that figure the circuit of the drive. This fascism of the baby's face that encourages parents, gay or straight, to join in a mighty chorus of "Tomorrow Belongs to Me" suggests that if few can bring up a child without constantly bringing it up—as if the future the child secured, the one true access to social security, could be claimed only for the other's sake and never for one's own—then that future can belong only to those who purport to feel for the other (with all the appropriative implications such "feeling *for*" suggests): can belong only to those who accede to the fantasy of a compassion in which they shelter the infant future from *sinthom*-osexuals who do not.

But who would choose the "gravediggers of society" over the guardians of its future, *sinthom*-osexuality's voiding of meaning over Savage's "something more meaningful"? What might we learn from

Leonard about refusing what must always hang in the balance and de-
ciding—against the rhetoric of compassion, futurity, and life—to topple the scales that are always skewed, to put one's foot down at last,
even if doing so costs us the ground on which we, like all others, must
stand? To figure out how to answer such questions, let us think about
Leonard as a figure, one figured metonymically by his metonymic relation to the figure or figurine—"a pre-Columbian figure of a Tarascan warrior" (p. 90), the screenplay tells us, referred to throughout the
Mount Rushmore episode simply as "the figure" (pp. 138 ff)—that
contains, like a secret meaning, the secrets on the microfilm hidden
inside it. In Leonard, to be sure, the figure of the *sinthom*-osexual
is writ large-screen, never more so than when, in the midst of his
anti–Sermon on the Mount, he lowers the sole of his shoe and thereby
shows that he has no soul, thus showing as well that the shoe of the
sinthom-osexual fits him—and that he's wearing it—insofar as he
scorns the injunction to put himself in the other's shoes. But the gesture by which he puts his stamp on *sinthom*-osexuality—by stamping
on the fingers with which Thornhill clings to the monument's ledge
with one hand while clinging to Eve with the other as she dangles
midair above a sheer drop—constitutes, as the film makes clear, a response to an appeal.

After giving Eve the "vicious shove" that sends her down the
mountainside to almost "certain death" (p. 145), Leonard starts to
back away, the figure now firmly in hand, while Thornhill, by contrast,
takes Eve in hand as the ridge on which she had come to rest collapses
beneath her feet, leaving her hanging from Thornhill's arm as he
struggles at once to hold onto the cliff and the life he now holds dear.
Unable to save himself without plunging Eve into the void, unable to
lift her up without intervention from above, he calls out in anguish to
Leonard, calling him back to the fated encounter from which, in possession of the precious figure at last, he was ready to back away.
"Help," and then again, "help me," groans Thornhill, his face as ashen
as those on the monument itself. His sincerity, which banishes banter
here, his almost shocking plaintiveness as plainness displaces wit, all
index this as a moment of categorical transformation, as if, through
the love he bears for Eve and by which he bears her up, Thornhill

himself were born again, and borne away from the verbal games, the Madison Avenue playfulness and delight in linguistic control, that threatened to earn him the epithet—"a very clever fellow"—that served as the villain's epitaph in *Strangers on a Train*. As Thornhill's compassionate passion spirits the spirit of play away, Leonard, as if himself now inspired by Bruno, that "very clever fellow" from Hitchcock's earlier film, is moved to reply to Thornhill's call by calling upon the callousness that Bruno brought to bear on Guy when he stomped on the fingers with which Guy held fast to the merry-go-round-gone-mad. Deliberately trampling on Thornhill's hand, Leonard now channels Bruno by way of response to the painful sincerity with which Thornhill tunes Bruno out. And this strange exchange of attributes, this transference at the moment of Thornhill's heartfelt and desperate appeal, might lead us to wonder just what Thornhill wants when he calls upon Leonard for help.

No doubt he solicits compassion, as does Hitchcock here as well: the protracted notes of Hermann's score, their weightiness reinforced by the rolling thunder of percussion, add weight to the situation, as Thornhill waits for Leonard to act, feeling the weight of Eve who depends both on and from his hand. The reduction of Hitchcock's palette to an almost monochromatic slate, the blue-gray shade evocative of rock and rigor mortis, gives visual point to the near-complete encroachment of the void by drawing us into the depths already swallowing Thornhill and Eve. And the patently literalized suspense—which, after *Young and Innocent, Saboteur, To Catch a Thief,* and *Vertigo,* was patented in Hitchcock's name—names this as a moment where *mise-en-scène* writes Hitchcock *into* the scene as he forces the movie's viewers to suffer the other's pain as their own, to feel on their pulse the sensation of the characters's suspense.

Such control of the viewers's emotions produces compassion but does not reflect it. Dining with Ernest Lehman, who wrote the screenplay for *North by Northwest,* Hitchcock reportedly whispered across the table with delight:

> Ernie, do you realize what we're doing in this picture? The audience is like a giant organ that you and I are playing. At one moment we play *this* note on them and get *this* reaction, and then we play *that* chord and

they react *that* way. And someday we won't even have to make a movie—there'll be electrodes implanted in their brains, and we'll just press different buttons and they'll go "ooooh" and "aaaah" and we'll frighten them, and make them laugh. Won't that be wonderful?"[13]

In Hitchcock's vision, the machinery of cinema turns members of the audience into machines themselves, receptacles for stimuli compelling their performance of an automatic response. Enacting a scenario straight out of Sade, this Hitchcockian apotheosis of cinema would disarticulate the audience by reading them merely as some, no longer as *the* sum, of their parts. Instead of a Sadean catalogue of bodies reduced to their fetishized pieces, though, Hitchcock's quasi-pornography, his control of people by way of buttons that make their bodies go "ooooh" and "aaaah," imagines a cinema of neuronal compulsion in the face of a virtual reality, delighting in what *The Matrix*, in an act of bad faith, would years later denounce.

Such a view of the end of cinema engages the spectator's sense of compassion, of emotional investment in the image on-screen, with so little of its own that it fully acknowledges film as a form of Imaginary entrapment, of compulsory identification with the image of totality (one "implanted in [the viewers's] brains" no less than "electrodes" would be) that models as much as it mirrors the subject's sense of itself as whole, leaving that subject helpless before the coercions of the image, helpless to let go of the image that gives it the image of itself. When Hitchcock, then, like Thornhill, seems so genuinely to call forth compassion, when he moves the viewer to pain at the imaged threat to the image as such, he does so while engaging the *jouissance* of encountering something machinelike, automatic, beyond volition, internal to the very experience that compels us to compassion and to the pathos of the human itself: the *jouissance* of passing beyond the Imaginary limit of the human and dissolving into the drive that insists beyond the subject's desire. And so he calls upon Leonard, *sinthom*-osexual and Hitchcock surrogate, to step up to the challenge and answer the call for compassion as he hears it by putting his best foot forward and helping Thornhill learn to let go.

Thornhill may not intend his plea to be answered in quite this way, but our certainty about what he is asking for is what Leonard's act suspends. That Thornhill's first entreaty, "help," is followed by a second, "help me," suggests neither lack of commitment to Eve nor a failure of compassion. Thornhill's anxiety or suspense, much like ours, speaks to his identification with Eve, suspended as she is from the face of the cliff and pulling him into danger only as he tries to pull her out. "Help me," must mean "help me help her," and thus "help us" as well, or even, "help me change 'me' to 'us'; help me be joined to her." As such, his plea's sincerity speaks to the seriousness of coupling and the earnestness necessary in assuming the burden of reproductive logic (not for nothing is the woman named Eve). Leonard, of course, is not wild about this importance of being earnest or this strange request that comes to him, almost literally out of the blue, to drop his stance of enmity, along with the figure full of microfilm, lest Thornhill, dropping Eve, drop something more precious than all his tribe: the fantasy of heterosexual love, and the reproductive couple it elevates, as delivering us from the force of the Real, from the impossibility of sexual rapport, by virtue of delivering us, dialectically, from a knowledge with which we cannot live—the knowledge, as Lacan expresses it, "that the living being, by being subject to sex, has fallen under the blow of individual death."[14]

The *sinthom*-osexual, despite that blow, opposes the fantasy that generates our various narratives of generation. And Leonard, hearing what Joel Fineman might call the sound of "O" in Thornhill—the "O" that parades as Thornhill's initial to the extent that it stands for nothing—refuses the tragedy of desire that Thornhill's cry for help would sound.[15] Linked to the hollow figure with its belly full of film, *North by Northwest's* MacGuffin (Hitchcock's term for something invested with "vital importance" in the narrative that "is actually nothing at all"), Leonard would read Thornhill's tragedy as his *ceasing* to stand for nothing, his turning away from the "O" that turns the very globe to rot in order to stand for the law of desire to which he owes his standing as subject.[16] Leonard thus stands opposed to the desire for which Thornhill solicits support by standing on the hand he will not so much as lift in order to help him—or perhaps, to inflect that last phrase differently, will not lift precisely *to* help him: to help him slip free of fantasy and the clutches of desire, free of the hold by which love holds off his access to *jouissance* by offering, instead, the promise of totalization, of self-completion, in a future always to come.

Lacan provides some guidance here by recalling the legend of Saint Martin, who responded to a beggar on a cold winter's day by cutting his own warm cloak in two and sharing it with the man who had nothing. "Saint Martin shares his cloak, and a great deal is made of it," Lacan remarks about this touchstone of compassion; "We are no doubt touching a primitive requirement in the need to be satisfied there, for the beggar was naked. But perhaps over and above that need to be clothed, he was begging something else, namely that Saint Martin either kill him or fuck him. In any encounter there's a big difference in meaning between the response of philanthropy and that of love."[17]

The "love" Lacan refers to here, the love that exceeds "philanthropy" (etymologically, the "love of man"), disdains the Imaginary structure of the familiarly narcissistic love we love to love so much. This other kind of love exceeds the feel-good forms of altruism with which we tend to identify compassionate identification—the compassion that merely, as Lacan points out, reinforces the ego's narcissism: "my egoism is quite content with a certain altruism, altruism that is situated on the level of the useful," he observes; "what I want is the good of others provided that it remain in the image of my own."[18] Lacan, however, distinguishes such modes of altruism, philanthropy, or compassion from the love that the beggar, more disturbingly, may have been asking Saint Martin to give: "It is in the nature of the good to be altruistic. But that's not the love of thy neighbor."[19] Instead, at the heart of the neighborly love that Saint Augustine associates with the "counsel of compassion," Lacan perceives the function of "malignant *jouissance.*"[20] And this, he argues, accounts for the fact that confronted by the commandment to "love thy neighbor as thyself," Freud, Lacan tells us, "stops and retreats in understandable horror."[21]

Lacan, of course, is referring to *Civilization and Its Discontents,* in which Freud, after noting with understatement that "men are not gentle creatures," questions the dictate to "love [one's] neighbor," since, where most people are concerned, "their neighbor is for them not only a potential helper or sexual object, but also someone who tempts them to satisfy their aggressiveness on him, to exploit his capacity for work without compensation, to use him sexually without his consent, to seize his possessions, to humiliate him, to cause him pain, to torture and kill him."[22] One can hear in this a faint echo of Kant, who, maintaining "that our species, alas! is not such as to be found particularly worthy of love," insists that love as a feeling cannot be imposed upon us as duty, since what we do by constraint of duty is by definition not done from love. The injunction to love one's neighbor, therefore, cannot, as Kant puts it, "mean, 'Thou shalt first of all love, and by means of this love (in the first place) do him good'; but: 'Do good to thy neighbor, and this beneficence will produce in thee the love of men.'"[23] Lacan draws out the extent to which such a translation of "love one's neighbor," though appearing to support a compassionate love with its roots in the Imaginary—by virtue of which "I imagine [others's] difficulties and their sufferings in the mirror of my own"—has the effect to the contrary of rupturing the subject's Imaginary totalization, the image of self-completion that "love" as fantasy would sustain, by installing the abstract logic of duty as the submission to moral law, whereby pathos becomes pathological and reason the logical path.[24]

The command to love one's neighbor would thus unleash its negativity against the coherence of any self-image, subjecting us to a moral law that evacuates the subject so as to *locate* the subject through and in that very evacuation, permitting the realization thereby of a freedom beyond the boundaries of any image or representation, a freedom that resides, like the ground of God's power, according to Lacan, "in the capacity to advance into emptiness."[25] Kant's duty to conform to moral law without any pathological motive, for the sake of duty alone, thus trenches—and this marks the core of Lacan's elaboration of Kant with Sade—on the question of *jouissance:* "When one approaches that central emptiness, which up to now has been the form in which access to *jouissance* has presented itself to us, my neighbor's body breaks into pieces."[26] Here, however paradoxical it seems, psychoanalysis encounters the meaning of the command to "love thy neighbor," which, as Lacan reminds us, unlike altruism or philanthropy, "may be the cruelest of choices."[27]

Leonard, the *sinthom*-osexual, presses his foot into Thornhill's hand thereby to impress upon him as well that by breaking his hold on the cliff he would give him the break for which he was asking: the neighborly love sufficient to break him open with *jouissance* and launch him into the void around and against which the subject congeals. In the earnestness of Thornhill's cry, Leonard hears what Saint Martin was deaf to in the shivering beggar's plea: a request, beyond what the subject knows, for something beyond his desire. If that meant for Lacan where the beggar was concerned that "Saint Martin either kill him or fuck him," then Leonard, installed as the reified obstacle to (hetero)sexual rapport, enacts in his dealings with Thornhill the one as displacement of the other.[28] Treading on Thornhill's fingers, he takes on an allegorical aspect, as if he became an iconic response to the question posed by Lacan: "Does it go without saying that to trample sacred laws under foot . . . itself excites some form of *jouissance?*"[29] Bound to the law, whose potential transgression both elicits and inflames it, desire as lack lacks what it takes to let go of the law that it tramples—and hence what it takes to let go, *tout court.*

But Leonard, who goes beyond transgression and so beyond the law, engages the *jouissance* found only by going beyond desire. For the *sinthom*-osexual, by figuring a permanent access to *jouissance,* a continuous satisfaction like that peculiar to the drives, threatens the subject who inhabits the temporality of desire and knows nothing but the *non*satisfaction that *perpetuates* desire by staving off—through the narrative dilation that begets, by postponing, the future—any encounter with *jouissance.*[30] Thus aligned with the law's prohibitions that keep its object out of reach, desire is desire for no object but only, instead, for its own prolongation, for the future itself as libidinal object procured by its constant lack.

Paradoxically, then, the *objet a,* Lacan's object/cause of desire, does not partake of desire itself; instead, it consists of the *jouissance* that desire must keep at a distance insofar as desire *relies* on that distance, on that lack, for its survival. While desire as lack would forever put off the moment of satisfaction, the *sinthom*-osexual insistently exposes the availability of *jouissance,* revealing, perhaps most intolerably, its interiority to the very law of desire that would hold it at arm's length.

Sinthom-osexuality, in other words, finds something *other* in the words of the law, enforcing an awareness of something else, something that remains unaccounted for in the accounts we give of ourselves, by figuring an encounter with a force that loosens our hold on the meanings we cling to when, for example, we cry for help. The force thus figured is figured in the film by Leonard's relation, as I suggested before, to what the film represents as "the figure," the object surrounding an empty space in which we find something that revises our sense of what and how it "means." In this the figure would seem to serve as a figure for figure as such and not, as certain critics propose—including, most importantly, Raymond Bellour—as a figure for Eve, or even for Eve in her status as merely a figure herself for the "threatening body" of the mother.[31] Thornhill, in the scene at the auction house, fully cognizant that Eve has betrayed him, may refer to her contemptuously as "this little piece of—sculpture" (p. 90), but the figure that comes to figure the murderous duplicity intrinsic to figure passes—or rather is transferred, in a literalization of "metaphor"—into Leonard's hands from Eve's as the two of them struggle on Mount Rushmore, making him, not her, the one that the figure metonymically figures *as* figure.[32] And what a figure he cuts.

As a "gravedigger of society," as one who "care[s] nothing [for] the future," Leonard, the *sinthom*-osexual, annuls the temporality of desire, as a result of which futurity, like the heteronormative couple to whom the burden of bearing it falls, is "suspended, interrupted, disrupted," in the words with which Paul de Man describes the effect of irony on narrative.[33] And if irony leaves the "intelligibility of (representational) narrative disrupted at all times,"[34] if it induces, as de Man asserts elsewhere, "unrelieved *vertige,* dizziness to the point of madness," then irony, with its undoing of identity and refusal of historical progression, with its shattering of every totalized form (and of every form *as* totalization), names the figure as which Leonard's relation to the figure effectively figures him.[35] The shot of the falling figure we are offered just after Leonard is shot, which substitutes the breaking of that object for the shattering of his body at the end of its fall, thus portrays, in the *sinthom*-osexual's fate, the fatality he would inflict: the dissolution effected by *jouissance,* before which, as Lacan reminds us, "my neighbor's body breaks into pieces."

The Tarascan figure thus literally embodies—by endowing with the image *of* a body—an emptiness within that hollows out the image intended to contain it. And true to the radical groundlessness that irony effects, we can never decide if the pieces of film that emerge when the figure breaks open are the precipitates of that emptiness—images, that is, of the hollowing out that ruptures the image as lure—or images instead of the fantasy precipitated to *counter* such an emptiness: the fantasy of the image as negating that vertiginous negativity, as filling the void with the fantasy structure that constitutes desire. For the strips of film, like *North by Northwest,* image the emptying-out of the image as the sustaining form of fantasy; at the same time, though, and precisely *by* imaging the emptying-out of the image they fill it anew, reproducing the Imaginary fantasy of totalized form.

But note in this a paradox: this emptiness that breaks out from within the figure, suspending by means of irony all totality and coherence, expresses the constancy of *jouissance,* the insistence of the drive, and the access therefore to perverse satisfaction of which the drive is assured, while desire as enabled by fantasy, the structure that aims to fill up, to flesh out, and hence to substantialize that emptiness, substitutes absence for presence, endless pursuit for satisfaction, the deferral that conjures futurity in the place of *jouissance.* This, one might say, is the irony of irony's relation to desire; for just as compassion allows no rhetorical ground outside its logic, no place to stand beyond its enforced Imaginary identifications—by virtue of which, whatever its object or the political ends it serves, compassion is *always* conservative, always intent on preserving the image in which the ego sees itself—so irony's negativity spawns compassion to negate it and thereby marks compassion and all the components of desire, its defining identifications as well as the fantasies that sustain them, with the very negativity of the drive against which they undertake to defend.[36]

And nothing at the moment evinces more clearly this structuring irony of compassion than the discourse that persistently registers homosexuality as *sinthom*-osexuality. Consider, for example, that in July of 2000 Pope John Paul II unambiguously affirmed that I, like others outside the heterosexual norm, deserve nonetheless to be treated "with respect, compassion, and sensitivity"; but as one of those "homosexual persons who assert their homosexuality," I possess, or so his

Church insists, an "inclination . . . toward an intrinsic moral evil," an inclination said to constitute "an objective disorder" in itself that bars me from any legitimate claim to "civil legislation . . . introduced to protect behavior to which no one has any conceivable right."[37]

Certain that the Church, in thus trying to sniff out the scent of "moral evil," must be barking up the wrong tree, I may well decline such interpretations of my sexual inclination, but the decline of civilization itself, in the opinion of the Church, would be clinched were many twigs—or, heaven help us!—twigs in general to be bent as I am inclined. For if no one has "any conceivable right" to engage in homosexual acts, it is precisely insofar as homosexual acts cannot lead one to conceive; they violate so-called natural law, according to the Catechism, to the extent that they necessarily close off "the sexual act to the gift of life."[38] That gift, understood by the Church as the gift of compassion *par excellence,* compels the Church to resist any tempering of its sanctions against homosexuality. Only, from such a perspective, a deeply *misguided* sense of compassion leads "well-intentioned" persons to act "with a view to changing civil statutes and laws" in response to "the pro-homosexual movement['s] . . . deceitful propaganda."

The Church, by contrast, in the words of the Vatican, "can never be so callous,"[39] and therefore, as it declared in a letter of admonition to its bishops, deviation from official Church doctrine where homosexuality is concerned "in an effort to provide pastoral care is neither caring nor pastoral."[40] And this sentiment found more concise expression in a statement released by the "Concerned Families of Maryland," a nonsectarian organization devoted to "family-friendly" policies: "There is more compassion in truth than [in] deception, and more compassion in denouncing homosexuality than [in] endorsing it."[41]

That compassion can look like callousness, then, and callousness like compassion, that the bleeding-heart sob sister's tears can destroy what her tough-talking, tough-love-promoting twin's invective purports to redeem, suggests that compassion and callousness differ only by decree, as the Professor inadvertently told us near the outset of *North by Northwest.* This irony must be lost, however—it is incumbent that it be lost—on all who would stand with Saint Peter's heir on the rock of compassionate love—and lost on them most through the loss of the Leonards, of all the *sinthom*-osexuals, whose loss is perceived as none at all since they represent loss itself: represent, more precisely, loss *of* self, of coherence, of life, and of heirs. "Gay activism is wholeheartedly determined," writes Father John Miller, the author of *Called by Love,* and editor of the *Social Justice Review,* "to do battle against human life." Therefore, Father Miller insists, "Mistaken compassion must not allow us to 'grant' civil rights to gays. . . . We have every natural, God-given right to discriminate against immoral, unhealthy, ugly, society-disturbing behavior."[42]

This negation of the negativity, the *jouissance,* of the *sinthom*-osexual, epitomizes the logic of compassion to which we are all of us called by love. In the process it determines dialectic, in its temporal elaboration, as always, to borrow a phrase from Lacan, a "dialectic of desire."[43] Or, to put that somewhat differently, the fantasy that desire subsists on requires dialectic as temporalization, as the production of sequence, of narrative, that moves toward an always unrealized end. Desire, that is, in opposition to the *sinthom*-osexual who figures the drive, necessitates the emergence of fantasy in order to screen the drive's insistence. That fantasy, always experienced as the very reality in which we live, installs the law's prohibition as a barrier to *jouissance* and opens the space of desire to an infinite future of failed pursuit through which desire, like Faust, refuses satisfaction or enjoyment, prolonging itself by negating the satisfaction at which it aims and only through that negation attaining the enjoyment it refuses to know.[44]

The relation of desire's dialectic, with its endless unfolding of the future, to the *sinthom*-osexual's death drive, with its enjoyment that is always "*at hand,*" echoes the relation of allegory to irony as theorized by de Man.[45] Allegory, as de Man explains it in "The Rhetoric of Temporality," enacts "the tendency of . . . language toward narrative, the spreading out along the axis of an imaginary time in order to give duration to what is, in fact, simultaneous within the subject" (p. 225). Hence, as he goes on to assert, "allegory exists entirely within an ideal time that is never here and now, but always a past or an endless future" (p. 226). Irony, on the other hand, reduces time to "one single moment" (p. 225) that allows "neither

memory nor prefigurative duration" (p. 226). It is, instead, "instantaneous like an 'explosion,'" de Man insists, and then he adds: "and
the fall is sudden" (p. 225).

If compassion for others moves us, as Reagan put it, to "reach out a
hand when they fall," could we think of compassion in terms of the
sequential narratives of allegory, resisting while carrying forward—
through and as the dilation of time—the negativity condensed in
irony's instantaneous big bang? And would not this form of compassionate love, intended to buck up the order of desire expressed as reproductive futurism, allegorize, to the profit of dialectic, the expense
of the unrecuperable irony that compassion is always compelled to
abject in the form of *sinthom*-osexuals, those who endanger the order
of desire insofar as their access to *jouissance* seems to give them more
bang for their buck?[46]

Consistent with this allegorization of irony, with this willful translation of irony into a moment in the allegory by (and within) which it
is dialectically overcome, *North by Northwest* gets rid of the *sinthom*-
osexual with a bang of its own, the irony of which gets voiced in the
mordant comment the shooting elicits from Leonard's superior, Vandamm: "That wasn't very sporting, . . . using *real* bullets." With this
brief ironic epitaph the film dismisses irony, discarding, along with
Leonard, Thornhill's single most obvious trait, or the trait that could
only be obvious so long as he himself remained single. Married—and
that marriage occurs, we might say, in the gesture that has him drop
irony in order to keep from dropping Eve—he drops, as if it were casually, one last line that would mark his change: "I'm sentimental," he
says to Eve in the final words of the film, his body now falling all over
hers as she, permitted to do so at last, falls backward onto the bed.
We need not, of course, accept that this statement expresses the wisdom won by escaping the force field of irony's violence; we need not,
in fact, accept that this statement is without irony itself. But the irony
then would be Hitchcock's or *North by Northwest*'s instead of Thornhill's and would ironize the sentimentality to which Thornhill lays
claim at the end of the film by ironizing the claim of sentiment,
which is allegory's claim as well, to have superseded irony—to have
pulled itself up by its bootstraps from under the *sinthom*-osexual's

boot to assure thereby the survival, in the future unfolded by desire, of the ego's Imaginary unity that compassion seeks to conserve.

Has any film imaged more elegantly the conservation of such an image or rendered more economically the dialectic of desire as it rewrites the fatal fall into the abyss of *jouissance* as an endless fall forward through time so as to keep *jouissance* at bay? Hanging from the face of the cliff inscribed with those massive, stony faces—images at once of the founding fathers and of the foundational fantasy that the law of the father, by barring our access to *jouissance* and confounding the *sinthom*-osexual, can safeguard the image we take as our own, can give us a ground to stand on—the film's reproductive couple procures its future as well as ours by enacting the movement of dialectic by which the self aspires to find itself, to borrow a phrase from de Man, "standing above its own experiences."[47] For the scene on Mount Rushmore can only conclude, the escape from the threat of the death drive as posed by Leonard can only take place through a sequence that joins the activities of suspending, annulling, and raising up and thus translates into visual terms the *Aufhebung* of dialectic.

No sooner has the pressure of the death drive that Leonard drives home been suppressed by the law than the film suppresses all reference to agencies external to the couple itself. Closing in tightly on their faces, which serve to procure our Imaginary totalization through identification with an image, the camera invites a suspension of logic as Thornhill lifts Eve up to safety, single-handedly in more ways than one, by raising her body directly from where it hangs above the void to the coziness of an upper berth in a bedroom coach on a train. And as Eve is borne up and into the berth so that the future itself may be born, the film engages a dialectic of continuity through disconnection, achieving, like allegory in the words of de Man, "the illusion of a continuity that it knows to be illusionary" and granting the reproductive couple the prolongations of desire across and by means of a break that has all the force of anacoluthon.[48]

For the strangeness of this moment, often eliciting a laughter that mingles disappointment with relief, centers on Hitchcock's willfulness—or even his perversity—in representing the escape from the pull of the void in a sequence that puts the space of that void at the center of its structure. Though the reproductive couple's joined hands join hands with Hitchcock's cinematic technique to insist on the logic of continuity here, the sequence marks the discontinuity of what its continuity editing joins. Strikingly, the temporal and spatial violations involved in the syntax of this movement, which replaces the particulars of an all-but-impossible rescue from the cliff with the act, both more plausible and more mundane, of hoisting Eve up to the berth, coincide with a violation of naturalism's insistence on the synchronization of sound as the words on the audio track cease to coincide with the movements of Thornhill's lips. In this momentary disconnection, itself a rendering, through displacement, of the ruptured temporality that the editing works to conceal, a voice that comes from somewhere else—the voice, to be sure, of Thornhill but coming from somewhere beyond the image we see, coming, we learn, from the future he labors to bear in the body of Eve—delivers them into that future with four simple words: "Come along, Mrs. Thornhill." With this the film raises all of us into that future along with Eve.

To the extent that it carries us forward, though, like the train onto which the couple suddenly finds itself transported, the engine of that movement here is fantasy alone: the fantasy, first and foremost, that this whole scene is *not* a fantasy but, rather, a return precisely to what is plausibly mundane; the fantasy, then, that futurity, the temporality of desire, can designate reality instead of screening out the Real. Thornhill's bandaged fingers may carry Leonard's imprint still (and the screenplay, after Thornhill's last words, calls them to our attention), but the film, only able to come to a close by opening onto desire, desires its way to survival by casting Leonard, now that it has cast him out, as a dream from which it has awakened into history, temporality, and the cycles of reproduction.

This is the compassionate destiny destined to keep the romantic couple, like every subject of desire, from ever reaching its destination, to keep it always traveling toward something at which it can never arrive: what Lacan has described as "the part of himself, lost forever, that is constituted by the fact that he is only a sexed living being, and that he is no longer immortal," no longer, in other words, whole, complete, untouched by division.[49] And this, of course, is the fate foretold in the familiar Lacanian anecdote concerning the logic of sexuation in which two children, a brother and a sister, are turned, by the signifiers of sexual difference, into strangers on a train.[50] "For these children," as Lacan informs us, "Ladies and Gentlemen will be henceforth two countries toward which each of their souls will strive on divergent wings, and between which a truce will be the more impossible since they are actually the same country and neither can compromise on its own superiority without detracting from the glory of the other."[51] Thus like Thornhill and Eve, they must book a berth on the train that is called Desire and that leads, like Tennessee Williams's play, to an end informed by the train of births that creates and sustains the illusion of its endless locomotion.[52]

North by Northwest will appear, then, to take its hero, as Raymond Bellour suggests, "from an ignorance to a knowledge," recalling in this the narrative logic of temporal succession whereby allegory sorts out and distributes sequentially, in an effort to resolve, the incompatible pressures that irony condenses into a single instant.[53] The film's last shot would seem to confirm such a triumph of allegorization by flattering the "knowingness" of an audience more than happy to give a hand—as much to itself as to the film—when the phallic symbol it did not see coming comes handed to it like a gift. And Hitchcock never tired of pretending to reveal what that last shot meant: "There are no symbols in *North by Northwest*," he told the *Cahiers du Cinéma*, "Oh yes! One. The last shot. It's a train entering the tunnel after the love scene between Grant and Eva Marie Saint. It's a phallic symbol. But you mustn't tell anyone."[54] As symbol of the Symbolic, of the law of the father as the law of desire that would protect us from *jouissance*, the phallic symbol would put its seal on the overcoming of irony; but to the extent that it does so by raising the order of meaning on a meaningless signifier, impelling us ever after to seek a "return" to the mythic coherence—the wholeness we "lost" through sexual difference—by riding the rails, like the brother and sister Lacan adduces in his fable, toward the part of ourselves forever lost in the place of Ladies or Gentlemen, those foreign places to which we can never hope to get from here, to that extent the phallic symbol reinstates the very irony, the simultaneity of contradictions, the "dizziness to the point of madness," that its promise of "meaning" is meant to transcend.

Those children, after all, as realizations of reproductive futurism—
toward which, as sure as night follows day, they are doomed to be
railroaded too—image the only answer permitted the question of desire in a signifying order whose elements admit no other totalization
except the one provided by the fantasy of futurity—a fantasy that
they, as children, may come to figure for a time, but one they will be
forced to figure out how to realize in time to come. The *mise en abime*
that reproductive futurism thus effects—figured by the child, enacted
by desire, and symbolized by the phallus—defends against the abyss
of irony it negates and preserves at once. In the process it reveals the
compassion for which Saint Martin provides the model, the compassion that nothing would contravene in the social field shaped by desire, as another name for castration, for the law that we, like Saint
Martin's beggar, solicit for the wool it pulls over our eyes in order to
blind us to the *jouissance* that would knock them right out of our
heads.

Leonard, the *sinthom*-osexual, loves his neighbor enough to say
no, to give him the kick that he is begging for and from which he gets
his kicks. Unlike Roy Batty (Rutger Hauer) in *Blade Runner* (1982),
a later *sinthom*-osexual who stands, in a comparable moment of
truth, looking down at his adversary, Rick Deckard (Harrison Ford),
with whom he has been paired in a life-and-death chase, as Deckard
desperately struggles to keep his grip above the abyss, Leonard, embodying the machinery of the drive more fully than his android
brother, resists, *in extremis,* the redemptive lure of sentimental hu-
manization. Not for Leonard identification with the image of the
other or nostalgia for a totalized self; not for him the aestheticized
elegies to which Batty, after rescuing Deckard, gives voice; not for
him the Symbolic survival in the bird that wings its way upward on
Batty's death, rewarding his act of compassion with the sign of a fully
humanized soul. Leonard's sole act is to grind his sole, like a brand,
into Thornhill's flesh, crushing the hand toward which, unmoved, he
refuses to reach out his own. Moved by the death drive's compulsion,
instead, he gets to the heart of the plea for help by helping the other
to get in touch with his ways of getting off. Batty's altruistic act, like
Saint Martin's generosity, may earn the spiritual seal of approval im-

plied by the wings of the dove, but Leonard's bespeaks the difference "between the response of philanthropy and that of love."

The *sinthom*-osexual, then, as saint? Saint Leonard, as Martin Landau plays him, usurping Saint Martin's place? But the *sinthom*-osexual will not offer a blessed thing by way of salvation, will not promise any transcendence or hold out a vision of survival. In breaking our hold on the future, the *sinthom*-osexual, himself neither martyr nor proponent of martyrdom for the sake of a cause, forsakes all causes, all social action, all commitment to a better tomorrow and the promised perfection of social forms. Against such activism, he performs an act: the act of repudiating the social, of stepping, or trying to step, with Leonard, beyond compulsory compassion, beyond the future and the trap of the images that work to keep us in its thrall. Insisting, with Kant, on a freedom from pathological motivation, on a radical type of selflessness that allegory will not redeem, the *sinthom*-osexual stands for the (im)possibility of an ethical act, and precisely to the extent that he stands both on and for that (im)possibility, the logic of social organization necessarily cannot stand him.

Alenka Zupančič, in *Ethics of the Real,* after noting that the Kantian ethical act "is denounced as 'radically evil' in every ideology," describes how ideology tries to defend against such an act: "The gap opened by an act," she remarks, "is immediately linked in this ideological gesture to an *image.* As a rule this is an image of suffering, which is then displayed to the public alongside this question: *Is this what you want?* And this question already implies the answer: *It would be impossible, inhuman, for you to want this!*"[55] The image of suffering so adduced is always the threatened suffering of an image: the image, precisely, onto which the face of the human has been projected such that, with it, we risk losing the face by which we (think we) know ourselves. For "we are, in effect," as Lacan ventriloquizes the normative understanding of self, "at one with everything that depends on the image of the other as our fellow man, on the similarity we have to our ego and to everything that situates us in the imaginary register."[56]

To be anything else—to refuse the constraint, the inertia, imposed by the ego as form—would be, as Zupančič rightly puts it, "impossible, inhuman." As impossible and inhuman as a beggar who implores us to kill him or to fuck him; as impossible and inhuman as Leonard, who responds to Thornhill by crushing his hand; as impossible and inhuman as the *sinthom*-osexual who shatters the lure of the future and, for refusing the call to compassion, surely merits none himself. To embrace the impossibility, the inhumanity of the *sinthom*-osexual: that, I suggest, is the ethical task for which queers are singled out. Leonard affords us no lesson in how to follow in his footsteps but calls us, beyond volition or desire, to a *sinthom*-osexuality of our own—one we assume at the price of the very identity named by "our own." To those on whom his ethical stance, his act, exerts a compulsion, Leonard leaves only the irony of trying to read him as an allegory, as a figure in whom we encounter the *sinthom*-osexual's concretization: the formalization of his resistance to the conservation of forms, the substantialization of his negativity that dismantles every substance. He leaves us, in short, the impossible task of trying to fill his shoes—shoes that were empty of anything human even while he was wearing them but that lead us, against our own self-interest and in spite of our desire, toward a *jouissance* from which everything "human," to have one, must turn its face.

Notes

1. Saint Augustine, *On Christian Teaching,* Book II, chap. 7, sec. 11, trans. R. P. H. Green (New York: Oxford University Press 1997), pp. 34, 35.
2. Ronald Reagan, "First Inaugural Address," in *Speeches of the American Presidents,* 2nd ed., ed. Janet Podell and Steven Anzouin (New York: H. W. Wilson Company, 2001), p. 873.
3. I take this use of "disfiguration" from the work of Paul de Man, for whom it signifies the reduction of a perceptual reality to a rhetorical construct. See, for example, the essays collected in *The Rhetoric of Romanticism* (New York: Columbia University Press, 1984). For a fuller account of disfiguration and the face, see my essay "Imagining the Homosexual: *Laura* and the Other Face of Gender" in *Homographesis: Essays in Gay Literary and Cultural Theory* (New York: Routledge, 1994).
4. Ernest Lehman, *North by Northwest: The MGM Library of Film Scripts* (New York: Viking, 1972), pp. 45, 46. All subsequent references to this screenplay will be to this edition and will appear in parentheses after the citation in the text.
5. See Lee Edelman, "*Sinthom*-osexuality" in *Aesthetic Subjects,* ed. David McWhirter and Pamela Matthews (Minneapolis: University of Minnesota Press, 2003); and "Hitchcock's Future" in *Hitchcock: Centenary Es-*

says, ed. Richard Allen and Sam Ishii Gonzalez (London: BFI Press, 1999).

6. This is not to say, of course, that those persons who are read as figures of *sinthom*-osexuality are themselves incapable of love, but only that the figure of the *sinthom*-osexual materializes the anxiogenic force of a compulsion whose mechanical quality is posed against the spiritualizing— and "humanizing"—ideology of "love."

7. Jacques-Alain Miller, "On Perversion," in *Reading Seminars I and II: Lacan's Return to Freud*, ed. Richard Feldstein, Bruce Fink, and Maire Jaanus (Albany, NY: State University of New York Press, 1996), p. 313.

8. Jacques Lacan, *The Four Fundamental Concepts of Psychoanalysis* (New York: W. W. Norton & Company, 1981), p. 205. Earlier in this volume, Lacan contrasts the fundamental narcissism of love with the function of the drive when he notes that he himself has come close to what Freud "articulates when he distinguishes between the two fields, the field of the drives on the one hand, and the narcissistic field of love on the other, and stresses that at the level of love, there is a reciprocity of *loving* and *being loved*, and that, in the other field, it is a question of a pure activity *durch seine eigene Triebe*, for the subject" (p. 200).

9. Lacan, *Four Fundamental Concepts*, p. 205.

10. For a fuller account of this logic in relation to the death drive, see Richard Boothby, *Death and Desire: Psychoanalytic Theory in Lacan's Return to Freud* (New York: Routledge, 1991).

11. "Party Ousts 'Phobe French Senator," Yahoo News, August 3, 2000, at http://dailynews.yahoo.com/h/po/20000803/co/2000903002.html.

12. Dan Savage, "The Baby," *New York Times Magazine*, November 15, 1998, p. 95.

13. Cited in Donald Spoto, *The Dark Side of Genius: The Life of Alfred Hitchcock* (New York: Ballantine Books, 1983), p. 440.

14. Lacan, *Four Fundamental Concepts*, p. 205.

15. With this reference to Joel Fineman's analysis of Othello, I mean to suggest that Thornhill, who, like Othello, is associated with the "O" of desire—though a desire that *North by Northwest* describes as standing for "nothing"—becomes a figure through whom our faith in desire, our confidence in its world-making logic, can be confirmed as the ground of futurity. See Joel Fineman: "The Sound of 'O' in *Othello:* The Real of the Tragedy of Desire," in *The Subjectivity Effect in Western Literary Tradition: Essays toward the Release of Shakespeare's Will* (Cambridge, MA: MIT Press, 1991), pp. 143–164.

16. Alfred Hitchcock, cited in François Truffaut, *Hitchcock*, rev. ed. (New York: Simon & Schuster, 1985), p. 138.

17. Lacan, *The Ethics of Psychoanalysis 1959–1960, The Seminar of Jacques Lacan: Book VII*, ed. Jacques-Alain Miller, trans. Dennis Potter (New York: Norton, 1992), p. 186.

18. Lacan, *The Ethics of Psychoanalysis*, p. 187.

19. Lacan, *The Ethics of Psychoanalysis*, p. 186.

20. Lacan, *The Ethics of Psychoanalysis*, p. 187.

21. Lacan, *The Ethics of Psychoanalysis*, p. 193.

22. Sigmund Freud, *Civilization and Its Discontents, The Standard Edition of the Complete Psychological Works of Sigmund Freud,* vol. XXI, pp. 109, 111.

23. Immanuel Kant, *Introduction to the Metaphysical Element of Ethics,* trans. Thomas Kingsmill Abbott, in *Great Books of the Western World,* vol. 42 (Chicago: Encyclopedia Britannica, 1952), p. 376.

24. Lacan, *The Ethics of Psychoanalysis,* p. 187.

25. Lacan, *The Ethics of Psychoanalysis,* p. 196.

26. Lacan, *The Ethics of Psychoanalysis,* p. 202.

27. Lacan, *The Ethics of Psychoanalysis,* p. 194.

28. Ernest Lehman's screenplay introduces Leonard as follows: "A man is playing croquet all by himself in the fading light. His name is LEONARD. Later, we will see him at closer range and perhaps be slightly repelled. He is about thirty, but looks much younger, for he has a soft baby-face, large eyes, and hair that falls down over his forehead. His attitudes are unmistakably effeminate" (p. 11). Note that the substitutive relation of killing to fucking can also be seen in the enactment by Leonard of the "murder" of Vandamm with Eve's blanks-filled gun.

29. Lacan, *The Ethics of Psychoanalysis,* p. 195.

30. See, for example, Jacques-Alain Miller's formulation of this aspect of Lacan's thought: "What Freud calls the drive is an activity which always comes off. It leads to sure success, whereas desire leads to a sure unconscious formulation, namely, a bungled action or slip: 'I missed my turn,' 'I forgot my keys,' etc. That is desire. The drive, on the contrary, always has its keys in hand." Jacques-Alain Miller, "Commentary on Lacan's Text," in *Reading Seminars I and II: Lacan's Return to Freud,* p. 426.

31. Raymond Bellour, "Symbolic Blockage," trans. Mary Quaintance, in *The Analysis of Film,* ed. Constance Penley (Bloomington, IN: University of Indiana Press, 2000), p. 191.

32. The figure, of course, is linked to Leonard before this final struggle. It is he, of course, who directs VanDamm's attention to it in the auction house, and it appears in the frame a number of times while Leonard, with Eve's gun behind his back, enacts what his boss first interprets as his jealousy of her.

33. Paul de Man, "The Concept of Irony" in *Aesthetic Ideology,* ed. Andrzej Warminski (Minneapolis: University of Minnesota Press, 1996), p. 184.

34. Paul de Man, "The Concept of Irony," p. 179, n. 21.

35. Paul de Man, "The Rhetoric of Temporality," in *Blindness and Insight: Essays in the Rhetoric of Contemporary Criticism,* 2nd ed. (Minneapolis: University of Minnesota Press, 1983), p. 215. All subsequent references to this essay will be to this edition and will appear in parentheses after the citation in the text.

36. When Lacan calls attention to the subject's retreat from *jouissance* and the transgression it entails, he gestures as well toward the logic according to which altruism, the realization of compassion, would necessarily carry with it the trace of the negativity it negates:

> We retreat from what? From assaulting the image of the other, because it was the image on which we were formed as an ego. Here we find the con-

vincing power of altruism. Here, too, is the leveling power of a certain law of equality—that which is formulated in the notion of the general will. The latter is no doubt the common denominator of the respect for certain rights—which, for a reason that escapes me, are called elementary rights— but it can also take the form of excluding from its boundaries, and therefore from its protection, everything that is not integrated into its various registers. (Lacan, Seminar VII, 195)

> The *sinthom*-osexual figures what must be excluded from protection, denied certain "elementary rights," insofar as it threatens the boundaries securing the form of the social subject and thereby denies the authority of social organization or the "general will"—the will, that is, to articulate itself in an image whose totalization must be secured precisely by means of the meaning that futurity affirms.

37. "Some Considerations Concerning the Catholic Response to Legislative Proposals on the Non-Discrimination of Homosexual Persons," June 1992 letter to American bishops, available at http://www.polarnet.ca/~prince/dignity/rights.html.

38. *Catechism of the Catholic Church*, "Chastity and Homosexuality," [2357] (Mahwah, NJ: Paulist Press, 1994), p. 566.

39. Letter to the Bishops of the Catholic Church on the Pastoral Care of Homosexual Persons (October, 1986), sec. 9, available at http://www.polarnet.ca/~prince/dignity/halloween.html.

40. Letter to the Bishops of the Catholic Church, sec. 15.

41. "Homosexuality," Concerned Families of Maryland, http://www.us2000.org/cfmc/poshomosex.htm. The nonsectarian nature of this group reflects the universality of the dogma of reproductive futurism: "We believe the family is the heart of our nations and the key to any true progress to restoring our moral bearings and building a better future for our children."

42. Reverend John Miller, "Homosexuality: What? How? Dangers and Remedies," *Social Justice Review*, http://www.txdirect.net/users/dgreaney/homosex.htm, pp. 3, 5.

43. See Lacan's essay, "The Subversion of the Subject and the Dialectic of Desire in the Freudian Unconscious" in *Écrits: A Selection*, trans. Alan Sheridan (New York: W. W. Norton & Company, 1977). Note especially the oft-cited penultimate sentence of this essay: "Castration means that *jouissance* must be refused, so that it can be reached on the inverted ladder of the Law of desire" (p. 324).

44. See Johann Wolfgang von Goethe, *Faust: A Tragedy*, trans. Walter Arndt (New York: W. W. Norton and Company, 2001), p. 47:

> You heard me, there can be no thought of joy.
> Frenzy I choose, most agonizing lust,
> Enamored enmity, restorative disgust.
> Henceforth my soul, for knowledge sick no more,
> Against no kind of suffering shall be cautioned.
> I mean to savor to my own self's core,

Grasp with my mind both highest and most low,
Weigh down my spirit with their weal and woe,
And thus my selfhood to their own distend,
And be, as they are, shattered in the end.
(*Faust* Part I, lines 1765–1775).

45. I take this phrase from Jacques-Alain Miller, who writes of "the pervert" that "he has an immutable, constant share that is always ready to use—it is *at hand,* an *at hand* enjoyment." "On Perversion," in *Reading Seminars I and II: Lacan's Return to Freud*, p. 310.

46. Note that Lacan traces the dialectic of history back to the advent of Christianity:

> It is also Christianity that associates that death [of God in the crucifixion of Christ] with what happened to the Law; namely, that without destroying the Law, we are told, but in substituting itself for it, in summarizing it, and raising it up in the very movement that abolishes it—thus offering the first weighty historical example of the German notion of *Aufhebung,* i.e., the conservation of something destroyed as a different level—the only commandment is henceforth "Thou shalt love thy neighbor as thyself."
>
> (Lacan, *The Ethics of Psychoanalysis,* p. 193)

47. Paul de Man, "The Concept of Irony," p. 177.
48. Paul de Man, "Rhetoric of Temporality," p. 226.
49. Jacques Lacan, *Four Fundamental Concepts,* p. 205.
50. Lacan recounts this anecdote in "The Agency of the Letter in the Unconscious": "A train arrives at a station. A little boy and a little girl, brother and sister, are seated in a compartment face to face next to the window through which the buildings along the station platform can be seen passing as the train pulls to a stop. 'Look,' says the brother, 'we've arrived at Ladies!'; 'Idiot!' replies his sister, 'Can't you see we're at Gentlemen'" (*Écrits,* p. 152).
51. Lacan, *Écrits,* p. 152.
52. That the train is the vehicle of temporal, and hence of narrative, dilation, may be reinforced by the fact that the train on which Thornhill encounters Eve is expressly identified as the "Twentieth-Century" (see Lehman, *North by Northwest,* p. 48).
53. Raymond Bellour, "Symbolic Blockage," p. 81.
54. Cited by Raymond Bellour in "Symbolic Blockage," p. 81.
55. Alenka Zupančič, *Ethics of the Real: Kant, Lacan* (New York: Verso, 2000), p. 95.
56. Lacan, *The Ethics of Psychoanalysis,* p. 196.

8

Cosmetic Surgeons of the Social

Darwin, Freud, and Wells and the Limits of Sympathy on *The Island of Dr. Moreau*

NEVILLE HOAD

Not to go on all-Fours; that is the Law. Are we not men?
Not to suck up drink; that is the Law. Are we not men?
Not to eat flesh or fish; that is the Law. Are we not men?
Not to claw bark of trees; that is the Law. Are we not men?
Not to chase other men; that is the Law. Are we not men?[1]

This essay revisits an imperialist Gothic novel of terror in a time and place in which the terror returns home, though where or what home can be must for the time being remain an open question. How might a quite (in the British rather than American sense of the word) white African post(settler) colonial turned queer diasporic literary critic teaching in Texas attempt such an encounter? I perform this situational hand-wringing at the outset in order simultaneously to claim and resist the impersonal, universal, academic voice, a voice not unrelated to the central problem in *The Island of Dr. Moreau* of making humans out of nature in one's own image.

I. Feasting with Panthers[2]

H. G. Wells states that the 1895 trials and subsequent imprisonment of Oscar Wilde provided the impetus for *The Island of Dr. Moreau:*

> There was a scandalous trial . . . the graceless and piteous downfall of a
> man of genius, and [my] story was the response of an imaginative mind to

the reminder that humanity is but animal, rough-hewn to a reasonable shape and in perpetual internal conflict between instinct and injunction. The story embodies this ideal, but apart from this embodiment has no allegorical quality. It was written just to give the utmost possible vividness to that conception of men as hewn and confused and tormented beasts.[3]

The novella is a first-person account of a sojourn on an island in the tradition of *Robinson Crusoe* or the first book of *Gulliver's Travels*. The narrator and protagonist, Prendick, is shipwrecked somewhere off the Pacific coast of South America. He and two other companions are adrift without food or water when they flip a coin to ascertain which one of them will serve as food for the other two. A fight ensues, and his two companions topple into the sea and drown. Prendick, revealingly an amateur natural historian, is then rescued by a medical man, Montgomery, who is traveling with a mysterious servant and a cargo of animals, including a caged puma, to the as-yet-unnamed island of Dr. Moreau.

Upon arrival at the island, the captain of the rescue ship refuses to have anything more to do with Prendick. Montgomery and Moreau do not want him on the island, and he is cast adrift; however Montgomery takes pity on him and he is invited ashore. An atmosphere of foreboding, secrecy, and terror pervades the island. Prendick gradually works out that Moreau is a disgraced London vivisectionist who is continuing his experiments on the island. Prendick explores the island and learns the ways of the beast-folk and the central law to which they subscribe. The puma is Moreau's new animal subject for experimentation, and as she is being surgically altered, her screams allow Prendick to realize that the strange human population is composed of various animals that Moreau through surgery has transformed into humans of sorts. Prendick begins to fear for his life: either he will become an object for Moreau's experimentation and be taken into the House of Pain, the name given to Moreau's laboratory by the inhabitants of the island, or the beast-folk will ignore the prohibition on eating flesh or fish, and attack him.

One night the puma breaks free and is chased by Moreau. She kills him, but dies herself. Prendick manages to maintain some order on the island by denying the death of Moreau and persuading most of the beast-men that the Law still stands. However, gradually the beast-men revert to their original animal natures. Montgomery is killed and the House of Pain goes up in flames. Eventually, Prendick manages to build a raft and escapes to sea, where he is rescued and taken back to London—a place of apparent civilization that he finds unbearable as the urban populace reminds him too much of the beast-people. So he retreats to the countryside, where he spends his days in his library and his nights studying the night sky. The island experience hence limits Prendick to perceiving only the animality of humanity. Prendick's time on the island is a persistent memory, which underwrites the truth of whatever else may come after it.

As this narrative summary suggests, *The Island of Dr. Moreau* offers its readers a series of competing speculations on the meaning of the term "human" in the wake of the Oscar Wilde trials of 1895.[4] Are its "beast-folk" folk or monsters or animals? Do the inhuman practices of the vivisectionist, the eponymous Moreau, render him less than human? How may our narrator, Prendick, experience his humanity on the island? Wells writes that the story is itself an embodiment. In addressing these questions, it becomes apparent that the unhuman[5] is frighteningly proximate to the human, as the novel struggles to distinguish the human from the previously human, the potentially human, the almost human. The novel produces the human as both a historical and a spatial problem. In mapping the island back onto Britain and seeing beast-folk everywhere, Prendick suggests that humans exist nowhere. In presenting Moreau—a white, technologically sophisticated scientist—as the cause of monstrosity, the narrative implies that imperial modernity is not particularly helpful to the existence of humanity in the full semantic range of humanity, either at home or abroad.

The novella is uncertain of what criteria can be used to distinguish the human from its proximate others, as it shuttles between a biological definition of the human as simply a distinguishable species and a definition of the human as the carrier of certain attributes that might be called ethical—the human as the humane. As Wells's acknowledgment of the inspiration of the Wilde trials confirms, sexuality is a critical arena for the task of distinguishing the human in both the biological and ethical senses of the term. The stakes of this task of distinguishing the human for the novella can be reduced to the following: ethically, the unhuman cannot make equivalent claims on both the narrator's and the reader's sympathy. The human, in contrast, produces ethical imperatives around the claims, not always reconcilable, of sympathy and justice.

I will intersplice my reading of the novella with readings of snippets of Darwin and Freud in the hope of seeing how their respectively authoritative definitions of the human can be used to unpack the im/possibility of an ethical relation between humans, and between the human and its proximate others, on the island of Dr. Moreau. This paper does not set out to track a pattern of influence between the three authors it discusses. It is well established that Sigmund Freud (1856–1939) read and was deeply influenced by Charles Darwin (1809–1882), as was Wells (1866–1946). Freud and Wells were roughly contemporaries and, given their shared voracity as readers, may very well have read each other, though problems of timing interpose and lines of influence become tenuous. *The Island of Dr. Moreau* is published in 1896. Freud's story of the primal horde is elaborated in *Totem and Taboo,* first published in 1911. Darwin's brief but generative positing of the primal horde is found in Chapter 21 of *The Descent of Man* of 1871. Paradoxically conceptual innovations, which we might call Freudian, are sustainedly anticipated in the novella in terms of both the Freudian rewrite of the primal horde and the Freudian theorizing of an event called the primal scene.

I yoke these three authors together across borders of genre, discipline, and language in the interest of investigating what, in shorthand, I will call *Victorian human origin narratives,* and as speculative material for pondering the meaning of humanity in the wake of the tragedy in New York and the wake of the ongoing tragedy in Afghanistan.[6] I am particularly interested in locating the place of an entity called "homosexuality" in such narratives.[7] These narratives are all attempts to produce definitions of the category "human" in the throes of the Darwinian revolution. Like Freud and unlike Darwin, Wells works in both an ontogenetic and a phylogenetic register. The novella is both a warped creation narrative and an investigation into the inner workings of the narrating subject—Prendick's desires and terrors and what ethical relations he may have with the island's inhabitants. It is hence both psychodrama and allegory. I will read it in both registers; first as a failed allegory of human evolution (phylogeny) and then as a screen memory of the primal scene (ontogeny). The dialectic between these two registers of "origin"—the "human" as species produced by a long evolutionary process and the "human" as individual produced by heterosexual intercourse and normative socializing—is the driving problem of Wells's novella and at the core of much of Freud's oeuvre. By organicizing the social, Darwin avoids the pole of the "human" as individual. The origins and nature of the *individual* human psyche are questions that *The Descent of Man* can only beg. The human as the subject of ontogeny, as individuated subject, is potentially the ethical agent for both Wells and Freud.

In *The Island of Dr. Moreau*, this reader can sympathize with all the inhabitants of the island yet remains reluctant to use sympathy as an alibi for the evasion of judgment. The narrator, Prendick, is structurally the character with the most narrative space to make a claim on a reader's sympathy, but he refuses to commit to any action beyond self-preservation. He does nothing to help the puma-woman even though he is acutely aware of and sympathetic to her plight. His feelings of repulsion for the beast-folk precludes any sympathy with them, let alone forging community with them after the death of Moreau. Only the witness stands outside the freak show which is *The Island of Dr. Moreau*. Sympathy as a human attribute also seems caught, like Prendick, in the space between doing and watching. Prendick may allow readers to experience sympathy as a self-consolidating experience—the horror on the island is rendered palpable throughout—but he never experiences sympathy as a way of putting himself at risk, as a way of redefining himself, as an invitation to an action that may involve some self-sacrifice in the interest of a collective rather than individual good.

Judging the narrator's actions is not the only way to read the novella in terms of the ethical relations it works through. Certain contradictory allegories have proved irresistible to this reader, despite Wells's explicit warnings against allegorizing. If the Wilde trials provide the inspiration for the writing of *The Island of Dr. Moreau*, homosexuality, a thing of uncertain lineaments in the Europe of this moment, yet considered deeply, if not constitutively, unnatural in the literary, religious, and scientific discourses of his day, is partially

aligned with the animal, the natural. Moreover, vivisection, sign of
European rationalist science's refusal of ethical limits in pursuit of
knowledge, starts to look like going native, barely two years before
Conrad sends Kurtz to dance a similar two-step. If Moreau's crime
consists of too much investment in the interiors of bodies, some unspeakable desire to arrange their innards to make them human, why
would Wells pick on a writer whose critical praxis is relentlessly dedicated to the expressiveness of surfaces? The fact that the beast-folks
revert to beastliness after the death of Moreau suggests that the tor-
turous surgery was only the play of surfaces. Wilde and Moreau coincide not only in their "scandalous and graceless downfalls" but also as
cosmetic surgeons of the social.

Reading the narrative in this minimally contextualized way may
require that readers perform contradictory identifications in imagining the differences between the unhuman, the inhuman, and the
human. We need to identify with the agent of harm, Moreau, and his
victims, the beast-folk, while identifying at one remove with the sexually deviant Wilde, who is paradoxically allegorized as both Moreau
and beast-folk. The Wilde trials may well have provided the impetus
for the novella, but the identifications map in confounding ways.
Wilde is Moreau, the great man undone by unsanctioned practices.
Vivisection is declared illegal[8] a decade or so before unspecified acts
of gross indecency between men in private are criminalized by the
Labouchere Amendment of 1886. Wells could assume some famil-
iarity with both these legal contexts. Homosexuality and vivisection
mark unsanctionable intimacies with bodies, and while the twentieth
century saw massive intellectual and legal work to disentangle them,
there are still ways in which the rubric of "crimes against nature" per-
sists in linking the two. Yet at another level of abstraction, Wilde is a
beast-folk tormented by his animal sexual nature and destroyed by
the injunctions against his sexual instincts, and the suffering of both
Wilde and the beast-folk invites our sympathy.

II. Primal Hordes

I will begin with phylogeny, because it is here that the politics of being
human are rendered more visible and ethical relations are foreclosed,

as there are no individuated human beings in the phylogenetic narrative. Consequent to the Darwinian revolution, humanity is first and foremost part of nature. It thus becomes difficult to account for human particularity, except in developmental terms. Man is an animal, just a more advanced one. Human sexual behavior occupies a slippery place on this reconfigured border between the animal and the human. This new beginning of "Man" results from the insertion of the human subject into a raced, gendered, and strangely homosexualized society, which both may and may not be read as imperialist allegory. For Darwin, originary human society could not contain promiscuity of intercourse and the first human groups were probably ruled by an alpha male who monopolized the women and drove his male progeny from the group as soon as they reached sexual maturity. Freud reworks this tale in having the brothers bind together through "homosexual feelings and acts" in order to kill the father.

The problem of who or what is to take the *place of the father* then emerges. As a solution to this problem, the brothers institute the incest taboo, from which the Oedipus complex and the consequent psychological development of the individual are elaborated. The brothers make a blood pact to ensure their freedom and their equal access to the women the father had monopolized.[9] *The Island of Dr. Moreau* refuses the primordialism of both these narratives by situating its scenario in the present. Yet the novella almost compulsively repeats and reworks evolutionary and psychoanalytic *topoi* in the production of the human as a category for philosophical, scientific, and ethical inquiry. It posits the Law as both supplement to and finally replacement for the rule of Moreau, the putative father of the island's queer inhabitants.

Bracketing the problem of influence but without entirely dispensing with chronology, let us go back to *The Descent of Man,* and see if we may productively splice elements of the narrative of Dr. Moreau into Darwin's seminal text:

> judging from the social habits of man as he now exists, the most probable view is that he aboriginally lived in small communities, each with a single wife or if powerful with several, whom he jealously guarded against all other men. Or he may not have been a social animal, and yet have lived with several wives like the gorilla; for all the natives "agree

that but one adult male is seen in a band; when the young male grows
up, a contest takes place for mastery, and the strongest, by killing and
driving out the others, establishes himself at the head of the community." The younger males, thus expelled and wandering about, would,
when at last successful in finding a partner, prevent too close inter-
breeding within the limits of the same family.[10]

An unaccounted-for, resolutely naturalized heterosexual desire both
underpins and continually threatens the emergence of society in this
rendition of the tale of the primal horde. An animalesque competitive heterosexuality is the marker of animality *par excellence* for Darwin. *The Island of Dr. Moreau* reverses the temporal sequence of the
story of the primal horde in its second half. It is equally concerned
with the degeneration of the beast-folk back into beasts, for after the
death of Moreau, they lose the appellation beast-folk or beast-men
and are referred to as beast-monsters. The degeneration of the beast-
folk or their unbecoming human is what most concerns our narrator
after Moreau's death.

The markers of this fall back into animality are not the unbridled
natural heterosexual passion of Darwin, but cannibalism and other
unspeakable desires for human flesh. Wells's novella is clearer than
most that cannibalism was as much a problem for stranded U.S. and
European sailors[11] as it was for "the savages" such people encountered. Near the beginning of the novel, Prendick and his fellow shipwrecked sailors are drawing lots to see which one will serve as food
for the others when a fight ensues and Prendick's two companions
topple into the sea and drown:

> The lot fell upon the sailor, but he was the strongest of us and would
> not abide by it, and attacked Helmar with his hands. They grappled to-
> gether and almost stood up. I crawled along the boat to them, intending
> to help Helmar by grasping the sailor's leg, but the sailor stumbled with
> the swaying of the boat, and the two fell upon the gunwhale and rolled
> overboard together. They sank like stones. (p. 3)

In Wells's novella, the threat of cannibalism, the problem of men
eating each other, is part of the civilized world as much as it produces
anxiety for Prendick on the island. More generally, in the Victorian
phylogenetic story of the human, what are the respective develop-

mental places of homosexuality and cannibalism? In *Totem and Taboo*, the very crucible of the social, the foundational moment for the possibility of human civilization, may be predicated on the incorporation and transcendence of a developmentally homosexual phase phylogenetically, followed by the cannibalizing of the murdered father in the totemic meal:

> Sexual desires do not unite men but divide them. Thus, the brothers had no alternative if they were to live together, but not perhaps, until they had passed through many dangerous crises—to institute the law against incest, by which they all alike renounced the women they desired and who had been their chief motive in despatching their father. In this way, they rescued the organization that had made them strong— and which may have been based on homosexual feelings and acts, originating perhaps during the period of their expulsion from the horde.[12]

The precursor to the founding moment of human society—the beginning of the incest taboo, which is what separates us from the animals for Freud—may be speculatively predicated on the movement from the homosexual to what Eve Kosofsky Sedgwick terms the "homosocial," or what Luce Irigaray terms the hom(m)osexual.[13] The organization that made the brothers strong may have been tentatively "based on homosexual feelings and acts." Phylogenetically, before savages can even be savages they have to have been and transcended being homosexuals.

It is possible to suggest that this Freudian phylogenetic narrative of homoerotically engaged sons bonding together to kill the father in order to institute a homosocial order may function ideologically as imperialist allegory. Running the psychoanalytic version of the story of the primal horde through some representative and representational axioms of imperialism, it is possible to produce the following sentences: White men, having descended from the apes via the savages, and having successfully sublimated their homosexual desire for each other (though a touch paranoid about its possible return) cooperate with each other in the sharing of women, whose bodily destinies are necessarily subordinated to the men.[14] The men are also working hard to ensure that the murdered savage father from whom they have descended does not return.

For Wells, the process of unbecoming human on the island is marked by the narrator's deep terror that the beast-folk are out to eat him, something that would be natural to their animal natures but profoundly inhuman. We are left with the paradox that to become human, we are cut up; to unbecome human, we dismember and ingest. Here Wells parts with the Freudian origin myth of the primal horde, in which, after killing the father, the brothers partake in the totemic meal by eating him. For Freud, we need to be cannibals after being homosexuals before becoming human, at least phylogenetically.

The Island of Dr. Moreau fails and succeeds more spectacularly as imperialist allegory. A white scientist cuts up and reassembles animals in the attempt to create people. He is killed by one of his creations, and his creations revert to their animal natures. European science is the agent of monstrosity and humanity and quite literally constructs the natives of the island. It is possible to find a nascent anti-imperialism in this part of the narrative, in that Moreau, apparent agent of European rational, technological progress, is actually the cause of suffering and the maker of monsters, effectively giving the lie to the civilizing-mission rationale of imperialism. However, the imagining of the difference of the beast-folk in terms of reversion and degeneracy could not avoid racist implications in the 1890s, any more than it can now. The fact that the demise of Moreau brings about social chaos on the island suggests that once white men—and it does not matter how cruel they are—are no longer in charge, barbarism and savagery will necessarily ensue. This is clearly an important imperialist fantasy. However, the novella consistently sets up Moreau's cruelty as equivalent to if not morally more repugnant than the cannibalistic impulses of the beast-folk. The island, while a particular place, appears to the narrator as a microcosm of metropolitan society when he returns to London:

> I see faces keen and bright, others dull and dangerous, others unsteady, insincere, none that have the calm authority of a reasonable soul. I feel as though the animal was surging up through them, that presently the degradation of the Islanders will be played over again on a larger scale. (p. 155)

For Wells, post-Darwin, the civilizing mission, whether at home or abroad, seems destined to failure. Our animal natures will win out, and like the Freud of *Civilization and Its Discontents*, the cost of civilization is high, requiring significant sacrifices.[15] With its confidence in the meanings of animality, *The Island of Dr. Moreau* does not entirely escape primordialism by setting itself in the present. In its assertion that we are all savages, it both repeats and confounds the racist common sense of its time.

III. Eavesdropping on a Woman in the (Imperialist) House of Pain

It is in its ethical moment that the novella offers its deepest challenge to and reveals its frightening complicity with the axiomatics of imperialism. In the three chapters at the center of the novel, revealingly entitled "The Crying of the Puma," "The Thing in the Forest," and "The Crying of the Man," Prendick must struggle with the screams of pain of the puma as she becomes human. The crying of the puma drives Prendick from his room:

> The crying sounded even louder out of doors. It was as if all the pain in the world had found a voice. Yet had I known such pain was in the next room, and had it been dumb, I believe—I have thought since—I could have stood it well enough. It is when suffering finds a voice and sets our nerves quivering that this pity comes troubling us. But in spite of the brilliant sunlight and the green fans of the trees waving in the soothing sea-breeze, the world was a confusion, blurred with drifting black and red phantasms, until I was out of earshot of the house in the stone wall. (p. 40)

"It was if all the pain in the world had found a voice." As she becomes human, the puma makes noises that Prendick is able to hear as the cumulative voice of world-pain. The external world, in the full beauty of its tropical plenitude, becomes, in a kind of paranoid transfiguration, "blurred with drifting black and red phantasms"—peopled with imaginary figures of indeterminate terror and threat. The voice plays on his viscera, rendering the world unintelligible to Prendick's senses. Only when the sound of the animal in pain can no longer be heard can the world cease to be "a confusion."

What is Prendick to do in this situation? He is not responsible for the inflicting of the pain. Moreau is. Too disoriented to act, he must run away. Here Prendick, who overhears trauma, behaves as if he were the subject of trauma. Running away from the pain-saturated cost of making humans out of animals (hewing culture from nature?), Prendick is stalked by the leopard-man: "And presently a shapeless lump heaved up momentarily against the skyline and vanished again. It was assured now that my tawny-faced antagonist was stalking me again" (p. 48). In a turnabout that almost defies understanding, after this ordeal in the face of cannibalistic/homosexual panic, Prendick attributes radically different affect to the cries of the puma:

> And presently, with the positive effect of relief, came the pitiful moan-
> ing of the puma, the sound that had originally driven me out to explore
> this mysterious island. At that, though I was faint and horribly fatigued,
> I gathered together all my strength and began running again towards
> the light. It seemed to me a voice was calling me. (p. 51)

What had driven him away by its sheer awfulness brings him back, saves him. The screams of the puma-woman are less terrifying, they may even promise relief in comparison to an encounter with the heaved up lump of the leopard-man. Reading this as phylogenetic al-legory, an encounter with the leopard-man would represent the return to primitivism or homosexuality, the connected precursors to the entry into human subjectivity that the tale of the primal horde, as phylogenetic bolster to the Oedipus complex, describes. Primitivism, marked *par excellence* by cannibalism, and homosexuality (if I may riskily extrapolate from "homosexual feelings and acts") are the re-spective sublated terms in the phylogeny and ontogeny of the civilized for Freud. The desublimation, the fall back into the homosexual and primitive position represented by the leopard-man's interest in Pren-dick, is somehow worse than overhearing the pain of the puma be-coming human.[16] The encounter with those drifting black and red phantasms does not allow for sympathy. Once he has eaten[17] and calmed down, a new voice makes a call on him:

> Presently I heard something else very faint and low. I sat as if frozen in
> my attitude. Though it was faint and low, it moved me more profoundly
> than all that I had hitherto heard of the abominations behind the wall.
> There was no mistake this time in the quality of the dim broken sounds,
> no doubt at all of their source; for it was groaning, broken by sobs and

gasps of anguish. It was no brute this time. It was a human being in tor-
ment. As I realised this I rose, and in three steps had crossed the room,
seized the handle of the door into the yard and flung it open before me.
(p. 56)

The moaning of the animal first prompts Prendick to flee, then it
guides him home, then it almost instantaneously demands that he
act. This new voice freezes him. Fleeing is not an option. Previously
the overheard voice had been unrecognizably indeterminate—"all the
pain in the world." As the voice becomes recognizable as a human
voice—"it was no brute this time"—even though the voice is "faint
and low," this new voice can make a claim on his sympathy. It would
seem that ethical relations for Prendick need a nuanced balance between commonality and difference, spatial proximity and distance.
The pain of the alien, the animal, the world in the abstract, the clearly
not-me can be escaped. The pain of the near-me, the perhaps-me,
must be attended to. It is only projective recognition that produces the
imperative to act. As long as Prendick can hear the voice as the voice
of a brute or as world-pain in the abstract, the call of the other produces the escape imperative. When the voice is recognizable as potentially his own, when the projective identification with the beast as
human can be made, intervention becomes a necessity, a moral imperative. However, this moment is short-lived. The chapter ends:

I picked myself up and stood trembling, my mind a chaos of the most horrible misgivings. Could the vivisection of men be possible? The question
shot like lightning across a tumultuous sky. And suddenly the clouded
horror of my mind condensed into a vivid realisation of my danger. (p. 56)

This trauma can more accurately be read in the realm of the ethical.
This is, after all, the response of one human to another. There is no
self-shattering desublimation here. This is evident in the shift from
the Lear-like pathetic fallacy of the transmutation of "of the brilliant
sunlight and the green fans of the trees waving in the soothing sea-
breeze/ [to] drifting black and red phantasms" to the ordinary metaphor "like lightning across a tumultuous sky." Having entered the site
of trauma, the House of Pain, having moved from listening to acting,
he can no longer flee. Identification is clearly a double-edged sword
for Prendick. It forces him to act to save the puma-woman, only to

realize his own danger. The irony of the moment of identification is that it is a misrecognition. It is a beast-folk in the House of Pain, not another human. The demands of survival and altruism, momentarily one, became shatteringly competitive. Whom is he obliged to save?

Prendick can experience no solidarity with the puma-woman here, no relation to her pain that does not threaten to destroy himself, no relation to otherness that could be called ethical. This failure to reach the ethical may be an ongoing historical one. Prendick's shifting reading of the meanings and claims of the voice are difficult to historicize within the framework of Victorian human-origin narratives, but historicizing may allow the impediments to an ethical Prendick to become visible. Some axioms of the ideological edifice of European imperialism may assist in finding responsibility for Prendick's failure not in his psychology nor within the idea of the ethical itself, but may suggest that change in the historical grounding of subjects is necessary to produce a subject capable of behaving ethically.

The missionary impulse in imperial endeavors is strong. It was deemed that the natives needed to be saved from themselves. The call of the colonizable was heard as the call of the human in the making. The plethora of colonial justifications in the form of civilizing missions is by now well known. To invoke a resonant abolitionist sentence from the earlier part of the nineteenth century: Is the African not a man and a brother?[18] Theories of imperialism that rely on economic rationality run into trouble. Economic historians have struggled to prove that in the long run the British Empire was profitable.[19] Imperialism was for the most part undertaken with the best of intentions, prompted precisely by the imperatives of saving, rescuing, improving, uplifting that Prendick is partially experiencing in this scene. What does the voice in the House of Pain need to be saved from? The cruelty of modern science? The agony of becoming human? What is the meaning of torture in this scene? Does the moment of becoming human belong to the puma or does the ability to respond to the call of the other mark the moment in which Prendick, near-cannibal, uninvited guest, potential meal, almost laboratory rat, fleetingly becomes human?

In other words, whom are we saving when we open the doors of the House of Pain? Are missionaries or colonial administrators or human rights activists, human representatives of the historically specific humane, just, and fair—all those who speak for the human and the civilized—saving natives or saving themselves as they intervene? The immediacy of identification that perceptions of shared pain permits prohibits this question. We cannot enter alterity through the House of Pain. The groans, the cries of the puma-woman are never given content. Prendick acts because he knows: "there was no mistake this time, no doubt at all." Pain in this logic is irreducible. The body knows. The listener recognizes. There can be no other histories, there can be no other way of being human except the listener's.

Yet can we exit the House of Pain, or like Prendick, will we, as human subjects, be pulled back to it, with "the positive effect of relief," hearing voices calling us, voices that we hear only as they become our own voices? Sympathy is thus constructed as the scene of identification with oneself and begins to look indistinguishable from its negation—self-absorption, indifference to the suffering of others. Shared species-being appears essential for sympathy, and even then, the risk that sympathy may require action makes Prendick's experience of sympathy fleeting.

Prendick flings open the doors to the House of Pain perhaps with the intention of ending the suffering of the puma-woman, but upon encountering the resistance of Montgomery and Moreau begins to fear for his own life and resolves to flee. Prendick is able to experience sympathy with the puma-woman as long as he only overhears her cries. When forced into a shared experience of her danger by imagining that he too could become a victim of Moreau's vivisection experiments, he loses the requisite distance for sympathy and, unable to make common cause across the gender and hybridized species divide, can only fall back into self-preservation, itself an undoubted ethical good, but at a terrible price. He experiences the cries of the puma-woman as an incitement to sympathy and then as a rationale for fleeing.

Thinking ontogenetically, that is, about the emergence of the human being as an individual member of a species rather than about the human as a species, the content of the cries of the puma-woman is never specified. They may be birth pangs. She is giving birth to her human self. Her pain may also mark the appropriation of her reproductive power by our white scientist, Moreau. As Gayatri Spivak has written about another maker of monsters: "Frankenstein's antagonist is God himself as Maker of Man, but his real competitor is also woman as the maker of children."[20] The House of Pain becomes a womb of sorts. With God gone, the origin moment for the making-of-men story is the fable of the primal horde. If Moreau's transgression is this severing of gender and reproduction, and readers remember Wells's inspiration for *The Island of Dr. Moreau*, a resonant asymmetry emerges. Wilde's transgression, as the public embodiment of homosexuality for a Victorian audience, is the severing of sexuality and reproduction. Moreau stands up as the bad queer patriarch; his unsanctionable intimacies with the bodies of the animals both support and destroy the order of things.

IV. Primal Scenes

Freud can help us here. Freud too has a collection of beast-folk, most famously the Wolf-Man and the Rat-Man. Moreover, Freud's insistence on the humanity of the aberrant and the proximity of the normal and abnormal is no small ethical contribution. It is in "From the History of an Infantile Neurosis" (1918), popularly known as the Wolf-Man, that Freud offers the lengthiest and most substantial discussion of what he calls the "primal scene." The word primal—and the translation offers no difficulties here—has two critical senses. The primal scene or primal phantasy is the real or imagined image the child has of parental sexual intercourse; it is primal because it is this scene that is the source for any number of screen memories. It is also primal in the sense that it is the scene that may allow the child to deduce his or her origin. As the case of the Wolf-Man illuminates, the significance of primal scenes is irreducibly individual. In his primal scene the wolf-child learns that his mother is indeed castrated, that the castration is the price of sexual gratification from the father.

Many problems attend viewing the central scene in *The Island of Dr. Moreau* as a primal scene of sorts. First, Prendick does not witness the making of the puma into a human being; he overhears it. Second, the web of identifications map in complicated ways. The puma is strictly speaking self-mothering of her human self. The literal, if generative, trauma of vivisection is not coextensive with the symbolically generative trauma of castration. What Wells's fable and Freud's schema share is an insistence that the making of humans involves violence and pain. The observers of the primal scene "adopt what may be called a sadistic view of coition. They see it as something the stronger participant is forcibly inflicting on the weaker."[21]

Moreover the entry into subjectivity through the primal scene is inevitably gendered. The puma is an "it" until it is operated on. Splendidly obviously, the acquisition of subjectivity through the primal scene is also sexualized, and if we think back to the Wolf-Man, it is possible to locate a prior if not originary homosexual desire in this irreducibly singular primal scene. Within the late-nineteenth-century European bourgeois family, the representational content of the primal scene is necessarily heterosexual, and the conflict between the homosexual desire of the Wolf-Man for his father and his resistance to the castration of his mother, which may or may not be misrecognition, is generative of his neurosis. In order for the wolf-boy to learn that castration is the price of sexual gratification from his father, his desire for his father precedes his primal scene.

I fixate on this because of the significant ethical difference between the narration of homosexual desire in the tale of the primal horde and in the positing of the Wolf-Man's primal scene. Homosexual desire is not present only as a superceded moment in becoming human as it is in the tale of the primal horde. Narratologically, homosexual desire is troped in the Wolf-Man's primal scene as an agent encountering gender as a complication. In the tale of the primal horde, homosexual desire appears as that which must be incorporated and transcended by homosocial heterosexuality. That the Wolf-Man ends up neurotic may, in another temporal frame, undermine my case here, but let us not privilege narrative closure and freeze the moment of the primal scene in order to see the wolf-boy's homosexual desire run into problems rather than being posited as an *a priori* problem in his entry into gendered and sexualized subjectivity. The wolf-boy can be read as engendering a paradigm of sexuality trouble, in skewed relation to gender trouble, which is induced by anxiety generated by the contradiction between the homosexual desire he already has and the antithetical gender he learns he has to take up in order to have it. A more robust notion of sexuality difference may be at play here, compromised as it is by femininity troped as castration.[22]

To return to *The Island of Dr. Moreau,* is Prendick Wolf-Man or puma-woman? What scene or screen memory produces his trauma?

The logic of the narrative almost collapses here. The narrative implies that Prendick is terrified because he fears that Moreau will cut him up too. Yet it is already clear that Moreau only cuts up animals to make them human. Prendick is already human. Moreau emerges as a god not entirely able to make humans in his own image. He produces an accelerated version of the phylogenetic narrative by moving animals across the species border into humans. He remains indifferent to the individual qualities of the creatures he mutates, unlike Montgomery, who forges friendships with M'Ling and the Dog-Man. Moreau is mostly equally indifferent to Prendick, only wanting him not to interfere with his scientific work. Prendick's terror that he is about to be cut up appears anticipatory but cannot be. It must be a remembered one. In shorthand, he re-members himself in earshot of the puma's cries as she experiences the bodily violence of becoming human, whether we recode vivisection as castration or the "sadistic view of coition." Prendick anticipates shared victimhood with the puma-woman here, briefly risking a shattering identification with a woman and a beast-folk, but cannot follow through on this imagined commonality. He can read the difference of the beast-folk only in terms of the logic of castration, mutilation, and reworked racism. As repugnant as he finds the other white men on the island, he must remain one of the masters:

> It was after this that we met the Satyr and the Ape Man. The Satyr was a gleam of classical memory on the part of Moreau, his face bovine in expression—like the coarser Hebrew type—his voice a harsh bleat, his nether extremities Satanic. . . .
>
> "Hail," said they, "to the Other with the whip!"
>
> "There's a third with a whip now," said Montgomery. "So you'd better mind!"
>
> "Was he not made?" said the Ape Man. "he said—he said he was made."
>
> "The Satyr Man looked curiously at me. "The Third with the whip, he that walks sweeping into the sea, has a thin white face."
>
> "He has a thin long whip," said Montgomery.
>
> "Yesterday he bled and wept," said the Satyr. "You never bleed nor weep. The master does not bleed nor weep." (p. 98)

The Ape Man and the grotesquely anti-Semitically rendered Satyr seek an identification with Prendick in ways that allow them to claim the human in the sense that they wish to align Prendick with themselves in terms of the creator/creature distinction and because he, like them, bleeds and weeps. The whip remains the favored answer to the call of the other(ed) human. We are back in the resistance of imperialist allegory to an ethical sympathy. Despite his bleeding and weeping, Prendick will not relinquish the privileges of his "thin white face," content to let Montgomery recode it as "a thin, long whip."

Can I read *The Island of Dr. Moreau* as imperialist allegory, proto-psychoanalytic speculation, and ethical instantiation at the same time? In moving from the primal horde to the primal scene, will I lose sight of my homosexual cannibal, the beast-folk, the primal horde of *Totem and Taboo,* the submerged figures I speculate may be paying the price for Prendick's entry into human society. The primal scene allows for the object of homosexual desire—the father—to be loved, if feared, and it is precisely the subject's passing through identification into love that may ground an ethics of homosexual desire in the tale of the Wolf-Man. The primal horde allows the father only to be envied and murdered, through the sons' identification with the father. They want to be him, to have what he has. While the primal scene may paradoxically be a potential ethical site for the figuring of male homosexual desire, its inscription of gender through castration and female passivity, even as it is registered as pleasurable by the Wolf-Man, if not by Prendick, remains under the signifying regime of the phallus. Yet the drama of recognition and misrecognition in the House of Pain is being played out over the body of the animal/woman whose desires populate Freud's dark continent. Woman, animal, homosexual, cannibal, are all definitional buttresses to the term human, with their own particular conceptual trajectories, uneven embodiments, and incommensurate histories.

Returning to the island of cannibals and homosexuals and hoping that the metaphor of island and continent may mark the difference in scale of the problems of homosexuality and femininity respectively, let us be haunted by both the desiring little wolf-boy and the screams of the puma-woman. The falling away from the state of being human in

The Island of Dr. Moreau is marked by an anxiety around falling back not only into cannibalism but through if not into unsanctionable sexual desires—many of them registered in language suggestive of homoerotic content. Except for the puma-woman, who kills Moreau and hence occupies a uniquely privileged space in the narrative, the predatory creatures that threaten our narrator are male. He is stalked by the leopard-man and the hyena-man. The taboo instituting human society on the island is explicitly the taboo on cannibalism rather than incest or homosexuality—the other unspeakable desires for human flesh. Early on, Prendick is stalked by the leopard-man. As he flees, he notices "it was no animal, for it stood erect." What does he fear/desire from these other men? What moment in the fantasy of the phylogeny of the human may he be revisiting?

The simplicity of the surface of the prose of *The Island of Dr. Moreau* is deceptive, and while the narrator pretends to be providing a straightforward, almost journalistic account, many metaphors and names invite further allegorical complications. While never as explicitly engaged in narrative terms as is Darwin's primal horde or as explicitly anticipated as is Freud's primal horde, previously hegemonic biblical accounts of the nature and origin of man are at play. This is evident in the name, "the man who walked in water," given by the beast-folk to Prendick after Moreau's death. The name Moreau is evocative: death plus water, diluted death? What vulgar Franglais speculations may Prendick invite?

It is at the level of the surface of the prose that I locate the homosexual panic and desire on the island. In Freud's tale of the primal horde, the homoerotic must be sublimated for the homosocial (and arguably, for Freud, there is no other social—at least phylogenetically) to emerge.[23] The surface of Wells's prose reveals considerable anxiety that this process is now being reversed, that the descent back into savagery will entail a descent into homoeroticism and a desublimation. The final commandment in the Law of the beast-folk reads: "Not to chase other men; that is the law. Are we not men?" The third commandment prohibits the eating of flesh. If cannibalism is already prohibited, why would the beast-folk wish to chase other men? Is the desire for food the only desire for male flesh?

V. Psychoanalysis in the Wild[24]

If *The Island of Dr. Moreau* marks the backward tracking of the origin myth of the primal horde, what innovations may it make in its anticipation of the Freudian fable? Readers are over three quarters of the way through the novella before a feminine pronoun is encountered. We meet the puma in the second chapter. The female animal is constantly referred to as "it." Only when it moves halfway into becoming human does the puma acquire a gender. After the relentlessly male milieu of the first seventy-five pages of the novella, we encounter the pronoun "her" with something like shock. If Dr. Moreau can turn animals into humans, surely he could also turn males into females and vice versa, though interestingly this is something the novella never broaches. Ungendered, regendered monstrosities lurk on the edges of the island even if they do not make it to the shore. Gender remains natural in a way that species does not. Freud is explicit about refuting the third-sex theorists of homosexual embodiment, and psychoanalysis allows for male homosexuality to remain masculine-identified in the last instance, but anxieties about gender and racial hybridity hide on the species border for Wells as they do for Darwin. *The Island of Dr.Moreau* frequently uses racialized images to describe the beast-folk, expressing the social-Darwinist commonplace that other races mediated the evolutionary gap between white folk and animals:

> They seemed to me to be brown men, but their limbs were oddly swathed in some thin dirty white stuff down even to the fingers and the feet. I have never seen men so wrapped up before, and women so only in the East. They wore turbans too, and thereunder peered out their elfin faces at me, faces with protruding lower jaws and bright eyes. They had lank blank hair almost like horse-hair and seemed, as they sat, to exceed in stature any race of men I have seen. (p. 26)

These beast-men appear unable to bond together against Moreau—their father, maker, and master. In terms of the tale of the primal horde, it is the puma-woman rather than the band of "homosexual" brothers who is the agent of the murder of the father. Here it is primal femininity that kills the father and institutes the law as abstraction rather than rationale/instrument for punishment by the father. Simultaneously, in killing Moreau, the puma-woman makes him "bleed and weep," thus marking his kinship with the beast-folk in a shared frailty of the flesh. Once Moreau, giver of the law, is revealed as subject to pain and mortality—conditions of animal/human embodiment—it follows that in Wells's fable, the death of the father figure is the precursor to social collapse rather than human sociality. Unbridled female power is clearly understood as less recuperable for civilization than sublimated homosexual bonds in the Victorian imagination. Femininity represents a kind of alterity marked by lack in the Freudian schema that must be domesticated rather than passed through in the Freudian account of the human. The killing of Dr. Moreau (God/Enlightenment science/white colonial rule?) by the puma-woman may encourage a very different kind of reading. Moreau is the builder and keeper of the House of Pain. He is the agent of pain and suffering on the island. The narrative suggests that his death exacerbates the terror on the island—for Prendick, at least.

However, if we sympathize with the puma-woman and the beast-folk/monsters, the weakening of the old law on the island may mark an opening for something to come into being that is not just the reversion to animality and savagery. Paradoxically, the death of Moreau marks something like the shift Foucault notes between forms of sovereignty that rely on punishment and those that require the internalizing of abstractions like the law, or more significantly in terms of the political dispensation on the island, the distinction Gramsci makes between coercion and hegemony.[25] The beastliness of the puma-woman's action can be rethought as an act of justice—she gets rid of the agent of harm on the island. The narrative works hard to refigure what may be the revenge of the oppressed into a return of the repressed—the animal in the human that must be repressed or at best sublated to make humans civilized.

The problem of femininity for Freud is posed more in supplemental narratives; questions of homosexuality are inflected by *developmental* ones. That Wells grasps that the undoing of the self in the imperial symbolic may involve moments of both homosexual desire and panic and attendant desublimations, a good decade before *Totem and Taboo*, suggests that this idea of homosexuality as a kind of preorigin of the social is not simply a psychoanalytic invention and that Darwin's theory of the primal horde was almost waiting around for someone to come and (homo)sexualize it. Simultaneously, the novella engages an earlier and equally problematic definition of the human as that which is born of woman. Not of woman born is a common Gothic designation of the monstrous. Woman, in this logic, at once is the maker of humans and needs to precede them, rendering her access to the rights and responsibilities of being human more complicated than that of male humans. The refrain of the law of the beast-folk is not "are we not women?" It is closer to "Thank God I was not born a woman," though in being forced to self-mother themselves, the beast-folk become monstrous and feminine in the same maneuver. Interestingly, the puma-woman is the only female being granted any narrative prominence. Women have no access to the (homo)social and attendant individuation on the island.

Nevertheless, in many ways, the puma-woman is the only ethical agent on the island. The human inhabitants are hardly humane. Wells called *The Island of Dr. Moreau* an early exercise in blasphemy, and the human inhabitants display the indifferent cruelty of gods who live above and beyond the pain and struggle of human existence. The unlikely trio parodies the holy trinity: Moreau as God the Father, Prendick—"the Other who walked in the sea"—as a feeble, sympathetic Jesus (though redeeming self-sacrifice is the task of the puma-woman), and Montgomery as a wittily debased Holy Spirit, dispensing spirits of another sort. Moreau is entirely indifferent to the pain he causes. While Montgomery rescues Prendick, he is only too willing to abandon him. Prendick can allow for sympathy only through projective identification and, even then, fears for his own safety soon mitigate against this. Moreover, his feelings of repulsion towards the beast-folk on the island, repeated in his sense of horror at the humans back in England, hardly mark him as a model for fellow feeling. The puma-woman at least finds her own pain and the pain of the beasts in the House of Pain intolerable and makes the ultimate sacrifice in her bid for freedom. While it is not easy to establish what critical distance the novella takes from the misanthropy of its narrator, humans hardly inspire optimism on *The Island of Dr. Moreau.*

The motley collection of beast-folk liberated into their degeneration by the puma-women may offer the representation of a community that can cope with difference, not needing to think difference in terms of lack, hierarchy, telos, development. The beast-folk represent a far-from-homogenous community:

> Beyond these general characters their heads had little in common; each preserved the quality of its particular species; the human mask distorted but did not hide the leopard, the ox, or the sow, or other animal or animals from which the creature had been moulded. The voices, too, varied exceedingly. (p. 94)

Though with the exception of the Dog-Man, they seem to want to eat and fuck men. The novella thus offers us civility as the rule of a cruel father or collectivity as romantic and dangerous return to Nature. Within this collectivity across the hybridized differences of the beast-folk, certain utopian moments emerge as failed opportunities for imagining a new social order after the death of Moreau. The beast-folk need not degenerate into creatures ruled only by "Nature—red in tooth and claw." Prendick is invited to become one of the beast-folk but is too invested in his superiority and too disgusted by the differences between himself and the beast-folk. This is the Dog-Man:

> Even now they talk together beyond there. They say, "The master is dead; the Other with the Whip is dead. The Other who walked in the sea is—as we are. We have no master, no Whips, no House of Pain any more. There is an end. We love the Law and will keep it; but there is no pain, no Master, no Whips for ever again." (p. 145)

The novella rebuts the possibility of new ethical collectivities on the island but is equally clear that there is ultimately no escaping the condition that events on the island emblematize. The ostensible civilization that Prendick returns to is no different. As terrifying as the House of Pain is, it seems that it is the only place where humans can live on the island, though the beast-folk can fleetingly imagine community not contingent on masters, whips, and houses of pain.

To get home from t/here, or more precisely, to try to escape the House of Pain as home, I could take a detour through the uncanny, *das Unheimlich*—literally, the unhomely in Freud—the place where one has been but cannot quite remember—the civilian dead of U.S. imperialism transformed into the dead in New York, the "not here, the anywhere but here" response of so many American nationals to the events of September 11, the terrifying return of the export of terror. But the chain of equivalences keeps breaking. Can one speak of the victims of September 11 as the collateral damage of globalization?[26] September 11, 2001, may simply be the historical event of its date or it may mark a rupture in the national/imperial symbolic, as Americans learn the terror of the death that comes from the sky, unknown, unannounced, from elsewhere. My hope is that this terror may teach Americans the ethical lesson of calculating the cost of global ascendancy, the price of prosperity (the human costs of cheap gasoline, for example), the connections between the freedoms here[27] and the oppressions elsewhere, the wars that sustain *Pax Americana*, to ponder the ease with which populations of men are sacrificed to the law in order to question what *The Island of Dr. Moreau* never does, namely, the law itself. *The Island of Dr. Moreau*'s reworking of the obviously fallacious or objectively preposterous story of the primal horde can be allegorized to render visible not simply the return of the repressed but the foundational violence of the civilized. The subject of Stone Age bombing is up for grabs: which is more Stone Age, to be bombed back into the Stone Age, or to bomb someone else back into the Stone Age? The pressing problem becomes one of how both to sympathize with the wounded but far-from-dead Moreau as agent of imperial modernity by realizing that he too is a creature riddled by difference, contains multitudes, as a national poet would have it; and to sympathize with the demonized agents of terror, the puma-woman, the leopard-man, those hybridized creatures,[28] like Moreau, created by imperial modernity but subject almost invariably to the punishment of its laws and never the beneficiaries of them.

Viewing the carnage in the House of Pain with Prendick, one asks why the experience of alterity must be one of terror; How might we own those drifting red and black phantasms that emerge when world-pain finds a voice that is close enough to the listener's to be recognized as human and consequently as requiring action? Prendick

performs for us the double-edgedness of the attribution of barbarism. He deplores Moreau and his actions on the island yet, once
Moreau is dead, is desperate to pretend that he is still alive. He needs
to assimilate to the barbaric, inhumane position of pure instrumen-
tality in the name of defending freedom and civilization. This kind of
autoinversion of the human and the beastly is produced in the interest of the continued survival of the powerful as the powerful. There
can be no ethical figuration of human differences there. Risking the
desublimation work that allows a recognition of those proximate,
half-subjectified others—the primitive and the homosexual in the
case of psychoanalysis—as something other than sublated stages in
the emergence of the civilized, no longer using the figure of woman
as the originary matrix for the emergence of the human may allow
cultural, political, symbolic work to help Prendick, the guest of
Moreau, the biter of the hand that feeds him, to move from witnessing to solidarity into a history that is more rupture than repetition.

Acknowledgments

I would like to thank Lauren Berlant for her editorial generosity and
brilliance. Candace Vogler's many readings of the essay improved it
enormously and she has my heartfelt gratitude, and Vic McWherter
helped me to finish it. Joseph Massad's comments helped me think
through the political stakes of this essay.

Notes

1. H. G. Wells, *The Island of Dr. Moreau* (New York: Bantam, 1994), p. 65.
   All subsequent references will be in the main text.
2. This is Wilde's description of his "rough trade" sexual excursions. See Ru-
   pert Croft-Cooke, *Feasting with Panthers: A New Consideration of Some
   Late Victorian Writers* (New York: Holt, Rhinehart and Winston, 1967).
3. H. G. Wells on the impulse/inspiration to write *The Island of Dr.
   Moreau.* Cited in Elaine Showalter, *Sexual Anarchy: Gender and Culture
   in the Fin de Siecle* (London: Penguin Books, 1990), p. 178.
4. For accounts of the Wilde trials, see Harford Montgomery Hyde, *The
   Three Trials of Oscar Wilde* (Harmondsworth, UK: Penguin, 1962); Ed
   Cohen, *Talk on the Wilde Side* (New York: Routledge, 1993).
5. "Unhuman" captures better the unearthly quality of the beast-folk. Humans can be "inhuman"; it is harder for them to be unhuman. The beast-

folk are "nonhuman," but so are tables and chairs, and the beast-folk are both animal and animate.

6. Wake is an interesting word: the break in the surface of water following the passage of a boat, the social event following a funeral, the emergence from sleep.

7. The London *Times* reports the following in an article entitled: "Kandahar Comes out of the Closet":

> Our correspondent sees the gay capital of South Asia throw off strictures of the Taleban. Now that Taleban rule is over in Mullah Omar's former southern stronghold, it is not only televisions, kites and razors which have begun to emerge. Visible again, too, are men with their ashna, or beloveds: young boys they have groomed for sex. . . . Kandahar's Pashtuns have been notorious for their homosexuality for centuries, particularly their fondness for naive young boys. Before the Taleban arrived in 1994, the streets were filled with teenagers and their sugar daddies, flaunting their relationship. It is called the homosexual capital of south Asia. Such is the Pashtun obsession with sodomy locals tell you that birds fly over the city using only one wing, the other covering their posterior, that the rape of young boys by warlords was one of the key factors in Mullah Omar mobilizing the Taleban. . . . Once the boy falls into the man's clutches, nearly always men with a wife and family, he is marked for life, although the Kandaharis accept these relationships as part of their culture.
>
> When driven around, ashna sit in the front passenger seat. The back seat is simply for his friends. Even the parents of the boys know in their hearts the nature of the relationship, but will tell people that their son is working for the man. They, like everyone else, will know this is a lie. "They say birds flew with both wings with the Taleban," Muhammad said. "But not any more." (Tim Reid, "Kandahar Comes out of the Closet," London *Times*, January 12, 2002)

The article is fascinating in the ways it relentlessly exposes the fault lines in western representations of Islam. The Taliban, supposed agents of repressive traditionalism, are actually agents of modernization; they get rid of old traditions, such as the "homosexual practices" of the Kandahari Pashtuns. Now, the public visibility of these practices is both ancient and a result of the U.S. liberation of Afghan society. Homosexuality is modern, like television, and traditional, like kites. The West here frees people from what it stages as Islamic tradition in order that they can be more traditional. The article reads like something Sir Richard Francis Burton could have written in his notorious terminal essay to his translation of *A Thousand and One Nights* (1886) and sustainedly ignores the history of imperialism in the area, including western complicity in the coming to power of the Taliban.

8. For historical discussions of the implications of the 1876 Cruelty to Animals Act, see Nicolaas Rupke, "Pro-vivisection in England in the Early 1880s: Arguments and Motives," in *Vivisection in Historical Perspective,* ed. Nicolaas Rupke (London: Croom Helm, 1987), pp. 188–208; and Stewart Richards, "Drawing the Life-Blood of Physiology: Vivisection and the Physiologists' Dilemma 1870–1900," *Annals of Science,* 43, 1 (1986), pp. 27–56.

9. For a nuanced defense of the tale of the primal horde against the "just-so story" allegation of incompetent ethnography, see Joan Copjec:

> to call it crackpot is to miss the point that if this father of the primal horde is indeed preposterous, then he is objectively so. That is to say, he is unbelievable within the regime in which his existence must be unthinkable if relations of equality are to take hold. . . . What Freud accounts for in Totem and Taboo is the structure, the real structure, of a society of equals, which is thus shown to be irreducible to the labile relations of equality that never pertain absolutely. *(Read my Desire: Lacan against the Historicists* [Cambridge, MA: MIT Press, 1994], p. 12)

As should be clear, I read psychoanalysis as symptom of subject formation under western capitalism as well as the most brilliant diagnosis/description we have of this historical process. My tireless allegorizing is a way of getting at this.

10. Charles Darwin, *The Descent of Man* (New York: Prometheus Books, 1998), p. 612.

11. See Caleb Crain. "Lovers of Human Flesh: Homosexuality and Cannibalism in Melville's Novels," *American Literature,* 66, 1 (1994), pp. 25–53.

12. Sigmund Freud, *The Standard Edition of the Complete Psychological Works of Sigmund Freud,* ed. and trans. James Strachey, vol. 12 (London: Hogarth, 1950), p. 144. In German:

> Das sexuelle Bedürfnis einigt die Männer nicht, sondern entzweit sie. Hatten sich die Brüder verbündet, um den Vater zu überwältigen, so war jeder des anderen Nebenbuhler, bei den Frauen. Jeder hätte sie wie der Vater alle für sich haben wollen, und in dem Kampfe aller gegen alle wäre die neue Organisation zugrunde gegangen. Es war kein Überstarker mehr da, der die Rolle des Vaters mit Erfolg hätte aufnehmen können. Somit blieb den Brüdern, wenn sie mit einander leben wollten, nichts übrig, als— vielleicht nach Überwindung schwerer Zwischenfälle—das Inzestverbot aufzurichten, mit welchem sie alle zugleich auf die von ihnen begehrten Frauen verzichteten, um deren wegen sie doch in erster Linie den Vater

beseitigt hatten. Sie retteten so die Organisation, welche sie stark gemacht hatte, und die auf homosexuellen Gefühlen und Betätigungen ruhen konnte, welche sich in der Zeit der vertreibung bei ihnen eingestellt haben mochten. Sigmund Freud. Gesammelte Werke: Chronologisch geordnet, v. 19, eds. A. Freud et al. (Frankfurt am Main: Fischer, 1961–1978) p. 174.

Interestingly, the section on "homosexual feelings and acts," which is rendered parenthetical by Strachey, is not grammatically subordinated in the same way in the original German. What is equally clear in the original and the translation is that the real interest in these "homosexual feelings and acts" is the way in which they may have been necessary in the constitution of the social. They are understood as instrumental rather than as ends in themselves. They are represented as feelings and acts, not as *Triebe* or *Instinkte*—the terms with explanatory force in Freud's lexicon.

13. See Eve Kosofsky Sedgwick, *Between Men: English Literature and Male Homosocial Desire* (New York: Columbia University Press, 1985), pp. 1–5. Luce Irigaray's positing of patriarchy as a *hom(m)osexual* relation does similar conceptual work to the idea of the homosocial: "Which means that the possibility of our social life, of our culture, depends upon a hom(m)osexual monopoly. The law that orders our society is the exclusive valorization of men's needs/desires, of exchanges among men. What the anthropologist calls the passage from nature to culture amounts to the institution of the reign of hom(m)osexuality." *This Sex Which Is not One,* trans. Catherine Porter (Ithaca, NY: Cornell University Press, 1995), p. 171.

14. The success of this sublimation is up for grabs, considering the information on the sex lives of many of the leading lights of empire that has recently emerged. Gordon, Kitchener, and Rhodes, three central and very public figures in the expansion of the British Empire in Africa, all shared a soft spot for handsome young men. Judd makes the argument that the isolation from "racial" peers, particularly women, and the relative power and status of the colonizer over the colonized could prove attractive to young men whose sexual desires were taboo in the metropolis, and that a career in the imperial service opened up opportunities for such men to explore their nonnormative desires with far greater impunity; Donald Judd, *Empire: The British Imperial Experience, from 1765 to the Present* (London: Harper, 1996), pp. 172–173.

15. "If civilization imposes such great sacrifices not only on man's sexuality but on his aggressivity, we can understand better why it is hard for him to be happy in that civilization. In fact, primitive man was better off in knowing no restrictions of instinct. . . . Civilized man has exchanged a portion of his possibilities of happiness for a portion of security. Sigmund Freud, *Civilization and its Discontents,* trans. and ed. James Strachey (New York: Norton, 1961), p. 73.

16. Here, *The Island of Dr. Moreau* almost moves from a preemptive Freudianism to a Lacanian parable. As subjects move into the human, infantile/animal (the ontogeny/phylogeny recapitulation again) plenitude is

cut away, experiencing the loss, which, within the temporal frame of the human, becomes the structuring lack of the subject in language, the engine of desire.

17. I am somehow charmed by Wells's tendency to offer food as compensation for trauma. The first thing the time traveler requests upon his return to the present, after his near-death food experience at the hands of the Morlocks in *The Time-Machine*, is some mutton.

18. "Abolitionist discourse [was] organized around the notion of 'negroes' (their terminology) as younger brothers and sisters." Catherine Hall, *White, Male and Middle Class: Explorations in Feminism and History* (New York: Routledge, 1992), p. 211.

19. John Gallagher and Ronald Robinson, "The Imperialism of Free Trade," Economic History Review, 1953, vol. 6, no. 1, pp. 1–15.

20. Gayatri Spivak, *A Critique of Postcolonial Reason: Toward a History of the Vanishing Present* (Cambridge, MA: Harvard University Press, 1999), p. 133.

21. Freud, Sigmund. "On the Sexual Theories of Children." *Standard Edition of the Complete Works of Sigmund Freud*, vol. 9, p. 220.

22. My wider claim here is a simple and practical one. What is interesting about homosexuality—both male and female—for having the fantasy of desire without gender hierarchy, for thinking the impossibility of gender as symmetry, is that women fuck and men get fucked. Normative heterosexuality would look a little different if it could imagine *Bend over Boyfriend* as a new primal scene. Let me suggest, in passing, the normative literal fucking of men on a massive scale as a utopian gender project.

23. This is one of Irigaray's main points of contention. See footnote xi.

24. I riff here on Freud's "wild psychoanalysis." See *Freud*, vol. 11, pp. 219–227.

25. Michel Foucault, *Discipline and Punish: The Birth of the Prison*, trans. Alan Sheridan (New York: Vintage, 1979); Antonio Gramsci, "The Intellectuals," in *Selections from the Prison Notebooks*, ed. and trans. Quintin Hoare and Geoffrey Nowell-Smith (New York: International, 1971), p. 12.

26. See Madeleine Albright's comments on the 500,000 dead Iraqi children as a result of Operation Desert Storm and the subsequent U.S.-led sanctions. "In 1996, Madeleine Albright, the then U.S. secretary of state, was asked on national television what she felt about the fact that 500,000 Iraqi children had died as a result of U.S. economic sanctions. She replied 'that it was a very hard choice,' but all things considered, 'we think the price is worth it.'" Arundhoti Roy, "The Algebra of Infinite Justice," *The Guardian*, September 29, 2001. To invoke the great animal fable in English of the twentieth century, George Orwell's *Animal Farm*, and the inverted echo of Moreau's Law in Orwell's "Four legs good, two legs bad," it is clear that some lives are more equal than others.

27. My own participation in the freedoms here has been drastically curtailed due to the U.S. Congress passing draconian measures restricting the civil liberties of non–U.S. citizens in the United States in the Patriot Act. These measures include arrest and indefinite detention without any need to provide cause, and deportation. Nevertheless, while I am legally im-

plicated, I suspect that my own "thin white face" was not envisaged by the authors of this act as a potential victim, and the vast majority of those who have been harassed and persecuted under the provisions of the Patriot Act have been Arabs and Muslims in the United States. See http://www.thenation.com/thebeat/index.mhtml?bid=1&pid=69

28. Here, one of the risks of the attempt to read *The Island of Dr. Moreau* as ongoing imperialist allegory becomes nastily visible: one needs to engage ongoing racist nineteenth-century evolutionary and degeneracy tropes of racial difference without giving them credence. It is perhaps more useful in our current moment to think of the beast-folk not only in terms of the inevitable hybridity of the colonized but also as protocyborgs, as another eerie instance of Wells's prophetic genius—creatures part biological, part technological. The beast-folk, while troped in terms of nineteenth-century degeneracy theory, anticipate postmodern theories of subjectivity. The unhuman meets the posthuman here.

Suffering and Thinking

The Scandal of Tone in *Eichmann in Jerusalem*

DEBORAH NELSON

*The German text of the taped police examination . . . each page corrected by
Eichmann, constitutes a veritable gold mine for a psychologist—provided he is wise
enough to understand that the horrible can be not only ludicrous but outright funny.*
—————Hannah Arendt, *Eichmann in Jerusalem*[1]

*Eichmann really figured, you know, "The Jews—the most liberal people in the
world—they'll give me a fair shake." Fair? Certainly. "Rabbi" means lawyer.
He'll get the best trial in the world, Eichmann. Ha! They were shaving his leg
while he was giving his appeal! That's the last bit of insanity, man.*
—————Lenny Bruce, "The Jews"[2]

I. Introduction

By many accounts, the 1961 trial of Adolf Eichmann in Jerusalem
coincided with and accelerated the emergence of the Holocaust into
the collective memory of the twentieth century. The word "Holocaust" was coming into popular use; its historians were publishing in
noticeably greater numbers with the benefit of broader archival and
ethnographic research; personal testimony about the Holocaust was
losing its stigma, significantly as an effect of the trial itself; and a new
generation, particularly in Israel, was stirring up controversy by asking difficult questions of survivors, who had been reluctant to discuss
in public the atrocity that had defined their lives. Because we have
grown so accustomed to the Holocaust as a fixture of the public
imagination and because testimony to trauma *per se* became so prominent a feature of late-twentieth-century culture (at least in the
United States), we may need to remind ourselves of the emotional
intensity and intellectual uncertainty that attended these changes in
public discourse.

Into this very sensitive moment came the often ironic and, for many, scandalously *in*sensitive *Eichmann in Jerusalem: A Report on the Banality of Evil* by Hannah Arendt. The reputation of this esteemed political philosopher, a German Jew who had herself fled the Nazis, assured readers of the book's seriousness; serialization in the *New Yorker* and publication by Viking Press shortly thereafter guaranteed exposure of the story to a wide audience. It is hard to imagine conditions under which a book would receive more notice, and, indeed, it enjoyed extraordinarily broad coverage and criticism: scores of reviews, radio programs, interviews, mentions in gossip columns, extended essays, private book club discussions, public symposia, and hundreds of letters to the editors of the *New York Times,* the *New Yorker,* and newspapers and magazines around the world. No one, neither contemporary reviewers nor recent critics, discusses Hannah Arendt's report on the trial of Adolf Eichmann without first touching on the intense and protracted controversy that it generated. In fact, as Dan Diner has argued, the controversy became as much a subject for commentators as the book itself, giving to the debates around Arendt's work an iconic status apart from their source.[3]

There have been many attempts to understand precisely why *Eichmann in Jerusalem* was and remains so disturbing, but it has yet to be fully examined how Arendt's treatment of suffering catalyzed a discussion of sympathy in relation to the Holocaust. While *Eichmann in Jerusalem* engendered a great deal of acclaim for Arendt, its reception was more profoundly marked by the bitterness, anger, hurt, and disappointment, primarily but not only among her Jewish readers. The outrage over the book arose largely around two questions: the first was Arendt's sensitivity, the second her factual accuracy. Scholars more knowledgeable than I have treated the question of Arendt's accuracy, currently deemed a notable but less troubling issue than the initial accusations of pervasive error and distortion predicted.[4] Instead, I want to concentrate on the problem of Arendt's tone, because the debates over her book suggest that among the many controversial ideas that she expounded, *Eichmann in Jerusalem* violated conventions of sympathy that were still incoherent, though deeply felt, and only later formalized. The book continued to irritate readers because the late twentieth century was a period when psychic pain became one of the most prominent features of political and aesthetic discourse.

Her critics have been much more inclined to interrogate her rhetoric than her supporters have, though the problem has often been cast as one of personality or psychology. According to this line, Arendt was simply herself unsympathetic, cold, even brutal; she hated herself for being a Jew and therefore accused the Jews of their own murder; she identified with the German persecutors. Her supporters, however, have never presented a very satisfying case for the virtues of Arendt's writing style.[5] Often praising her cool impartiality, wry pleasure, and wit, these reviewers sometimes acknowledged the frank and occasionally caustic comments and seeming coldness and harshness of tone without speculating on the potential injury—let alone the strategic deployment—of such rhetoric. Arendt was certainly aware of the terrible history of those who would find her arguments most urgent, and to be deliberately, or even carelessly, tactless would have been cruel. It is not that I want to rescue Arendt from this charge so much as that I want to restate the question in order to derive a meaningful philosophical and political answer from it. I prefer, that is, to pose this question to Arendt's ideas rather than her personality.

To restate the question: Does the rhetoric of *Eichmann in Jerusalem* derive from Arendt's political philosophy? And does this political philosophy presuppose a relationship to suffering? The issues that *Eichmann* addresses are central to Arendt's work as a whole, though they are not explored systematically; she was, after all, acting as a journalist, providing a report on a trial by telling a story. Too often *Eichmann* is taken out of the context of Arendt's other work, but it would be a mistake to imagine that her recourse to irony was made without calculation. Arendt had reflected on how to think about extremity for a more than a decade, and her views on it were typically idiosyncratic. In fact, published only a month before *Eichmann in Jerusalem* was *On Revolution,* which contains her most sustained discussion of sympathy and the politics of misery. The writing of *On Revolution* was temporarily interrupted by Arendt's attendance at the trial, and the manuscript was completed just before she began to work on her report. Naturally, then, her ideas about emotion—specifically compassion, love, pity, and sympathy—and, as she put it, their "disastrous " effects on politics and public discourse would have been very much present to her as she arrived at her analysis of the

Eichmann trial, and the Eichmann trial very much on her mind in the revising of *On Revolution*.[6]

In particular, the chapter "The Social Question" is noteworthy because she gestures toward it in her famous post-*Eichmann* exchange with Gershom Scholem, the scholar of Jewish mysticism who had been her longtime friend. Equally important, the last work of her life—the posthumously published *The Life of the Mind*—attempted to resolve the question that she declared her consuming topic after witnessing the display of what she called Eichmann's *thoughtlessness*. Once we see Eichmann as posing a problem of thinking, however, it also becomes clear that this investigation did not begin after *Eichmann* but considerably earlier, in *Rahel Varnhagen* and *The Origins of Totalitarianism*. What remained for Arendt to develop was a conception of thinking that would avoid the traps and delusions she dissected in those two earlier works.

Therefore, though they have taken their own paths in the reception of Arendt's work, the questions of sympathy and thinking cannot be entirely separated, as *Eichmann in Jerusalem* demonstrates. In this work we see the relationship between sympathy and thinking rendered incoherent when Arendt attempts what she called "the unpremeditated, attentive facing up to, and resisting of, reality—whatever it may be" (viii) in *The Origins of Totalitarianism*. "Facing up to reality" appears repeatedly in slightly different phrasing throughout Arendt's entire body of writing, often in terms that recognize only metaphorically its exorbitant price. Thinking and suffering, the motivation for sympathy, also come together in Arendt's figure of the pariah. Not only a figure for the Jew, the pariah is also the thinker who refuses the myriad safeguards against reality, some of which offer themselves as types of thinking. The foundation of individual conscience and political common ground, Arendt's notion of thinking seems to require suffering the painfulness of reality without consolation, compensation, or communion with others. Arendt's employment of irony in *Eichmann*, I want to suggest, is less a product of her character (though no doubt it is enabled by her psychological makeup) than part of an implied philosophy of suffering, one that violated the assumptions and expectations of many postwar readers, both the "professional thinkers" and the nonprofessional alike.

II. The Pain Dialogues

Sorting through the reception of *Eichmann in Jerusalem* is a massive undertaking. Nevertheless, two sets of reviews and responses point in the general direction of the sympathy discussion and begin to suggest its contours. The first exchange, now the most widely noted of any, consisted of letters written by Arendt and Gershom Scholem that were initially published in *Mitteilungs Blatt* and then translated for publication in *Encounter* (the letters were collected later in *The Jew as Pariah* in 1972). Though she was one of the rare individuals whom he had addressed with the informal "Du" in his correspondence (that is, until her writing on Eichmann),[7] Scholem's response to *Eichmann in Jerusalem* was deeply wounded and fiercely critical. The second moment, arguably the most influential in the popular press in the 1960s, began with Michael Musmanno, Pennsylvania Supreme Court justice, Nuremberg prosecutor, and witness for the prosecution in the Eichmann trial, whose indignant review on the front page of the *New York Times Book Review* was followed little more than a month later by almost three pages of letters from readers (roughly 10 percent of the issue)[8] and an exchange between author and reviewer.[9] William Shawn, the *New Yorker* editor, also weighed in, defending Arendt in his magazine after corresponding at length with Musmanno.[10] Both sets of exchanges take issue primarily with Arendt's tone and her treatment of suffering, Scholem explicitly so and Musmanno less directly.

Scholem begins by suggesting that her work is "not free of error and distortion"[11] but turns directly to the heart of the matter, her tone, especially with regard to the role of the Jews in the catastrophe. "At each decisive juncture . . . your book speaks only of the *weakness* of the Jewish stance in the world. I am ready enough to admit that weakness; but you put such emphasis upon it that, in my view, your account ceases to be objective and acquires overtones of malice" (241). The depth of Scholem's anger becomes evident in his conclusion:

> Insofar as I have an answer, it is one which, precisely out of my deep respect for you, I dare not suppress; and it is an answer that goes to the root of our disagreement. It is that heartless, frequently almost sneering and malicious tone with which these matters, touching the very quick of our life, are treated in your book to which I take exception. (241)

Accusing Arendt of "heartlessness," especially given the evidence of personal friendship in the letters (they address one another by first name and exhibit a somewhat strained and formal intimacy), might appear to the reader as a chilling but perhaps merely *ad hominem* attack. Scholem, however, has in mind a very specific definition: heartlessness is the lack of particular kinds of emotion for which he uses the Hebrew *Ahabath Israel,* "the love of the Jewish people," and German *Herzenstakt,* the "tact of the heart."[12] Taken in tandem, these two definitions of heart comprise a relationship to sufferers and suffering that is both general (it extends to the Jews as a people) and generalizable (it is decorum motivated by sympathy for anyone else's pain). He concludes: "to speak of [the suffering of our people and the 'questionable figures who deserve, or have received their just punishment'] . . . in so wholly inappropriate a tone—to the benefit of those Germans in condemning whom your book rises to greater eloquence than in mourning the fate of your own people—this is not the way to approach the scene of that tragedy" (242). Her heartlessness is, then, united with her intellectual and moral priorities not just as a question of tone but as one of vision: it permits Arendt to look at tragedy without looking through suffering.

Arendt responds by decisively embracing heartlessness as Scholem defines it. While she claims that she had never denied her own Jewishness, she asserts in a much-quoted passage that she does not have a "love of the Jewish people." She answers:

> You are quite right—I am not moved by any "love" of this sort, and for two reasons: I have never in my life "loved" any people or collective— neither the German people, nor the French, nor the American, nor the working class or anything of that sort. I indeed love "only" my friends and the only kind of love I know of and believe in is the love of persons. (246)[13]

She concludes "I do not 'love' the Jews, nor do 'I believe' in them; I merely belong to them as a matter of course, beyond dispute or argument" (247). Later, she dismisses "the tact of the heart" as a political liability and an intellectual fraud:

> Generally speaking, the role of the "heart" in politics seems to me altogether questionable. You know as well as I how often those who merely

report certain unpleasant facts are accused of lack of soul, lack of heart, or lack of what you call *Herzenstakt*. We both know, in other words, how often these emotions are used in order to conceal factual truth. (247)

At issue in heartlessness for Arendt is the devotion to the concrete, which stands in for reality as such. The love of a people, like many abstractions for Arendt, is dangerously vague; the love of a person, like all concrete matters, is like a fact, specific and difficult to generalize into illusion. Heartlessness would therefore be a necessary component of Arendt's most fundamental charge to her readers: face reality.

Like Scholem, for whom suffering must remain in the foreground out of an ethics of attention, Musmanno obligates Arendt to attend to suffering because its sheer enormity makes it impossible to ignore. While Musmanno never makes broad claims about Arendt's tone with respect to the suffering of the victims, his own rhetoric is an implicit rebuke to her lack of sympathy.[14] Musmanno's review supplies the emotion he evidently found lacking in Arendt, at one moment speculating:

> If, in recalling the period, one could shut one's eyes to the scenes of brutal massacre and stop one's ears to the screams of horror-stricken women and terrorized children as they saw the tornado of death sweeping toward them, one could almost assume that in some parts of the book the author is being whimsical. (1)[15]

Musmanno's rhetoric dramatizes the engulfment in misery that Arendt finds "disastrous" in *On Revolution*. So overwhelming is the horror, recollection literally reproduces suffering and compels even the witness to participate in it: scenes and sounds become so real that only by becoming insensate (shutting eyes, stopping ears) can one avoid confronting them. Nevertheless, his sentimental invocation of "women and . . . children" in his censure of Arendt's whimsy suggests some mistrust of the fact of suffering, that the "tornado of death" is insufficient on its own. His apparent need to amplify the suffering that, in his own terms, is beyond intensification refers us not to the victims' but to his own distress at witnessing the scene.

Arendt's refusal of the obligation to attend to suffering rests precisely on its power to blind and deafen and to shift emphasis from an event to feelings about the event. The suffering of the Jews, Arendt argued in *Eichmann in Jerusalem,* had no place in the trial because it was not in dispute, rather Eichmann's responsibility for it was. But in *On Revolution,* Arendt banishes suffering from the public realm in more general terms, not because one can be indifferent to it, but because one cannot. Precisely for this reason, *On Revolution* is an extended defense of coldness and heartlessness. Drawing her metaphors almost always from bodies of water, Arendt repeatedly describes suffering and the emotion it stimulates as "boundless." As she says of Robespierre's sympathy for the destitute masses of Paris: "he lost the capacity to establish and hold fast to rapports with persons in their singularity; the ocean of suffering around him and the turbulent sea of emotion within him, the latter geared to receive and respond to the former, drown all specific considerations, the considerations of friendship no less than considerations of statecraft and principle" (90). In the context of this loss of boundaries, Arendt's heartlessness refuses the generalizing tendency upon which Scholem's definition rests. Moreover, the ocean of sympathy pulls into the public realm the necessities of life, which are the most immediate and urgent concerns there are: the reproduction and maintenance of life.

> Where the breakdown of traditional authority set the poor of the earth on the march, where they left the obscurity of their misfortunes and streamed upon the market-place, their *furor* seemed as irresistible as the motion of the stars, a torrent rushing forward with elemental force and engulfing the whole world. (113)

Once having entered the public sphere, necessity and the rage that accompanies its frustration will swamp all other concerns, just as suffering in Musmanno's description threatens to do. Because misery is so compelling, because it is impossible to look beyond it once it has shown itself, it must not be revealed in public. Sympathy, therefore, must be contained because its very nature is to overwhelm.

In the writing of her own account Arendt sought to hold back the tide of suffering that she felt threatened to overwhelm the trial. Her most characteristic rhetorical technique, especially in her report of Eichmann's testimony, is abrupt understatement. For instance, when Eichmann defended himself from the charge of "base motives" by ar-

guing that he "remembered perfectly well that he would have had a
bad conscience only if he had not done what he had been ordered to
do—to ship millions of men, women, and children to their death
with great zeal and the most meticulous care," Arendt concedes
"This, admittedly, was hard to take" (*EJ*, 25) and moves on with her
analysis. By explicitly naming Eichmann's duties, which certainly he
did not, Arendt pauses to make his crime concrete, but in tersely
confessing the pain his defense inflicts, she hurries past the emotional reaction while also minimizing it. When she retells Eichmann's anecdote of his "normal human encounter" in Auschwitz with
a man named Storfer, one of the representatives of the Jewish community he had worked with for years, she concludes: "Six weeks after
this normal human encounter, Storfer was dead—not gassed, apparently, but shot" (51). It is not that Arendt denies this story its horror,
but rather that she attempts to suggest its horror by *not* dwelling on
it, instead letting the rhythm of her prose convey the weight of the
evidence. This lengthy story told in complex, concatenated sentences
ends almost literally with a bang.

And yet, she is not able to resist completely the power of the victims' stories. The testimony of Zindel Grynszpan, one of the very few
she records, produces a moment of both engagement and resistance:

> This story took no more than perhaps ten minutes to tell, and when it
> was over—the senseless, needless destruction of twenty-seven years in
> less than twenty-four hours—one thought foolishly: Everyone, every-
> one should have his day in court. Only to find out, in the endless ses-
> sions that followed, how difficult it was to tell that story, that—at least
> outside the transforming realm of poetry—it needed a purity of soul, an
> unmirrored, unreflected innocence of heart and mind that only the
> righteous possess. (229)

Everything in the sentence, even the self-mocking "foolishly," refuses
momentum. Arendt's awkwardly placed dashes interrupt the flow of
her sentence and return us to the story. Her references to time inter-
vals between the dashes—twenty-seven years, twenty-four hours—
belie the brevity of the ten-minute testimony. Moreover, the two
repetitions in the first sentence—the slant repetition "senseless/need-
less" and the doubling of "everyone, everyone"—not only halt the

progress of the sentence, but also mark perhaps the only eruption of sympathy in the prose of *Eichmann in Jerusalem.* This passage is noteworthy not only for its rarity but for its style. If one eliminated these repetitions, the line would be voided of affect and transformed into a statement rather than an expression of anguish. Sympathy is conveyed in the micropauses of the commas, which produce a hitch between the repeated words. There is a momentary refusal to move on or pass over, a dwelling in the horror if only for the space of a breath.

Nonetheless, she takes these sympathetic pauses back immediately in the next sentence with her depiction of the tedium (the "endless sessions") when these stories are neither aesthetically satisfying nor pure of heart, by which she means un-[self]-reflecting (unconscious of one's effect on others). Indeed what most impresses Arendt about Zindel Grynszpan's testimony is its refusal of rhetorical emotion: "he spoke clearly and firmly, without embroidery, using a minimum of words" (228). It is his economy even more than his "shining honesty" (230) that tempts Arendt to abandon her strict refusal of survivor testimony, if only "foolishly." Combining the purity of heart with an aesthetic of the concrete, Grynszpan allows the facts to speak for themselves; it is as if he disappears behind or into them, which allows the listener to confront not the emotion produced by suffering, but the reality of suffering itself. The boundlessness of emotion in the sufferer and the witness is contained by an implied agreement not to share it—either the pain of suffering or the sympathy of witnessing.[16]

With Jewish suffering in the Holocaust making its appearance in public in the early 1960s, Arendt's defense of heartlessness in *On Revolution* looks both defensive and prescient. I think it is worth speculating that in addition to developing her analysis of totalitarianism in *On Revolution,* this time with respect to the Left, Arendt might have been moved to ponder the vicissitudes of compassion for the very reason that the extreme suffering of the camps was beginning to be explored in public, particularly in the Eichmann trial. Her admonition that "History tells us that it is by no means a matter of course for the spectacle of misery to move men to pity" (*OR,* 70) suggests some concern that miseries are asymmetrically compelling. The American revolutionary leaders were not moved by the spectacle of slavery and black labor and misery, seeing nothing of the possibilities of solidarity in suffering that the French revolutionaries did with the *sans-culottes* of Paris. So the possibility that misery is not a direct line to compassion, that it may indeed be overlooked no matter how visible it is, sits adjacent to its overwhelming power to sustain interest and obliterate all other considerations of justice. Moreover, the exposure of the heart carries its own dangers:

> Whatever the passions and emotions may be, and whatever their true connection with thought and reason, they certainly are located in the human heart. And not only is the human heart a place of darkness which, with certainty, no human eye can penetrate; the qualities of the heart need darkness and protection against the light of the public to grow and to remain what they are meant to be, innermost motives which are not for public display. However deeply heartfelt a motive may be, once it is brought out and exposed for public inspection it becomes an object of suspicion rather than insight; when the light of the public falls upon it, it appears and even shines, but, unlike deeds and words which are meant to appear, whose very existence hinges on appearance, the motives behind such deeds and words are destroyed in their essence through appearance; when they appear they become "mere appearances" behind which again other, ulterior motives may lurk, such as hypocrisy and deceit. (*OR*, 96)

For a combination of reasons—the capacity to be mesmerized by suffering or indifferent to it, the obscuring of fact by emotion, the corruption of motivation in the witness/reporter—Arendt pushes the heart and suffering out of the light of public display. She could not have been more out of step with the times.

If Arendt's sympathy, or lack thereof, for the Jews constituted one pole of the debate over her heartlessness, the other would be that she extended whatever sympathy she had to Eichmann himself. William Shawn links Musmanno's reading of her sympathy to his misunderstanding of her irony:

> he accused Miss Arendt of an excess of sympathy for Eichmann (her condemnation of the Nazi leaders was far more withering than any that had been made before) and of a lack of sympathy for the Jews (her sorrow over their suffering was far more eloquent than the Justice's own).

He ignored all Miss Arendt's ironies (referring to her "Alas, nobody believed him," unmistakably ironic in context, as a "lament" for Eichmann). (*New Yorker*, "Talk of the Town," July 20, 1963)

This "alas" was meant not for Eichmann, but for the court—prosecutors, counsel for the defense, and the judges—who "missed the greatest moral and even legal challenge of the whole case," that "an average, 'normal' person, neither feeble-minded nor indoctrinated nor cynical, could be perfectly incapable of telling right from wrong" (*EJ*, 26).

Another example will make the point more broadly and suggest the value Arendt might have found in irony. Musmanno states: "she says that Eichmann was a Zionist and helped the Jews get to Palestine." *New York Times*, May 19, 1963, Section 7, 1. Arendt's version is considerably less straightforward. In her account, when Eichmann began working for Himmler's security service, he was required to read

> *Der Judenstaat*, the famous Zionist classic, which converted Eichmann promptly and forever to Zionism. This seems to have been the first serious book he ever read, and it made a lasting impression on him. From then on, as he repeated over and over, he thought of hardly anything but a "political solution" (as opposed to the later "physical solution," the first meaning expulsion and the second extermination). (*EJ*, 40–41)

As ambivalent as Arendt's own relationship to Zionism was,[17] clearly she is not equating Zionism with Eichmann's "idealism," nor his belief with anything a Zionist would espouse.

It was, on the one hand, simpler. Eichmann's and the Zionists' goals overlapped: Eichmann was ordered to rid Europe of the Jews; the Zionists wanted a homeland. On the other hand, it was much more complicated. Eichmann's conversion to Zionism demonstrates the extent to which he understood himself as an "idealist":

> The reason he became so fascinated by the "Jewish question," *he explains,* was his own "idealism" . . . an "idealist," *according to Eichmann's notions,* was not merely a man who believed in an "idea" or someone who did not steal or accept bribes, though these qualifications were indispensable. An "idealist" was a man who *lived* for his idea—hence he could not be a businessman—and who was prepared to sacrifice for his

idea everything and, especially, everybody. *When he said* in the police examination that he would have sent his own father to death if that had
been required, *he did not mean* merely to stress the extent to which he
was under orders, and ready to obey them; *he also meant to show* what an
"idealist" he had always been. (41–42, emphasis mine)

As we can see in the passage, Arendt is not, as Musmanno claims, defending Eichmann "against his own words," but conversely, attempting to take Eichmann *at* his word, which for many reasons is
enormously difficult to do: he lied, boasted outrageously, and worst
for Arendt, demonstrated a staggering incompetence in the use of
language (his utter dependence on his own stock phrases and clichés,
"winged words" as he called them; his "heroic fight with the German
language, which invariably defeats him"; and his inability to speak
anything but "officialese" [48]). Nonetheless, her attempt to take him
at his word, which produces the irony so characteristic of her depiction of him, is crucial to both her sense of his moral failing and her
own attempt to do what Eichmann so conspicuously failed to do: view
the world through the eyes of others.

"It was all irony," Arendt said, and while many have commented on
her choice to characterize Eichmann primarily through irony, it has
remained an open question as to why she might have done so. One of
the consistent elements of the reception of *Eichmann in Jerusalem* is
the extent to which this irony backfired. As one commentator noted in
Dissent, "*If this is irony, at whom is it directed?* One does not have to be
a Zionist to be shocked, or to 'misunderstand' the author's intent."[18]
Shawn, too, argues that both the *Times* and Justice Musmanno were
"insensitive" to her irony, though Shawn insists that Musmanno
"chose" to misread. Whether deliberate or inadvertent, the misreading
of Arendt's irony seems to have derived from her attempt to commu-
nicate, mostly ironically, Eichmann's view of himself, which suggests
the extent to which the grammar of reported speech can itself convey
sympathy. Arendt's taking Eichmann at his word often struck her
readers as an act of solidarity rather than a testing of reality.

Why would Arendt take such a risk? Arendt's commitment to her
idea of "plurality," which Seyla Benhabib called her "political principle
par excellence,"[19] outweighs the risk of irony. Instead of evil, hatred, or

sadism, Arendt identifies Eichmann's most "decisive flaw" as the "almost total inability ever to look at anything from the other fellow's point of view" (EJ, 47–48). This solipsism is a failure "merely [to make] present to oneself what the perspectives of others involved are or could be," which pointedly is "not empathy . . . for it does not mean assuming, accepting the point of view of the other" (Benhabib, 190). It is not that Eichmann could not feel for others (though nothing in his testimony suggested that he could) that disabled his conscience and permitted him to transport the Jews to their death, Arendt argues, but that he could not imagine their having a perspective other than his own. Therefore, her irony can be viewed as an attempt at plurality, as mocking as it was. By taking him at his word, Arendt is able to display his self-understanding and its ludicrousness at the same time. That irony is an affectless rhetoric suggests the distance between plurality and empathy. It was a distance, however, that many of her detractors could not perceive, not because they were poor readers necessarily, but because their habits of reading and their preference for an emotional explanation for Nazi evil overrode her intervention.

Shifting the Nazi moral breakdown into the register of cognition rather than emotion, however, registered as a banalization of their crimes and an exoneration of Eichmann. As Ernest Piske was to claim in the *Christian Science Monitor,* "Using rationality where only experience and compassionate imagination could have been proper guides she has pushed herself into a position where she appears to adopt a thesis proclaimed by Franz Werfel that not the murderers but the murdered are guilty." *Newsweek's* reviewer, while calling her a "profound and brilliant political philosopher," nonetheless wonders whether thinking itself had gone too far in her attempt to understand the trial:

> Miss Arendt has the kind of courage which only first-rate intelligences have—the courage not only of her convictions, but also of the power of her thinking processes. It is here that she runs tragically afoul of her fellow Jews, who like most of mankind, have merely the courage of their convictions. They *know* what has happened to the Jews in recent history; Miss Arendt is constantly struggling to find out, to break through what appears to be the congealed surface of events to the life below. On

her side, the difficulty is that she sometimes dives too deep and not only loses contact with the surface, but also with the human oxygen that makes common-sense breathing and thinking possible.

—*Newsweek*, June 17, 1963

And yet it is precisely losing "common sense" and "contact with the surface" that Arendt finds so morally suspect in *Eichmann*. The foundation of Eichmann's thoughtlessness is his failure to remain in contact with reality and to share and dispute it with others, which is her definition of common sense:

> The longer one listened to him, the more obvious it became that his inability to speak was closely connected with an inability to *think*, namely, to think from the standpoint of somebody else. No communication was possible with him, not because he lied but because he was surrounded by the most reliable of all safeguards against the words and the presence of others, and hence against reality as such. (*EJ*, 49)

Eichmann demonstrates the moral collapse of Germany because he resists the kind of thought that would force him to face reality, which is the fact of his own guilt and the criminality of the regime on whose behalf he acts. Arendt's efforts to distinguish between Eichmann's thoughtlessness and his lack of intelligence or education makes thoughtlessness a product of will rather than of nature or socialization. His use of language protects him from contact with the concrete, verifiable, sharable facts of the world. Plurality and concreteness in language work together as the safeguards *of* rather than *against* reality, plurality because it is unpredictable in its tendency to mirror a person back to himself, concreteness because it, as she sees in Zindel Grynszpan's testimony, brings one face to face with reality without distortion or evasion.

Like the complete incapacity for plurality in Eichmann, who cannot recognize otherness because he cannot extend beyond himself, the overwhelming sympathy of the revolutionary temperament as described in *On Revolution* also destroys plurality. The boundlessness of emotion and sympathy dissolves otherness by eliminating distance, which maintains the distinction between self and the other that makes plurality attainable. Between these two poles of "ideal-ism," the right and left incarnations of totalitarianism, stands the re-alist whose foremost obligation is to reality as such, which must always be guaranteed with plurality, that is, that we share the world with others. However, testing reality against the views of others, while it may corroborate our own, also may not, which is its value but also its risk. The thinker who would value plurality must also em-brace its unpredictability and uncertainty. And concreteness may make reality perceptible and shareable, but the very facts of reality may be extremely painful to bear. The safeguards of reality (plurality and concreteness), then, deserve more scrutiny because they are the pressure points in Arendt's philosophy of thinking and suffering. What allows one to confront reality without safeguards, to take the essential moral, political, and psychological risks that this entails, and what are the risks of failing to do so?

III. Reality Bites

Arendt is far more explicit about the risks of failing to confront re-ality than she is about the capacities that must be nurtured in order to do so. Her decision to banish painful feelings from public life, theorized in *On Revolution* and put into practice in *Eichmann in Jerusalem*, needs to be understood in relation to her conclusions about suffering and thinking in the work that preceded these. Her biographer, Elizabeth Young-Bruehl, argues that Arendt felt her-self to be "cured" of an intense emotional relationship to painful reality in the writing of *Eichmann in Jerusalem*.[20] While Arendt sur-vived the malaise brought on by the extraordinary painfulness of the Holocaust and the rise of totalitarianism, her work preceding *Eichmann* wrestled continually with the painfulness of reality and with the forms of thinking that provided a distraction from it. In particular, *Rahel Varnhagen* and *The Origins of Totalitarianism* prin-cipally revolve around the terrible costs of failing to face reality and the forms of thinking that permit its evasion. In extracting the compensations from these forms of thinking that shelter individu-als and even whole societies from reality, we can approach her phi-losophy of political heartlessness.

Arendt's concern with the relationship between painful reality and forms of thinking dates back to the biography of early nineteenth-century Jewish socialite, *Rahel Varnhagen,* which, like *Eichmann in Jerusalem,* is frequently characterized as unsympathetic, harsh, or pitiless.[21] In this biography, Arendt places a very different value on Lessing's "self-thinking" from that she attributed to it in her letter to Gershom Scholem. There she defined self-thinking as characteristic of the "conscious pariah"[22]:

> What confuses you is that my arguments and my approach are different from what you are used to; in other words, the trouble is that I am independent. By this I mean, on the one hand, that I do not belong to any organization and always speak only for myself, and on the other hand, that I have great confidence in Lessing's *selbstdenken,* for which, I think, no ideology, no public opinion, and no "convictions" can ever be a substitute. Whatever objections you may have to the results, you won't understand them unless you realize that they are really my own and nobody else's. (*The Jew as Pariah,* 250)

In her post-*Eichmann* reconciliation with reality,[23] Arendt viewed self-thinking as a part of the public exchange of ideas, one that guaranteed a plurality of thought by insuring the independence of individuals from what was often called "group-think" in the sixties. In contrast, in *Rahel Varnhagen,* "self-thinking" is a form of Enlightenment reason peculiarly susceptible to the distortions of introspection and, therefore, particularly appealing to Rahel, who wished to avoid her own status as a pariah. Cut off from the world, "'self-thinking,' which anyone can engage in alone and of his own accord" (*PHA,* 54), becomes a way of closing oneself off from plurality and the facts of experience.[24] "Self-thinking" for Rahel, as Arendt gleans from her letters, "brings liberation from objects and their reality, creates a sphere of pure ideas and a world which is accessible to any rational being without benefit of knowledge or experience" (54). This distortion of self-thinking, a "foundation for cultivated ignoramuses" (54) as Arendt bluntly puts it, is liberating, but only for "isolated individuals." Preferring to imagine past prejudices as mere relics, the isolated individual is not required to acknowledge "a nasty present reality," which is the lingering of prejudice in the minds of others.

The trajectory of Rahel Varnhagen's life is toward the acceptance of her pariah status, as the words she spoke on her deathbed attest: "The thing which all my life seemed to me the greatest shame, which was the misery and misfortune of my life—having been born a Jewess—this I should on no account now wish to have missed" (49). This shift entailed learning to think with reality rather than using her mind to distract, obscure, and cushion the reality that was too painful for her to bear: her status as a Jew. Arendt does not underestimate the agony of Rahel's dilemma; if anything there is an astonishingly visceral pain in Arendt's description of her exclusion. She asks how introspection can "be so isolated that the thinking individual no longer need *smash his head against the wall* of 'irrational' reality?" (55, emphasis mine), and "how can you . . . transform reality back into its potentialities and so *escape the 'murderous axe'?*" (55, emphasis mine), a metaphor Rahel used for acknowledging herself a "Schlemihl and Jewess" (54). Arendt argues that, "bound by this inferiority," Rahel "must avoid everything that might give rise to further confirmation, must not act, not love, not become involved in the world. Given such absolute renunciation, all that seemed left was *thought*" (53). Introspection in *Rahel Varnhagen* is principally a form of compensation for this worldlessness and a consoling method of consolidating self-image by refusing to subject it to contradiction, whether prejudiced or insightful.

Rousseau is here (and elsewhere in *On Revolution*) Arendt's prime target for the "mania for introspection" as a form of self-delusion (55). Freed from the conflict and contradiction of plurality, the individual is more guarded against reality than ever before. For Arendt, these various forms of avoiding reality in introspection have their temptations, which she names as the power and the autonomy of the soul. However, she argues that these are "secured at the price of truth, it must be recognized, for without reality shared with other human beings, truth loses all meaning. Introspection and its hybrids engender *mendacity*" (55). This avoidance of the facts leads inevitably to disaster for the world's pariahs. Not only is the painful condition left unchanged by the retreat from reality, but also the self is obliterated in the process. Rahel's choice to avoid her reality "requires an inhuman alertness not to betray oneself, to conceal everything and yet have no definitive secret to cling to" (57). Finally, her own refusal to confront reality created a vagueness that confused the object of her oppression. Not "blocked by individual and therefore removable obstacles, but by everything, by *the* world" (59), no sort of action seemed either useful or possible.

The political worldlessness of Rahel and her generation was given much greater amplification in *The Origins of Totalitarianism,* which is itself about the distortions of thinking that permitted the rise of National Socialism. Moreover, Arendt defines totalitarianism as an attempt to obliterate the capacity to think, which had become increasingly difficult under the conditions of modern alienation and loneliness: "As terror is needed lest with the birth of each new human being a new beginning arise and raise its voice in the world, so the self-coercive force of logicality is mobilized *lest anybody ever start thinking*—which as the freest and purest of all human activities is the very opposite of the compulsory process of deduction" (171) (emphasis mine).[25] The two distinctive features of totalitarianism—supersense and terror—are thus brought together as problems of thinking. Everyone in the totalitarian system is implicated in the problem of thinking and facing of reality: the perpetrators, both the masses and the elites in different ways, the outside observers in the international community, and the victims of domination. The first three represent the anxieties of thought—unpredictability, uncertainty, and doubt—that make totalitarianism attractive and plausible; the last represents the abyss of thought that closes the door on suffering and its display in public.

In Arendt's terms, the masses' submission to logical supersense, the nonthinking that looks like thought, is a consolation and one that she exhibits a certain sympathy for:

> Before the alternative of facing the anarchic growth and total arbitrariness of decay or bowing down before the most rigid, fantastically fictitious consistency of an ideology, the masses will probably always choose the latter and be ready to pay for it with individual sacrifices—and this not because they are stupid or wicked, but because in the general disaster this escape grants them a minimum of self-respect. (50)

The value of this ultimately murderous fantasy of ideology is that it provides not only meaning and a place in history, but also predictability. In adopting this logicality, however, the masses develop contempt for their own reality. For supersense and logicality to proceed, reality must be wished away or ignored, even when that process works to the detriment of the individual's self-interest or even survival. The promises of meaningfulness and predictability are compensations and consolations for a reality that is unbearable. We can conclude, then, that logic is itself a consoling form of thought when divorced from experience and that consolation as much as logic is to be regarded with suspicion, for the cost of predictability is an abdication of the world.

Like the masses, the Nazi elite also banished reality by regarding it as mere inconvenience, something utterly plastic and subject to the will. Power and time would remake reality into the fantasy of the leader. In this sense, thinking has stopped altogether. There is *a* thought married to power, and reality is transformed in order to conform to the idea. As Arendt explains, description becomes prediction: the "Jews are a dying race" means "kill the Jews." The elites, she says, "instinctively" understand this. Thought married to power means the destruction of plurality, something that the masses have already lost in their isolated loneliness. "It is chiefly for the sake of this supersense, for the sake of complete consistency, that it is necessary for totalitarianism to destroy every trace of what we commonly call human dignity. For respect for human dignity implies recognition of my fellow-men or our fellow-nations as subjects, as builders of worlds or cobuilders of a common world" (*T*, 139). Other human beings' perspective on the world becomes not only a matter of inconvenience to the elite but an obstacle to remaking reality. To the extent that the inconsistency, disruption, and discomfort of opposition inherent in plurality seemed to contradict Nazi "reality," plurality had to be destroyed.

The international community was unable to grasp the reality of totalitarianism, despite the evidence, because their assumptions about human nature remained unexamined in light of new evidence, protected from new data, new experience, and new realities. The unexamined "common sense" that self-interest governed human motivation undermined the apprehension of the danger of totalitarianism, which is always potentially *self*-destructive (in Arendt's argument, all men, not just the victims of the camps, were equally superfluous).

There is a great temptation to explain away the intrinsically incredible by means of liberal rationalization. In each one of us, there lurks such a liberal, wheedling us with the voice of common sense. . . . But wherever these new forms of domination assume their authentically totalitarian structure they transcend this principle, which is still tied to the utilitarian motives and self-interest of the rulers, and try their hand in a realm that up to now has been completely unknown to us: the realm where "everything is possible." . . . what runs counter to common sense is not the nihilistic principle that "everything is permitted," which was already contained in the 19th-century utilitarian conception of common sense. What common sense and "normal people" refuse to believe is that everything is possible. (*T,* 137–138)

Thinking that has forgotten its obligation to the world and the necessity of self-doubt and questioning represents not a failure of feeling or empathy but a failure of nerve, a preference for the comfort of certainty to the anxiety of self-doubt. The harshness of her characterization of the "wheedling" of the "liberal" that "lurks" in us all suggests the contempt Arendt had for this avoidance of self-interrogation.

We come finally to those terrorized into abandoning thought, the inmates of the concentration camp. Once again, Arendt poses this as a relationship between thinking and reality, though in this case she argues that the individual *must* flee reality because it is unbearable. Reducing a human being to a set of physiological reactions makes thought impossible. More interesting in terms of Arendt's own insistence on facing reality is the problem of thinking *about* total domination in light of the suffering of the Jews. Richard Bernstein suggests "it is by 'dwelling on horrors' of the concentration camps . . . that Arendt can provide a brilliant analysis of these institutions."[26] A closer examination of her analysis in *The Origins of Totalitarianism* reveals that the camps were the only reality that could not properly be faced in the sense that she had elaborated elsewhere. The death camps, which are in her terms the most significant feature of totalitarianism, its laboratory for "everything is possible," produce something like an abyss in thought. It is essential to think *of* them, because totalitarianism presents the single greatest threat to the future of human beings, but it is literally impossible to think *about* them.

If it is true that the concentration camps are the most consequential institution of totalitarian rule, "dwelling on horrors" would seem to be indispensable for the understanding of totalitarianism. But recollection can no more do this than can the uncommunicative eyewitness report. In both these genres there is an inherent tendency to run away from the experience; instinctively or rationally, both types of writer are so much aware of the terrible abyss that separates the world of the living from that of the living dead, that they cannot supply anything more than a series of remembered occurrences that must seem just as incredible to those who relate them as to their audience. (*T,* 139)

The experience of the concentration camps violates the prerequisites of thought. The testimony is unbelievable to the one experiencing it as well as to the one listening, and it is therefore unsharable. Because it is "as though he had a story to tell of another planet" (139), the horror also attains the status of the surreal, if not the unreal. Unthinkable, unsharable, and unreal, the memory of the camps is transformed into physical pain: the memory is "smitten in the flesh," a wound that the sufferer cannot dwell on. Arendt also bars the contemplation of this suffering by others: "Suffering, of which there has been always too much on earth, is not the issue, nor is the number of victims. Human nature as such is at stake" (139). And pity is an infliction of pain like misery: "In times of growing misery and individual helplessness, it seems as difficult to resist pity when it grows into an all-devouring passion as it is not to resent its very boundlessness, which seems to kill human dignity with a more deadly certainty than misery itself" (27). It is left to the "fearful imagination" of those "aroused by such reports" to speculate on the future reappearance of totalitarianism. In this sense, pain, suffering, and the wound of history are relegated to the private realm. They are neither the grounds of politics nor a subject of knowledge.

Arendt even denies that facing this reality has any value by suggesting that the experience of the camps has no future consequences. She makes the startling claim that horror changes no one and nothing:

> A change of personality of any sort whatever can no more be induced by thinking about horror than by the real experience of horror. The reduction of a man to a bundle of reactions separates him as radically as mental disease from everything within him that is personality or character. When, like Lazarus, he rises from the dead, he finds his personality or character unchanged, just as he had left it. (*T,* 139)

By limiting the power of terror to the moment of its infliction, Arendt eliminates the need to revisit it after the fact. Because it changes nothing and no one, because it cannot be thought or shared, it exists simply as a motivation, as a question, *the* question, that unites all political thinking. Erasing horror from the domain of thought leads us back to *Eichmann in Jerusalem*. Declaring the suffering of the Jews in the camps beyond thought in *The Origins of Totalitarianism* and the heart's motivations beyond scrutiny in *On Revolution,* what could she have examined but Eichmann's thoughtlessness when she arrived in Jerusalem for the trial?

If writing *Eichmann in Jerusalem* allowed Arendt to recover the *amor mundi* that grounded her political philosophy, it has been less obvious the extent to which this recovery depended on developing a relationship to suffering that was distinctly unconsoling and austere. Two recent intellectual biographies, Julia Kristeva's *Hannah Arendt* and Sylvie Courtine-Denamy's *Three Women in Dark Times: Edith Stein, Hannah Arendt, Simone Weil,* celebrate Arendt's love of the world, much as Young-Bruehl did twenty years ago, Kristeva focusing on the importance of love in Arendt's thinking and Courtine-Denamy on Arendt's efforts to "reconcile herself with reality." Both see her thought as motivated by what we might call a will to joy and both find Arendt's tough-mindedness with regard to painful feeling and public life scintillating. Nevertheless, in their optimistic appraisal of Arendt's love of the world, they have not calculated the tolerance of suffering that was a part of her newfound equilibrium. The realist who stands between the twin poles of totalitarian idealism—the solipsism of thoughtlessness and the boundarilessness of revolutionary sympathy—must tolerate, even embrace, what might be considered forms of psychological distress. The realist accepts the pain of reality; endures doubt; welcomes conflict; consents to unpredictability; takes up the isolation of the conscious pariah; and concedes control over the future. Facing reality means, therefore, living in a state of turmoil and upset. The only way to become a realist, and for Arendt we all must do so for our mutual survival, is to cultivate a suspicion of intellectual and psychological comfort in whatever forms we find them. Arendt hated illusions about the terrible facets of human existence and wished for herself and her "co-builders" of the world to accept willingly a wounding by them. Suffering is so much a part of her notion of thinking that only by feeling pain can one know that one loves the world properly.

Notes

1. Page numbers are taken from *Eichmann in Jerusalem: A Report on the Banality of Evil* (New York: Penguin Books, 1994), hereafter *EJ*.
2. *The Essential Lenny Bruce: His Original Unexpurgated Satirical Routines,* ed. John Cohen (Frogmore, UK: Panther Books Ltd, 1975), 50.
3. Dan Diner, "Hannah Arendt Reconsidered: On the Banal and the Evil in Her Holocaust Narrative," *New German Critique,* 71 (Spring/Summer, 1997), 178.
4. See Hans Mommsen, "Hannah Arendt's Interpretation of the Holocaust as a Challenge to Human Existence: The Intellectual Background," in *Hannah Arendt in Jerusalem,* ed. Steven E. Ascheim (Berkeley, CA: University of California Press, 2001), 224–231.
5. Elizabeth Young-Bruehl traces out the debate over *Eichmann in Jerusalem* and comments frequently on Arendt's style but does not speculate as to why Arendt employed the strategies she did. See *Hannah Arendt: For the Love of the World* (New Haven and London: Yale University Press, 1982).
6. Page numbers are taken from *On Revolution* (New York: Penguin Books, 1990), hereafter *OR*.
7. See *Gershom Scholem: A Life in Letters, 1914–1982,* ed. and trans. David Skinner (Cambridge, MA, and London: Harvard University Press, 2002), vi.
8. In the preface to the selection of letters, the *New York Times Book Review* reported receiving more than 100 letters in the month after Musmanno's review, mostly in support of Arendt and critical of the review. The pages themselves include a selection, roughly half in support of *Eichmann in Jerusalem* and half in support of Musmanno's review.
9. Printing this volume of responses was unprecedented in the *New York Times Book Review.* The *Book Review* had never (nor has to this date) devoted as much space to one controversy as it did with *Eichmann in Jerusalem.*
10. The response is in "Notes and Comments" and does not contain a byline for Shawn, though he did indeed write it.
11. As reprinted in *The Jew as Pariah,* ed. Ron Feldman (New York: Grove Press, 1978).
12. See the translation in *Gershom Scholem: A Life in Letters, 1914–1982,* 396.
13. Moreover, she claims that "I cannot love myself or anything which I know is part and parcel of my own person," by which she implies a kind of narcissism in the love of a people; *The Jew as Pariah,* 247.
14. He does note tone in reference to various other figures in the trial. For instance, Arendt "deals intemperately" with lead prosecutor, Gideon

Hausner, and "pours scorn" on Israeli Prime Minister, David Ben-
Gurion; *New York Times Book Review,* May 19, 1963, 40–41.

15. *New York Times Book Review,* May 19, 1963, Section 7, 1.

16. In *The Human Condition* (Chicago: University of Chicago Press, 1998),
which Arendt wrote in the mid-1950s, she had already developed a
theory of the public world that did not include pain and emotion. Her
primary examples of things that cannot be shared in public are physical
pain and emotion, namely love. Because internal states are not subject
to the verifications of plurality, pain and emotion cannot be seen and
heard, which is the fundamental condition of publicity—appearance.
Moreover, she claims that certain things cannot bear the light of day,
the exposure to many, and that one of these is the intensity that comes
with intimate feelings. This intensity, she argues, is always a threat to
reality (50–51).

17. See Moshe Zimmerman, "Hannah Arendt, the Early 'Post-Zionist'"
(181–193), and Richard Bernstein, "Hannah Arendt's Zionism?"
(194–202) in *Hannah Arendt in Jerusalem.* As Bernstein says: "To ask, in
an unqualified manner, 'Was Hannah Arendt ever a Zionist and when?'
obscures basic issues. We need to make more discriminating judgments.
We need to clarify what precisely attracted her to Zionism (especially
which version of Zionism, and when this occurred), as well as what repelled her about Zionist ideology and became the target of her stinging
criticism" (194–195).

18. Marie Syrkin, "The Clothes of the Empress," *Dissent,* Autumn 1963,
346.

19. Seyla Benhabib, *The Reluctant Modernism of Hannah Arendt* (London:
SAGE Publications, 1996), 190.

20. Arendt wrote to her close friend Mary McCarthy regarding her "*cura
posterior*": "You are the only reader to understand that I wrote this book
in a curious euphoria. And that ever since I did it I feel—after twenty
years—light hearted about the whole matter. Don't tell anybody: is it not
proof positive that I have no 'soul'?" (as quoted in *Hannah Arendt: For
Love of the World,* 337).

21. Moreover, this lack of sympathy is also linked to the similarities between
Arendt and her subject. As almost all critics do, Julia Kristeva reads
Rahel Varnhagen autobiographically, noting Arendt's especially harsh
treatment of her: "Far from empathizing with her heroine, Arendt appears to be settling scores with Rahel, a being held dear, an alter ego that
Hannah herself could never be although it threatened her, an alter ego
that she dislodged of any compassionate depth with a relentless severity
that was as ruthless as it was insightful"; *Hannah Arendt,* trans. Ross Gu-
berman (New York: Columbia University Press, 2001).

22. See a more extended discussion of the thinker as conscious pariah in the
first chapter, "The Conscious Pariah as Rebel and Independent
Thinker," in Richard Bernstein, *Hannah Arendt and the Jewish Question*
(Cambridge, MA: MIT Press, 1996).

23. See especially the epilogue to Sylvie Courtine-Denamy, *Three Women in
Dark Times: Edith Stein, Hannah Arendt, Simone Weil,* trans. G. M.

Goshgarian (Ithaca, NY: Cornell University Press, 2000), for an extended discussion of this attempt to reconcile with reality.

24. Page numbers are taken from *The Portable Hannah Arendt,* ed. Peter Baehr (New York: Penguin Books, 2000), hereafter *PHA.*

25. All quotations are taken from *Totalitarianism: Part Three of the Origins of Totalitarianism* (New York: Harvest Books, 1968), hereafter, *T.*

26. Bernstein, *Hannah Arendt and the Jewish Question,* 11.

Contributors

Lauren Berlant is Professor of English at the University of Chicago. She is the author of *The Anatomy of National Fantasy: Hawthorne, Utopia, and Everyday Life* (1991) and *The Queen of America Goes to Washington City: Essays on Sex and Citizenship* (1997), and edited a special issue of *Critical Inquiry* called *Intimacy* (1998), which was expanded into a book in 2000. She is also editor, with Lisa Duggan, of a book on the Clinton scandals, titled *Our Monica, Ourselves* (2001) and, with Laura Letinsky, *Venus Inferred* (2000).

Lee Edelman is Professor of English at Tufts University. He is the author of *Homographesis* (1994) and *Transmemberment of Song: Hart Crane's Anatomies of Rhetoric and Desire* (1987). He has recently completed *No Future: Queer Theory and the Death Drive*.

Marjorie Garber is William R. Kenan, Jr., Professor of English and Director of the Humanities Center at Harvard University. Her most recent work includes *Quotation Marks* and *The Medusa Reader* (coedited with Nancy Vickers).

Neil Hertz teaches in the Humanities Center at Johns Hopkins. He is the author of *The End of the Line: Essays on Psychoanalysis and the*

Sublime (1985) and *George Eliot's Pulse* (2003), of which his essay in this volume forms one chapter.

Neville Hoad is Assistant Professor in the English Department at the University of Texas at Austin. He has published articles in *Postcolonial Studies, GLQ: A Journal of Lesbian and Gay Studies, Development Update, Jewish Affairs,* and *Repercussions.* He is currently working on a project examining Victorian imaginings of the future of sex.

Deborah Nelson is Associate Professor of English and Gender Studies at the University of Chicago. She is the author of *Pursuing Privacy in Cold War America* (2002). Her current project is titled *Tough Broads: Suffering in Style.*

Mary Ann O'Farrell is Associate Professor of English at Texas A&M University. She is the author of *Telling Complexions: The Nineteenth-Century English Novel and the Blush* (1997) and coeditor of *Virtual Gender: Fantasies of Subjectivity and Embodiment* (1999). She is currently at work on a project about the text of manners.

Candace Vogler is Associate Professor of Philosophy at the University of Chicago, where she is also Codirector of the Masters of Arts Program in the Humanities. She is the author of *Reasonably Vicious* (2002), *John Stuart Mill's Deliberative Landscape* (2001) and various articles on ethics, literature, sexuality, Marxism, and feminism. She is currently at work on a manuscript about virtue.

Carolyn Williams is Associate Professor of English at Rutgers University, where she is also Codirector of the Center for the Critical Analysis of Contemporary Culture. Her publications on Victorian literature and culture include *Transfigured World: Walter Pater's Aesthetic Historicism* (1989). Recently she has been working on two projects in the field of nineteenth-century theater, one on the comic operas of Gilbert and Sullivan, and one on the form of melodrama.

Kathleen Woodward, Professor of English, is Director of the Simpson Center for the Humanities at the University of Washington. The author of *Aging and Its Discontents: Freud and Other Fictions* (1991) and *At Last, the Real Distinguished Thing: The Late Poems of Eliot, Pound, Stevens, and Williams* (1980), she is completing a book on the cultural politics of the emotions entitled *Statistical Panic and Other New Feelings.*